Hispanic American Biographies

Volume 5

Juncos, Manuel Fernández—Montez, Maria

GROLIER
an imprint of
SCHOLASTIC
www.scholastic.com/librarypublishing

First published 2006 by Grolier,
an imprint of Scholastic Library Publishing,
Old Sherman Turnpike,
Danbury, Connecticut 06816

Set ISBN-13: 978-0-7172-6124-6
Set ISBN-10: 0-7172-6124-7
Volume ISBN-13: 978-0-7172-6129-1
Volume ISBN-10: 0-7172-6129-8

Library of Congress Cataloging-in-Publication Data
Hispanic American biographies.
v. cm.
Includes bibliographical references and index.
Contents: v. 1. Acevedo-Vilá, Aníbal - Bocanegra, Carlos -- v. 2. Bonilla, Tony - Corretjer, Juan Antonio -- v. 3. Cortés, Carlos - Gálvez, Bernardo de -- v. 4. Gamboa, Harry, Jr. - Julia, Raul -- v. 5. Juncos, Manuel Fernández - Montez, Maria -- v. 6. Montoya, Carlos Garcia - Ponce, Mary Helen -- v. 7. Ponce de León, Juan - Seguín, Juan N. -- v. 8. Selena - Zúñiga, Martha.
ISBN-13: 978-0-7172-6124-6 (set : alk. paper) -- ISBN-10: 0-7172-6124-7 (set : alk. paper) -- ISBN-13: 978-0-7172-6125-3 (v. 1 : alk. paper) -- ISBN-10: 0-7172-6125-5 (v. 1 : alk. paper) -- ISBN-13: 978-0-7172-6126-0 (v. 2 : alk. paper) -- ISBN-10: 0-7172-6126-3 (v. 2 : alk. paper) -- ISBN-13: 978-0-7172-6127-7 (v. 3 : alk. paper) -- ISBN-10: 0-7172-6127-1 (v. 3 : alk. paper) -- ISBN-13: 978-0-7172-6128-4 (v. 4 : alk. paper) -- ISBN-10: 0-7172-6128-X (v. 4 : alk. paper) -- ISBN-13: 978-0-7172-6129-1 (v. 5 : alk. paper) -- ISBN-10: 0-7172-6129-8 (v. 5 : alk. paper) -- ISBN-13: 978-0-7172-6130-7 (v. 6 : alk. paper) -- ISBN-10: 0-7172-6130-1 (v. 6 : alk. paper) -- ISBN-13: 978-0-7172-6131-4 (v. 7 : alk. paper) -- ISBN-10: 0-7172-6131-X (v. 7 : alk. paper) -- ISBN-13: 978-0-7172-6132-1 (v. 8 : alk. paper) -- ISBN-10: 0-7172-6132-8 (v. 8 : alk. paper)
1. Hispanic Americans--Biography--Encyclopedias--Juvenile literature. I. Grolier Publishing Company.
E184.S75H5573 2006
973'.046800922--dc22
[B]
2006012294

For information address the publisher:
Grolier, Scholastic Library Publishing,
Old Sherman Turnpike,
Danbury, Connecticut 06816

FOR THE BROWN REFERENCE GROUP PLC

Project Editor:	Chris King
Editors:	Henry Russell, Aruna Vasudevan, Tom Jackson, Simon Hall
Design:	Q2A Solutions, Seth Grimbly, Lynne Ross
Picture Researcher:	Sharon Southren
Index:	Kay Ollerenshaw
Design Manager:	Sarah Williams
Production Director:	Alastair Gourlay
Senior Managing Editor:	Tim Cooke
Editorial Director:	Lindsey Lowe

ACADEMIC CONSULTANTS:

Ellen Riojas Clark, Division of Bicultural Bilingual Studies, University of Texas at San Antonio	Arnoldo de Leon, Department of History, Angelo State University

Printed and bound in Singapore

ABOUT THIS SET

This is one of a set of eight books chronicling the lives of Hispanic Americans who have helped shape the history of the United States. The set contains biographies of more than 750 people of Hispanic origin. They range from 16th-century explorers to 21st-century musicians and movie stars. Some were born in the United States, while others immigrated there from countries such as Mexico, Cuba, or Puerto Rico. The subjects therefore come from a wide range of cultural backgrounds, historical eras, and areas of achievement.

In addition to the biographical entries, the set includes a number of guidepost articles that provide an overview of a particular aspect of the Hispanic American experience. These guidepost articles cover general areas such as civil rights and religion as well as specific historical topics such as the Treaty of Guadalupe Hidalgo. These articles serve to help place the lives of the subjects of the biographies in a wider context.

Each biographical entry contains a box listing key dates in the subject's life as well as a further reading section that gives details of books and Web sites that the reader may wish to explore. Longer biographies also include a box about the people who inspired the subject, people the subject has influenced in turn, or the legacy that the subject has left behind. Where relevant, entries also contain a "See also" section that directs the reader to related articles elsewhere in the set. A comprehensive set index is included at the end of each volume.

The entries are arranged alphabetically, mostly by surname but also by stage name. In cases where the subject has more than one surname, he or she is alphabetized under the name that is most commonly used. For example, Héctor Pérez García is usually known simply as Hector P. Garcia and is therefore alphabetized under "G." Pedro Albizu Campos, meanwhile, is generally known by his full name and is alphabetized under "A." Both variants are included in the index. Where names are commonly spelled in a variety of ways, the most widespread version is used. Similarly, the use of accents is dictated in each individual case by general usage.

Contributors: Holly Ackerman; Jorge Abril Sánchez; Alma Alvarez-Smith; Robert Anderson; Kelvin Bias; Erica Brodman; P. Scott Brown; John Buentello; Francisco Cabanillas; Amalia Cabezas; Bec Chalkley; Alfredo Cruz; Gerardo Cummings; German Cutz; Anita Dalal; Zilah Deckker; Marilyn Fedewa; Stan Fedewa; Héctor Fernández L'Hoeste; José Gamez; Conrado Gomez; Susan Green; José Angel Gutiérrez; Luz Angelica Kirschner; Nashieli Marcano; Danizete Martinez; Elena Martinez; Luisa Moncada; Joseph Moralez; Carmen Nava; Eliza Rodriguez; Sara Elizabeth Scott Armengot; Melissa Segura; Iben Trino-Molenkamp; Angharad Valdivia; Emma Young.

CONTENTS

JUNCOS, Manuel Fernández

Journalist, Poet, Politician

The Spanish-born poet and writer Manuel Fernández Juncos is best remembered for having written the words to "La Borinqueña," the national anthem of Puerto Rico. The song was adopted officially only in 1977 but had been widely sung by nationalists since the first years of the 20th century. In Puerto Rico itself, where several schools and streets are named in his honor, Juncos is also remembered as an important patriot. He supported Puerto Rican independence when the island was under Spanish rule, and was a liberal nationalist whose ideas and writings contributed to the development of a Puerto Rican national identity. Juncos's daughter, Amparo Fernández Náter, was the cofounder of the Suffragist Social League, which during the 1920s struggled for Puerto Rican women's right to vote.

KEY DATES

1846 Born in Tresmonte, Asturias, in northern Spain, on December 11.

1847 Arrives in Puerto Rico.

1867 Writes the words to "La Borinqueña," which later becomes Puerto Rico's official anthem.

1877 Founds the popular Puerto Rican weekly newspaper *El Buscapié.*

1887 Founds *La Revista Puertorriqueña* (The Puerto Rican Magazine).

1897 Becomes a member of Puerto Rico's first autonomous government.

1928 Dies in San Juan, Puerto Rico, on August 18.

1977 "La Borinqueña" adopted as national anthem of Puerto Rico.

Early life

Juncos was born on December 11, 1846, in the small village of Tresmonte, near Ribadesella in Asturias, a province of northern Spain. In 1847, his well-to-do Puerto Rican parents returned to their homeland, which the young Juncos grew to love passionately. During the late 1860s, Juncos established himself as a popular poet and journalist, writing for such notable liberal newspapers as *El Progreso*, whose editor was the well-known abolitionist and civil rights campaigner José Julián Acosta. He also wrote for *Porvenir* and *Clamor del Pueblo*.

In his literary works, Juncos often examined the history, traditions, and culture of ordinary Puerto Rican people. Juncos's satirical but affectionate pen-portraits of the typical villagers and townsfolk of his homeland, found in such volumes as *Tipos y caracteres* (Types and Characters, 1882), earned him an enthusiastic readership.

In 1877 Juncos established the weekly arts and politics newspaper *El Buscapié* (*Firecracker*), through which he promoted socialist ideas such as universal free education. He also founded the *La Revista Puertorriqueña* (The Puerto Rican Magazine) in 1887, a specialized arts, science, and letters review.

Working for Puerto Rican independence

During the late 19th century, many liberal Puerto Rican thinkers such as Acosta pushed for their country to become more independent of Spanish rule. Junco became an active member of the pro-independence Autonomist Party, eventually acting as its secretary.

In 1897, when Spain finally gave way and a separate Puerto Rican parliament was formed, Juncos was elected to a seat in the new government. His political life proved short, however: In the following year, U.S. troops occupied Puerto Rico during the Spanish–American War, and the island subsequently became the territory of the United States.

After the U.S. invasion, Juncos retired from public life to concentrate on his writing. He wrote several influential essays and books. Juncos died on August 18, 1928, in San Juan, the Puerto Rican capital.

Legacy

Juncos was a civil rights activist, a patriot, and a humanitarian. He founded the Puerto Rican Red Cross, which still exists today. He is probably most remembered, however, for providing the lyrics to "La Borinqueña," which became the official anthem of Puerto Rico.

See also: Acosta, José Julián

Further reading: http://welcome.topuertorico.org/culture/famousprD-J.shtml (brief biography).

JURADO, Katy
Actor

Katy Jurado was a star of 1940s Mexican cinema who crossed over into the United States to make a memorable appearance in one of the greatest Hollywood Westerns of all time.

Born María Cristina Estela Marcela Jurado de García in 1924 in Guadalajara, Mexico, the actor was discovered at age 16 by Mexican director Emilio "El Indio" Fernández. He wanted to cast her in his next movie, but her wealthy landowning family disapproved of acting as a career. Undeterred, however, the teenager eloped with an actor and made her screen debut in 1943 in *No matarás*.

Jurado's acting ability and distinctive appearance gained her work with the leading Hispanic filmmakers of the period: Ismael Rodríguez used her in *Nosotros los pobres* (1948) and *El seminarista* (1949); Luis Buñuel later cast her in *El bruto* (1953). Between films she worked as a journalist, and while reporting on a bullfight, she was spotted by American director Budd Boetticher, who cast her in his *Bullfighter and the Lady* (1951). Although at the time Jurado spoke no English and had to learn her lines phonetically, she soon made herself fluent in the language. Her initiative led to her landing a part in Fred Zinnemann's Western *High Noon* (1952).

Crossing the border

For her performance as Helen Ramírez, the former mistress of Marshal Will Kane, played by Gary Cooper, Jurado won the 1952 Golden Globe award for best supporting actress. She then moved to Hollywood, California, and in so doing blazed a trail for other Mexican actors, who now saw that they could play roles in U.S. movies that were more than mere ethnic stereotypes.

KEY DATES

1924	Born in Guadalajara, Mexico, on January 16.
1943	Stars in her first film, *No matarás*.
1952	Plays Gary Cooper's mistress in *High Noon*.
1953	Appears in Luis Buñuel's *El bruto*.
1998	Appears in her last film, *El evangelio de las maravillas*.
2002	Dies in Cuernavaca, Mexico, on July 5.

▲ ***Katy Jurado showed that Mexican Americans could play roles that were more than ethnic caricatures.***

In 1954 Jurado became the first Mexican to be nominated for an Academy Award, as best supporting actress for her role in *Broken Lance*, but she lost to Eva Marie Saint who won for her role in *On the Waterfront*.

In 1959 Jurado married for the second time. Her new husband was Ernest Borgnine, her costar in *The Badlanders*, filmed the previous year. The couple separated in 1961, and divorced in 1964. In the latter part of her career, Jurado appeared mainly in Spanish-language films and several long-running soap operas for Mexican television. Among her American movies was Sam Peckinpah's *Pat Garrett and Billy the Kid* (1973), in which she played the formidable Mrs. Baker.

Late in life Katy Jurado suffered degenerative heart and lung problems. She died in 2002 at her home in Cuernavaca, Mexico. She has a star on the Hollywood Walk of Fame.

Further reading: Mora, Carl J. *Mexican Cinema: Reflections of a Society, 1896–1980*. Berkeley, CA: University of California Press, 1982.

http://www.imdb.com/name/nm0432827 (entry on Internet Movie Database).

KANELLOS, Nicolás
Publisher, Academic

Nicolás Kanellos is a prominent university professor. For over 20 years Kanellos has overseen the work of the Arte Publico Press, a Hispanic American publisher he founded at the University of Houston, Texas. The company prints books in both Spanish and English, and many of its titles promote the work of other Hispanic Americans.

Early life

Kanellos was born in 1945 to a Puerto Rican family living in New York. He studied at Woodbridge High School and graduated with a BA in Spanish from Fairleigh Dickinson University in New Jersey in 1966. Kanellos then attended a number of other universities including the Universidad Autonoma de Mexico, Mexico, and the Universidad de Lisboa, Portugal, before arriving at the University of Texas at Austin. There he earned an MA in Romance languages, followed by a PhD in Spanish and Portuguese in 1974.

Writer and professor

While studying for his doctorate in Texas, Kanellos joined the Teatro Chicano de Austin and put to use his talents at singing, acting, and playing the guitar. Kanellos took a position as professor of languages at Indiana University, Gary. There he cofounded the first of many important projects, *Revista Chicano-Riquena* (Chicano–Rican Review), a literary journal, and founded the Teatro Desengano del Pueblo. In 1979 Kanellos moved back to the University of Texas, this time basing himself in Houston. The journal's headquarters moved to Houston with him, where it became *The Americas Review*.

Publisher and editor

In 1979 Kanellos also began building the nation's largest nonprofit publishing house, Arte Publico Press, which is also based at the University of Houston. Today the organization publishes on average 30 titles annually. The press has abundant material in print for children and adults in both Spanish and English. Arte Publico also publishes the Hispanic Civil Rights Series, books about prominent Hispanic American events and leaders. As well as his work with Arte Publico, Kanellos also sits on the editorial boards of six journals and two university presses —Southern Illinois and the Sorbonne in Paris, France.

In 1992 Kanellos began a $20-million project entitled "Recovering the Hispanic Literary Heritage of the United States." The project is sponsored by the Rockefeller Foundation. Its aim is to collect Hispanic American literature produced before 1960. In 2006 Kanellos was the first Brown Foundation Endowed Chair of Hispanic Literature at the University of Houston, where he oversees the PhD program in Hispanic American literature.

▲ ***Nicolás Kanellos was appointed to the National Committee of Humanities by President Bill Clinton in 1994. He began a second term in that role in 2000.***

KEY DATES

1945	Born in New York City on January 31.
1979	Founds *The Americas Review* and Arte Publico Press.
1997	Named one of the 100 Most Influential Hispanics in the United States by *Hispanic Business* magazine.

Further reading: Kanellos, Nicolás, ed. *The Hispanic American Almanac: A Reference Work on Hispanics in the United States.* Detroit, MI: Gale Research, 1997.

http://www.uh.edu/ia/farfel/pages/nKanellos.html (Kanellos's citation as 17th recipient of Esther Farfel Award for excellence in teaching, research, and service at the University of Houston).

KAPP, Joe
Football Player, Coach

Joe Kapp has earned a reputation as a fierce competitor. The first Latino quarterback to lead a National Football League (NFL) team to the Super Bowl, Kapp led the Minnesota Vikings to the 1970 showdown in New Orleans. Earlier in his career, Kapp also steered the British Columbia Lions to the 1964 Canadian Football League's (CFL's) Grey Cup, and took the Cal Golden Bears to the 1959 Rose Bowl. He is the only player in football history to quarterback teams to the Super Bowl, Grey Cup, and Rose Bowl.

▲ ***Joe Kapp has dedicated much time to the Latino community, and he has highlighted the high number of Hispanic youth dropping out of school.***

Becoming a football player and coach

Born in Sante Fe, New Mexico, on March 19, 1938, Kapp was the son of a Mexican American mother and a German American father. He attended grade school in Salinas, California, and later moved to Newhall, California, where he excelled in football at Hart High School. Kapp then enrolled at the University of California at Berkeley (Cal) in the fall of 1955, and starred on both the football and basketball teams. Cal made its last Rose Bowl appearance under Kapp's leadership on January 1, 1959. Kapp was drafted in the 18th round by the Washington Redskins; he opted to play in the CFL, however, playing three years with the Calgary Stampeders and five years with the British Columbia Lions, winning the Grey Cup in 1964. In 1967 Kapp finally made it to the NFL, signing with the Vikings.

Having gotten into scuffles with teammates, Kapp's rough and tumble nature became widely known on July 20, 1970, when he appeared on the cover of *Sports Illustrated* next to the tagline "The Toughest Chicano." That fall, Kapp led the Vikings to the NFL title, but the team then lost to the AFL champion Kansas City Chiefs, 23-7, in Super Bowl IV. Kapp signed with the Boston Patriots in 1970, but when they asked him to take a pay cut, Kapp denounced the standard player contract as unconstitutional, and sued the NFL. The ensuing court fight ended his pro career. Soon afterward, Kapp began to appear on television and in films.

Although Kapp lacked experience, he was hired as a coach at Cal in 1982. He compiled an unimpressive 20–34–1 record in his five seasons at the helm of his alma mater, but he is remembered for coaching the Golden Bears when they pulled off a stunning 25–20 win over archrival Stanford in 1982, with what is referred to simply as "The Play." Trailing 20–19 with four seconds left in the game, Cal made five laterals and returned a kickoff 57 yards for the game-winning touchdown as the Stanford band marched onto the field. Nearly 25 years later, "The Play" is still shown nationwide on numerous sports highlight shows.

KEY DATES

1938 Born in Santa Fe, New Mexico, on March 19.

1959 Plays quarterback for the Golden Bears at the Rose Bowl in Pasadena on New Year's Day.

1964 Leads the Canadian Football League's British Columbia Lions to the Grey Cup.

1970 Leads the Minnesota Vikings to Super Bowl IV on January 11, losing to the Kansas City Chiefs, 23–7.

1982 Becomes head football coach at Cal.

Further reading: Klobuchar, Jim. *Knights and Knaves of Autumn: 40 Years of Pro Football and the Minnesota Vikings.* Cambridge, MN: Adventure Publications, 2000.
http://www.joekapp.com (Kapp's own Web site).

KID GAVILAN

Boxer

Kid Gavilan, one of the greatest Latino fighters ever, thrilled audiences with his legendary "bolo" punch, an arm circle followed by an uppercut that sometimes lifted opponents off their feet. Gavilan won 107 fights in a 15-year career.

Early life

Born Gerardo Gonzalez in 1926 in Camaguey, Cuba, Gavilan started developing his boxing skills long before he even knew what boxing was. As a child, Gavilan worked in sugar plantations. The circular sweeping motion he used to cut sugarcane with a machete was the same motion he would later use to punch his opponents.

At age 12, he competed in his first amateur fight. A team of boxing promoters saw him fight in Havana, Cuba, and took him to the United States to train. One of them, Fernando Balido, owned a café named El Gavilan—Spanish for "hawk"—and gave Gavilan the same nickname.

▼ ***Kid Gavilan poses before a fight against Peter Waterman in London, England, in April 1956. Gavilan won the bout in 10 rounds.***

KEY DATES

1926 Born in Camaguey, Cuba, on January 6.

1943 Turns professional.

1949 Loses his first world title bout against Sugar Ray Robinson in Philadelphia, Pennsylvania.

1951 Wins world welterweight title in New York City.

1990 Inducted into the International Boxing Hall of Fame.

2003 Dies of a heart attack in Florida.

Boxing success

After fighting 60 amateur bouts, Kid Gavilan defeated Antonio Diaz in his first professional fight on June 5, 1943. On July 11, 1949, Gavilan fought for the first time for the world welterweight title against Sugar Ray Robinson in Philadelphia, Pennsylvannia. The fight lasted a grueling 15 rounds, but ended in defeat for Gavilan. The Cuban would have to wait two more years to fight for the title again. On that day, Gavilan defeated Johnny Bratton in New York in another 15-round thriller. Gavilan successfully defended his title seven times.

By 1954, Gavilan decided to move up in weight and try his hand at the middleweight title. On April 2 he lost his middleweight title challenge against Carl "Bobo" Olson. Just seven months later, he also lost his welterweight title to Johnny Saxon in one of the most controversial boxing decisions in history. Even though 19 of 21 sports reporters at the fight thought Gavilan had won, the judges awarded the fight to Saxon. Many believe the fight was fixed.

Sad end

Gavilan continued fighting for four more years. At the end of his career, he had never lost by knockout and had been knocked down only twice. By the time Gavilan was inducted into the International Boxing Hall of Fame in 1990, his $2 million career earnings were gone. Although Gavilan married several times and fathered two children, he died estranged from his family in Florida.

Further reading: www.ibhof.com/gavilan.htm (biography). www.cyberboxingzone.com/boxing/kidgav.htm (Gavilan's boxing record).

LABOR ORGANIZATIONS

The history of Latino labor organizations is complex, and many of the facts are open to a wide range of different interpretations. One thing is clear, however: The working conditions and social status of Hispanic Americans have improved since unionization began in the late-19th century.

Exploitation

The annexation in 1848 by the United States of approximately one-half of Mexico's territory turned tens of thousands of residents of the Southwest overnight into U.S. citizens. Although their rights were theoretically guaranteed by the Treaty of Guadalupe Hidalgo, in practice Mexican Americans were regarded as an economic underclass by their new compatriots, and exploited accordingly. Their treatment was unfair, but they were powerless to prevent the abuses. Having been accustomed to much lower pay than that earned by people doing comparable work in the United States, they were attractive to U.S. employers. Their wages, while high by Mexican standards, were lower than the cost of living in the United States. Many Mexican Americans were thus caught in a classic poverty trap: They lived to work, rather than worked to live.

Their plight was made worse by the ease with which they could be identified as foreigners in their new environment: They often looked different, and spoke only Spanish among people who negotiated in English. As a result, they were at a disadvantage to make deals that would improve their lot, and were obvious candidates for exploitation: If the workforce needed to be reduced, it was often the Mexican Americans who were fired.

Rejection

Mexican Americans in the United States could probably have eased, if not actually solved, their problems by joining unions, but many established U.S. labor organizations would not have them. The largest such body, the American Federation of Labor (AFL), represented craftspeople, and was reluctant to admit into its ranks vast numbers of people who worked mainly as farm laborers, an activity that was categorized as "unskilled."

Latino and Latina garment workers in New York protest the 1994 NAFTA agreement, which they feared would cost U.S. jobs.

KEY DATES

1848	Treaty of Guadalupe Hidalgo.
1903	Sugar-beet workers strike in Ventura, California.
1917	Strike by Mexican American mine workers in Bisbee, Arizona.
1928	Strike by La Union de Trabajadores del Valle Imperial (The Imperial Valley Workers Union) in California.
1933	Strike by Latino cotton pickers in San Joaquin Valley, California.
1935	National Labor Relations Act (NLRA)—"the Wagner Act"—passed into law by U.S. Congress.
1942	Introduction of the Bracero Program.
1947	Taft-Hartley Act weakens NLRA.
1962	National Farm Workers Association (NFWA) union founded; it later becomes the UFW (United Farm Workers).
1964	Bracero Program ends.
1965	UFW instigates Delano grape growers strike in California.
1994	Implementation of NAFTA agreement.

That was the stated objection, but there were at least two other reasons for the exclusion of Mexican Americans from the AFL. One was racist: They were regarded as nonwhite. The other was the fear that the low wages Mexican Americans were prepared to accept would cost Anglo-Americans their jobs. From time to time, the prophecy fulfilled itself. When AFL members took industrial action, Mexicans and Mexican Americans were sometimes hired as strikebreakers. Such incidents reinforced preexistent prejudices on both sides, and further damaged already poor race relations.

Mutualistas

Unable to join established mainstream unions, Mexican Americans formed collectives of their own. The earliest such cooperatives were the *mutualistas* (mutual aid societies) that emerged in Texas in the mid-19th century, and soon spread to all the major cities of the Southwest and Midwest. *Mutualistas* helped Hispanic people orient themselves in an alien society. They offered help to Mexican Americans with education, health care, and insurance coverage. They also arranged legal assistance for Latinos and Latinas who had been defamed or accused of crimes, or who faced deportation to Mexico. The strength of the *mutualistas* was that they increased the Mexican American sense of community; their weakness was that they operated only locally.

Growing agitation

The *mutualistas* highlighted the need for more formal labor organizations, and paved the way for their creation. Among the most prominent worker bodies to emerge in the late-19th century was the Unión Federal Mexicana (Mexican Federal Union), which represented laborers on the rapidly expanding U.S. railroad network.

Mexican American labor organizations became increasingly proficient at protecting and furthering the interests of their members. In 1903, for example, an organized strike by sugar-beet workers in Ventura, California, led to two months of violent confrontation between growers and strikers. The employers eventually bowed to worker pressure, and granted the mainly Mexican American workforce the right to negotiate directly with the growers rather than with the Western Agriculture Contracting Company that had hired them. The moral was clear: While individuals might be powerless, group action could produce desired outcomes.

Industrial revolution

The growth of Latino union power was aided in the 1890s by the rapid industrialization of the U.S. Southwest. While Mexican Americans had been discouraged and often barred from entering established trades, the emergence of new industries enabled them to lay the foundations of their own economic power base. Few Anglo-Americans were eager to dig underground, so Mexican Americans were hired to extract valuable minerals. The most important deposit was coal, which fueled the new range of industries, and increased the economic and political power of the people who produced it. In the mid-1890s, the Western Federation of Miners was established. Chicanos made up an important segment of the mining population in the

THE PECAN SHELLERS' STRIKE

The pecan growers of San Antonio, Texas, hired more than 10,000 Mexican American workers a year to shell the nuts and pack them for shipment across the United States. Workers in the 1930s made less than $2.00 a week in crowded sweatshops without running water or toilets. Employers argued that they had an easy job: a warm place to work, time to chat with their friends, and all the free nuts they wanted to eat. They also claimed that low wages protected Mexican Americans from themselves: If they were paid more per hour, they would become lazy, work fewer hours, and waste their extra money on alcohol and other worthless items.

In 1938, at the height of the shelling season, workers at more than 100 plants walked off the job. Emma Tenayuca, a young activist, helped lead the strike. Workers won the battle but lost the war. They were successful in gaining the minimum wage required under the Fair Labor Standards Act, 25 cents per hour, but owners replaced them with machines, which they considered to be more efficient and less trouble. Mechanization of labor continues to be a tactic employed by bosses to undermine labor organization.

Southwest, and they provided the union's leadership. Another leading labor organization, the Western Federation of Miners (WFM), actively encouraged Mexican American membership.

Patchy performance

While increased union activity improved the position of Mexican American laborers in the United States, it did not solve all their problems. Indeed, isolated successes, such as the Ventura strike, distorted a much gloomier overall picture. Although the opposition of Mexican American laborers to discrimination and exploitation became more effective, much of their unionization lacked continuity. Many of their unions were formed to combat a particular abuse; once the immediate problem had been resolved, they disbanded. One of the outstanding success stories of the era was that of La Unión de Trabajadores del Valle Imperial (The Imperial Valley Workers Union), which in 1928 organized an action by cantaloupe workers in California, who struck for, and won, better pay and conditions. Typically, however, the union was never heard of again.

Employers, meanwhile, discouraged such activities by every means at their disposal, often including intimidation and violence. In 1917, for example, vigilantes hired by the owners of a mine at Bisbee, Arizona, rounded up more than 1,000 striking WFM workers and abandoned them in the desert.

Toward the slump

In the view of economists, the major factor in the relative improvement of Mexican American status in the early-20th-century labor market was the prosperity of the period, particularly in the 1920s. There was much work to be done, and it went to the people who offered to do it at the lowest price.

That all changed with the Great Depression (1929–1939), during the first five years of which unemployment rose by a factor of 8 to 12.8 million, 25 percent of the work force. With many Anglo-Americans out of work, there was a corresponding growth in antipathy to Mexican Americans, who were accused of taking their jobs. Almost 500,000 Mexican Americans were deported to Mexico, regardless of whether they were Mexican nationals or the descendants of people who became U.S. citizens in 1848.

Backlash

In response to such abuses, there was a revival of union activity by Mexican Americans who decided that the only way to survive was through collective action. They forged strong associations with the U.S. Communist Party and with established unions with communist links, most notably the Cannery and Agricultural Workers Industrial Union (CAWIU). In 1933, the CAWIU called a strike of 12,000 Latino cotton pickers in the San Joaquin Valley of California. The action lasted for several months before it was broken by a combination of government sanctions and vigilante violence.

Among the other unions that helped the Mexican American

workers' cause in the 1930s was the Congress of Industrial Organizations (CIO), which unionized many laborers in the Southwest, and its affiliated body, the Union of Mine, Mill, and Smelter Workers, which took on thousands of Hispanic employees at the metal-refining plants in El Paso, Texas.

Key legislation

Since there were so few jobs during the Great Depression, owners had the upper hand in disputes over pay and conditions. Strikes took place, but they were generally the last resort of desperate workers. Many companies allowed unions only if they themselves ran them; workers who tried to organize their own independent bodies were fired.

In an effort to halt such practices, in 1933 President Franklin D. Roosevelt obtained passage of the National Industrial Recovery Act (NIRA), which guaranteed employees the right to organize and bargain collectively. The NIRA was thwarted by corporate opposition, however, so in 1935 the U.S. Congress passed the National Labor Relations Act (NLRA), a law that effectively advanced the objectives of organized labor. It is also known as the Wagner Act for Robert Wagner, the U.S. senator appointed by Roosevelt to head the new National Labor Relations Board (NLRB) to mediate disputes.

Although the Wagner Act was a landmark in the history of U.S. labor relations, it did not immediately benefit Mexican Americans because most of them were farmworkers, a category excluded from the NLRA and Social Security.

Puerto Rico

By contrast, in Puerto Rico the Insular Labor Relations Act (ILRA), passed into law in 1945, although modeled after the NLRA, granted agricultural workers the right to organize and bargain collectively. Under the ensuing code of conduct, agricultural laborers of both sexes on the island were paid higher wages, and worked fewer hours per week in improved conditions.

César Chávez (in checked shirt, pointing) addresses a 1966 union rally in Delano, California. He successfully called for a nationwide boycott of nonunion-picked grapes.

On the U.S. mainland, the NLRA permitted urban workers to unionize, but the law was difficult to enforce. Latinos and Latinas who tried to exercise their rights still faced termination, threats, and violence.

Wartime revival

The U.S. economy recovered after the outbreak of World War II (1939–1945), as heavy industry became busy making munitions and other military equipment. When the United States entered the conflict in 1941, thousands of Anglo-American workers joined the armed forces to fight in Europe and the Pacific. Many of the jobs they vacated were filled by Mexican Americans. There was still resistance to the Latino presence, however, and the Pan-American Union was at the forefront of a campaign that persuaded the U.S. government to set up the Committee on Fair Employment Practice, which called for an end to racial discrimination in the recruitment of workers.

Invitation to return

As the war against Germany and Japan intensified, and more troops were drafted, the domestic labor shortage became acute. In 1942, an intergovernmental agreement between Mexico City and Washington, D.C., led to the introduction of the Bracero Program, a scheme that encouraged Mexicans to work in the United States. Over the 22 years of the program's existence, more than 5 million Mexicans found employment in 24 U.S. states. They were attracted by strictly defined terms of employment, guaranteed minimum wages and working hours, sanitary and affordable meals and housing, occupational safety, and exemption from military duty. Despite the undertakings, in practice the conditions were rarely honored.

After World War II, in 1947, the U.S. Congress passed the Taft-Hartley Act, which weakened the NLRA and the NLRB by allowing states to pass right-to-work laws, and by giving the president the power to end strikes if issues of national security were thought to be at stake. It allowed for forced cooling-off periods, loyalty oaths, and fines for strikers, all in an attempt to weaken collective bargaining and action. Taft-Hartley injunctions have been issued many times. For example, in 2001, President George W. Bush ended a strike by dock workers and longshoremen in which many Latinos were involved.

The lapse of the Bracero Program at the end of 1964 increased both the motivation and the freedom of Mexican Americans to organize and bargain collectively. In 1965, the United Farm Workers (UFW) union, founded three years previously by Dolores Huerta and César Chávez, began a series of legal actions on behalf of Mexican American workers. The first was the case of the Delano grape growers (*see box*). The UFW's nonviolent tactics drew support from other workers' institutions, including the AFL and the CIO, as well as from churches, students, and civil rights activists. Among the organizations that emulated the UFW approach was the Amalgamated Clothing and Textile Workers Union (ACTWU), which in 1972 organized a boycott of the Farah Manufacturing Company. The action secured improved conditions for the firm's female garment workers.

Loss of power

In the late-20th century, union membership and power declined, particularly under the administrations of presidents Ronald Reagan (1981–1989) and George H. W. Bush (1989–1993). Many of the gains made during previous decades, particularly through the militant years of the civil rights movements, were eroded. In 1981, Reagan fired 11,400 air traffic controllers and

DELANO GRAPE STRIKE

In 1962, Dolores Huerta and César Chávez left the Community Service Organization (CSO), and moved to California. In Delano, they formed their own union, the National Farm Workers Association (NFWA), the predecessor of the United Farm Workers (UFW).

In September 1965, after three years of groundwork, the NFWA voted to join a strike at Delano by Filipino grape workers belonging to the Agricultural Workers Organizing Committee (AWOC). A year later, the NFWA merged with AWOC to form the United Farm Workers Organizing Committee (UFWOC). They maintained the strike for five years.

Also in 1966, UFWOC farmworkers, guided by Huerta, completed an agreement with Schenley Wine: The contract was the first in U.S. history to be negotiated directly by workers with an agribusiness. That breakthrough resulted in landmark legislation, the 1975 Agricultural Labor Relations Act (ALRA) in California, the first law protecting farmworkers' rights to organize and collectively bargain in the continental United States.

In 2002, Huerta and UFW president Arturo Rodríguez forced California governor Gray Davis to add binding arbitration to the ALRA. Other major achievements of the UFW include the nation's first medical and pension plans for migrant farmworkers.

Dolores Huerta (right) watches intently as the California state assembly announces the outcome of its 2002 vote on proposed legislation to replace arbitrators with mediators in disputes between growers and farmworkers. The bill passed.

decertified their union, the Professional Air Traffic Controllers Organization (PATCO). Their replacements were workers without union affiliations, known by their critics as scabs. Strikes fell by 50 percent between 1980 and 1987, and there was a threefold increase in the number of nonunion workers in jobs that had previously been unionized.

Globalization

The decline of the unions was arrested in the last years of the 20th century. Their fortunes revived after the implementation of the North American Free Trade Agreement (NAFTA) in 1994. NAFTA removed trade barriers between the United States and Mexico, and in its wake there was a marked increase in the flow of immigrant workers from Mexico and other nations of Latin America to certain occupational sectors in the United States.

NAFTA was a symptom of globalization, a late-20th-century phenomenon that enabled companies to transcend national boundaries and produce their goods wherever materials and labor were cheapest. The development presented a new challenge to unions, and the most efficient of them adjusted their organizing strategies accordingly. Among the most proactive was the Farm Labor Organizing Committee (FLOC), which quickly changed its traditional focus from domestic growers to corporations and identifiable consumer products, such as Heinz pickles or Campbell's tomato soup. It organized transnationally to prevent companies from simply moving their operations from country to country at will. FLOC took the view that any abuse of the rights of workers in, for example, Mexico was not a local matter, but should be combated abroad by industrial action, if possible, or by boycotting the products of the exploitative company.

The future

By the first decade of the 21st century, Latinos had become the majority ethnic population in the United States. In some states, they are moving toward majority status. One of them, California, now has a holiday specifically devoted to a labor union leader: César Chávez Day (March 31) is a state holiday and a day of community service. The improvement in the status of Latinos within U.S. society as a whole, and in the labor market in particular, is reflected in the policy of the AFL and the CIO. Their earlier hostility to Latinos has been replaced by a recognition of the importance of migrant workers in the fabric of U.S. life. In 2001, the now amalgamated AFL–CIO called for an amnesty for all illegal Mexicans in the United States.

See also: Chávez, César; Guadalupe Hidalgo, Treaty of; Huerta, Dolores; Rodríguez, Arturo; Tenayuca, Emma

---

Further reading: Acuna, Rodolfo. *Occupied America: A History of Chicanos*. New York, NY: Pearson Longman, 2004.

Gómez-Quinones, Juan. *Mexican American Labor 1790–1990*. Albuquerque, NM: University of New Mexico Press, 1994.

Tatum, Charles M. *Chicano Popular Culture: Que hable el pueblo*. Tucson, AZ: University of Arizona Press, 2001.

http://pewhispanic.org/topics/index.php?TopicID=32 (Pew Hispanic Center research topic: Latino labor).

LAGUERRE, Enrique

Writer

Enrique Laguerre was one of Puerto Rico's leading writers. A novelist, essayist, playwright, professor, poet, and critic, Laguerre was one of the first people to link Puerto Rican nationalism to conservationism (*see box on page 16*).

Early life

Born on July 11, 1905 (some sources cite May 3, 1906), in the small northwestern mountain town of Moca, Puerto Rico, Enrique Arturo Laguerre Vélez was one of eight children of Antonia Vélez and Juan Laguerre. As a young child, Laguerre spent his time in the sugarcane fields that he would later write about in such books as *Solar Montoya* (The Montoyas' Plot of Land). Laguerre went to school in the towns of Isabela and Aguadilla. His interest in literature became obvious during his adolescence, when he began writing fiction and verse in his spare time.

In 1926, Laguerre took summer courses at the University of Puerto Rico. He took a teaching course in Aguadilla, which enabled him to teach in several schools around the island. Laguerre continued writing, beginning his first novel, *La Llamarada* (The Flare-up), in 1931. He registered at the University of Puerto Rico full time in 1934, and published the novel in the following year.

The beginning of the modern Puerto Rican novel

Many critics consider *La Llamarada* the foundation of the contemporary Puerto Rican novel. It deals with the struggles encountered by sugarcane workers under the domination of landowners—experiences that were common in the rural areas of the island. The book was very well received, and the Instituto de Literatura Puertorriqueña honored Laguerre in 1936.

Laguerre continued to study while writing; he graduated with a BA from the University of Puerto Rico in 1938, and received the Medalla Méndez Pidal recognition award for best literature student. Laguerre published his second novel, *Solar Montoya*, in 1941, and in the same year obtained a master's degree in Hispanic studies. *Solar Montoya* earned him a second award from the Instituto. It presents the socioeconomic problems that affected the agricultural zones in Puerto Rico.

In 1943, Laguerre published *El 30 de Febrero* (February 30), in which he changed his setting from the agricultural areas of Puerto Rico to the urban working-class areas of San Juan and the student residences at the University of Puerto Rico.

Laguerre started his doctoral degree at Columbia University in New York in 1949, but postponed finishing his thesis, entitled "El Ensayo en Puerto Rico" (Translation in Puerto Rico), since the university demanded that the work be written in English. Laguerre was completely opposed to the idea of writing a thesis on Hispanic studies in a language other than Spanish.

Man of many talents

Laguerre also developed an interest in writing plays, short stories, and essays. In 1944 he published *La Resentida* (Resentment), a three-act play, which opened at the Teatro de la Universidad de Puerto Rico.

Laguerre also wrote more than 20 short stories, which were published in several leading Puerto Rican magazines and newspapers, such as *Ambito, Brújula, Horizontes, Isla, El Mundo* (which collected his stories in the column "Hojas Libres"), *Puerto Rico Ilustrado, La Democracia, Alma Latina, El Diario de Puerto Rico,* and *Artes y Letras*. Among Laguerre's best known stories are "El Hombre Caído" (The Fallen Man), and "El Enemigo" (The Enemy).

Most of Laguerre's stories maintain a connection to his novels, stressing social conflicts and contrasting Puerto Rico's rural and urban societies. The characters are described in rich detail, highlighting their emotions and

KEY DATES

1905	Born in Moca, Puerto Rico, on July 11.
1935	Publishes his first novel, *La Llamarada*.
1942	Appointed professor of literature at the University of Puerto Rico.
1949	Publishes his novel, *La Resaca*; finishes his doctorate at Columbia University.
1956	Publishes *El Ceiba en Tiesto*.
1988	Retires as professor of literature.
1999	Nominated for the Nobel Prize for Literature.
2005	Accepts the Premio de Honor award from the Ateneo Puertorriqueño; dies in Carolina, Puerto Rico, on June 16.

INFLUENCES AND INSPIRATION

Enrique Laguerre believed that Puerto Rico's lack of sovereignty meant that it was very important to record the country's history and culture. He claimed that the record would be needed to form the basis of a future independent nation.

Hailed by conservationists for his outspoken advocacy of ecology in the country, Laguerre was one of the first people to link Puerto Rican nationalism to conservation. He argued that true nationalism was closely linked to an innate respect for the country's natural resources.

Laguerre was a fierce critic of the destruction of the mangroves and forests and the development of highways, housing complexes, and hotels for the rich. He argued against the building of shopping malls and for the protection of Puerto Rico's beaches. His books often dealt with important but controversial issues, such as the problems caused by industrialization and by overdevelopment.

their state of mind. Throughout his writing career, Laguerre was known by the pen names Tristán Ronda, Luis Urayoán, Motial, and Alberto Prado.

A new direction

With the publication of *La Resaca* (1949), Laguerre began a new period as a novelist, using innovative narrative techniques, such as interior monologue and flashbacks, to focus on the historical, political, and social experiences of Puerto Rico at the beginning of the 19th century. His other later publications include: *Los Dedos de la Mano* (The Fingers of the Hand; 1951); *El Laberinto* (The Labyrinth; 1959), *El Fuego y Su Aire* (The Fire and Its Air; 1970), and *Los Amos Benévolos* (The Benevolent Masters; 1976).

The teacher

Laguerre was also dedicated teacher. He was a professor at the University of Puerto Rico (1941–1988), and also taught at various universities in the United States, including the City University of New York (1969–1970). Laguerre was particularly interested in the development of his native country's education system. He worked as a research adviser to the Higher Council on Education, and as a special consultant to the Puerto Rican Department of Public Instruction.

Other interests and honors

Laguerre was a member of the Instituto de Cultura Puertorriqueña from 1955, and acted as its president in the 1970s. In 1975, the Instituto de Cultura Puertorriqueña honored Laguerre with the Premio Nacional de Literatura award. The Fundación Puertorriqueña de las Humanidades (Puerto Rican Humanities Foundation) declared Laguerre Humanist of the Year in 1985. Two years later, Laguerre became a member of the board of directors of the Centro de Bellas Artes (Center of Performing Arts), the Escuela de Artes Plásticas (School of Fine Arts), and the Centro de Estudios Avanzados (Center for Advanced Studies). Laguerre was also a founding member of the Academia Puertorriqueña de la Lengua Española (Puerto Rican Academy of the Spanish Language), and cofounder of the magazine *Palinque*. One of his greatest honors was being nominated for the Nobel Prize for Literature in 1999. The award that year went to the German novelist, Günter Grass.

Final years

On May 2, 2005, Eduardo Morales Coll, president of the Ateneo Puertorriqueño, recognized Laguerre's importance to Puerto Rico by awarding the author the Premio de Honor, the most prestigious prize given by the institution. In the same year, the film producer Ulises Rodríguez and the director Papo Nazario made a documentary entitled *Enrique Laguerre: Un Hombre Consciente de su Identidad* (Enrique Laguerre: A Man Aware of His Identity). The film included a detailed interview with the author, and testimonials by artists who were close to him. Laguerre remained active until his death in 2005 at age 99. He continued to publish articles of cultural, social, and political content in leading Puerto Rican newspapers such as *El Vocero.*

Influence

Enrique Laguerre is widely regarded as one of the most prolific Puerto Rican writers, and has influenced generations of Hispanic novelists. His experiments with new narrative styles and his concern for social issues made his novels, plays, and short stories classics in modern Latin American literature.

Further reading: http://books.guardian.co.uk/obituaries/story/0,,1518701,00.html (newspaper obituary).

LA INDIA

Musician

Puerto Rican–born musician La India, whose real name is Linda Viero Cabellero, is one of the best-known and most widely respected contemporary salsa singers. Her strong, distinctive voice, and assertive and independent personality have made her a prominent role model for Latinas all over the United States.

Early life

Born in Rio Piedras, Puerto Rico, on March 9, 1970, La India was raised in the South Bronx, New York City. As a child, her dark, exotic looks won her the nickname "India," which she later adopted as her recording name. La India grew up listening to a diverse range of music, from Celia Cruz to Ella Fitzgerald. She began singing and found that when she performed she was able to cast off the shyness that plagued her as a child. At school La India became friends with "Little" Louie Vega, who organized house parties in the local neighborhood. La India performed at these occasions. After a brief time modeling, aged 16 La India joined the pioneering Latin hip-hop group TKA as a backing singer.

From hip-hop to salsa princess

In 1989 La India married Vega, who was a well-known producer and DJ (the couple divorced in 1996). She recorded her first album, the freestyle *Breaking Night*. Unhappy with attempts to mold her into the "Hispanic Madonna," La India began to experiment musically in order to find her own style.

In the early 1990s, La India collaborated with the esteemed bandleader Eddie Palmieri, who wrote and coproduced her first salsa album, *Llego La India via Eddie Palmieri (*1992). The album was widely acclaimed and helped generate new interest in salsa.

KEY DATES

1970	Born in Rio Piedras, Puerto Rico, on March 9.
1985	Joins Latin hip-hop group TKA.
1989	Releases debut album, *Breaking Night.*
1992	Releases first salsa album. *Llego La India via Eddie Palmieri.*
1999	Releases *Sola,* a tribute to the singer La Lupe.

▲ ***La India is a leading member of the modern Nuyorican (New York–Puerto Rican) movement that pays tribute to the rich Puerto Rican culture and its New York urban roots.***

Throughout the 1990s, La India continued to experiment with Latin and Afro-Caribbean sounds. By the mid-1990s she was one of the leading Latina singers and was widely touted as the "Princess of Salsa." The feminist stance of many of her lyrics and her tough but glamorous image also made her a role model for many Hispanic American women. She recorded several albums, including *Yemaya y Ochun* (1994), an album of salsa dance tunes inspired by traditional Lukumí (Santeria) chants. In 1996 she collaborated with the legendary Latin jazz musician Tito Puente on the album *Jazzin'*, and in 1999 released the album *Sola*, a tribute to the iconic Cuban American singer La Lupe. A much respected artist, La India has been nominated for several awards, including two Grammys.

See also: Cruz, Celia; Palmieri, Eddie; Puente, Tito; Vega, "Little" Louie

Further reading: Obejas, Achy. "La India: She Adds a Feminist Fillip to Salsa's Macho Beat." *Chicago Tribune*, October 31, 1997.
www.geocities.com/laindiasworld/india.html (biography).

LARRAZOLO, Octaviano
Politician

Octaviano Larrazolo was the first Hispanic American to be elected as a U.S. senator. He campaigned for the protection of the rights of Hispanic immigrants throughout the early 20th century.

Early life
Larrazolo was born in El Valle de San Bartolo, Mexico, in 1859. He grew up in a comfortable upper-class family. Both his mother and his grandfather were well educated and wealthy.

In 1870 Larrazolo left Mexico for what was then known as Arizona Territory. (This was the southern portion of both the modern states of New Mexico and Arizona.) He moved to the United States under the guidance of Reverend Salpointe, the archbishop of Santa Fe, who sponsored his education. Larrazolo excelled in English and public speaking.

Professional career
After graduating, Larrazolo left for El Paso County, Texas. There he married Rosalia Cobos in 1881 and became a public-school teacher. In 1883 Larrazolo's father and first child died, and the direction of his life changed: He stopped teaching and decided to become an attorney. In 1884 Larrazolo became a United States citizen and a clerk at El Paso's District Court. He passed the bar in 1887. In 1889 he was elected as the district attorney of El Paso.

Known as the "silver-tongued orator," Larrazolo was also involved in civic and public affairs across the Southwest. Despite an initial failure to become a delegate member of Congress for the Democratic Party, Larrazolo continued to fight for better education for Hispanic Americans. His efforts paid off and he was appointed to the Board of Regents at New Mexico's Normal University in 1906. Soon after, Larrazolo changed his political platform, and was eventually elected as the first Republican governor of New Mexico in 1918.

◀ ***Octaviano Larrazolo used his political position and skills as a public speaker to promote bilingual education.***

KEY DATES

1859 Born in El Valle de San Bartolo (now part of Allende), Chihuahua, Mexico, on December 7.

1870 Moves to Arizona Territory.

1906 Appointed to Board of Regents of New Mexico's, Normal University.

1918 Elected as first Republican governor of New Mexico.

1926 Selected as a Republican candidate for House of Representatives.

1928 First Hispanic American elected to the Senate.

1930 Dies in Albuquerque, New Mexico, on April 7.

Groundbreaking achievements
By 1926 Larrazolo became a Republican candidate for the state House of Representatives. Two years later he became the first Latin American member of the U.S. Senate.

As he had done as district attorney, Larrazolo continued to work diligently to protect the rights of Hispanic American immigrants. He also fought selflessly for progress and against bossism. Bossism was a form of local politics that was dominated by a single powerful figure who controlled and profited from all aspects of public life.

Having been elected as the first senator of Mexican descent, Larrazolo fought for bilingual education, immigrant and labor rights, and women's suffrage. Larrazolo also worked on issues concerning problems related to the ceding of federally held public lands in the newly formed Southwestern states. He died in 1930.

Further reading: Zannos, Susan. *Octaviano Larrazolo*. Hockessin, DE: Mitchell Lane Publishers, 2004. http://www.montes-family.com/octaviano.shtml (biography of Larrazola and his family).

LAVIERA, Jesús
Poet

Jesús "Tato" Laviera is one of the leading Nuyorican literary figures. (Nuyoricans are people of Puerto Rican descent who live in New York City.) Laviera uses two languages and two cultural traditions to produce his poetry and plays.

The Nuyorican turn

Laviera was born Jesús Laviera Sánchez in Santurce, Puerto Rico, in 1951. His father, whose family came to the island from Maracaibo, Venezuela, was a contractor. His mother was a very religious housewife. In 1960, Laviera moved with his mother and sister to New York City, settling on the Lower East Side. Soon after, as Laviera began fifth grade, the seeds of his career as a poet were planted. A nun at school changed his name to Abraham. When he became a writer, Laviera took a third name, Tato. This third name change reflected how he felt stuck between the two cultures of his upbringing.

During the 1970s, Laviera attended Cornell University and Brooklyn College, but did not graduate. He taught basic writing skills in various educational programs including at Rutgers University, New Jersey. In 1979 Laviera joined the Puerto Rican Studies Department at Rutgers.

La Carreta Made a U-Turn was published the same year and made a substantial contribution to Nuyorican poetry. Written as the fourth act of a classic Puerto Rican play, *La Carreta*, in it Laviera argues that the destiny of Puerto Ricans in New York is not to return to the island, but to continue creating a new Puerto Rican culture in New York, outgrowing class, racial, linguistic, and political barriers.

Poet of the people

As a poet, Laviera considers himself a historian of the Hispanic American community of New York. In 1982 Laviera's *Enclave* put together a portfolio of the characters, real and imaginary, that populate Manhattan's El Barrio (also known as Spanish Harlem), underscoring the influences of the Nuyorican community. In 1986 *AmeRícan* showed Laviera's eye for words: An AmeRícan is a Puerto Rican in the United States in the process of negotiating equitable social conditions that would allow him or her to become a standard American. In 1988 *Mainstream Ethics / Ética Corriente* took Laviera's views one step further: Hispanic Americans constitute the ethical salvation of the United States, for their culture can only enrich that of the country in general.

▲ ***Tato Laviera uses both English and Spanish in his poetry to form hybrid Spanglish phrases. A Latino of African descent, Laviera also has strong links with the African American community.***

KEY DATES

1951	Born in Santurce, Puerto Rico, on September 5.
1960	Family moves to New York.
1979	Publishes his most important book, *La Carreta Made a U-Turn*. Invited to the White House Gathering of Poets.
1982	Wins American Books Award for *Enclave*.

Further reading: Rivero Marín, Rosanna. *Janus Identities and Forked Tongues: Two Caribbean Writers in the United States.* New York, NY: Peter Lang, 2004.
http://s91320770.onlinehome.us/laviera.html (biography).

LAVOE, Hector

Singer

One of the most famous figures in salsa music, Hector Lavoe was among the first singers to fuse salsa's Caribbean identity with the 1970s' urban music scene of New York City.

The New York sound

Lavoe was born Hector Juan Pérez in Ponce, Puerto Rico, in 1946. He belonged to a large and impoverished but musical family of singers and guitar players. Lavoe's mother and his older brother died when he was a child. Lavoe was therefore most influenced by his father, Luis, who was his first musical tutor.

Lavoe went to the Juan Morel Campos School of Music in Ponce to study the saxophone, yet singing was his true calling. At 14, he began singing professionally. Against his father's advice, Lavoe quit school and in 1963 went to New York City determined to become famous as a singer.

Once in New York, he was drawn into the musical circles of the Lower East Side and El Barrio, where the first Nuyorican generation was coming of age. Lavoe brought a fresh influence from traditional Puerto Rican music. In 1966 Lavoe met Willie Colón, a young Nuyorican bandleader. In 1967 the pair released their first record, *El Malo* (The Bad One). By 1973 the two had released a total of 14 albums and had defined the salsa sound coming from New York. Colon's harsh and daring trombone complemented Lavoe's street style and bravado.

The voice

For personal and professional reasons, Colón dissolved the alliance with Lavoe in 1973, but did not completely break off connections with him. It was Lavoe's time to assume the leadership of the band, and Colón eventually became his producer. Lavoe rose to the occasion. His first solo recording in 1975, *La Voz* (The Voice), and his second in 1976, *De Ti Depende* (It Depends on You), set him on course to stardom. Lavoe had achieved what he set out to accomplish when he left Puerto Rico.

Because of his excessive lifestyle and a battle with drug addiction, Lavoe had to interrupt his musical career in 1977. In 1978 he came back with a strong record, *Comedia* (Comedy), the last of his notable recordings.

KEY DATES

1946	Born in Ponce, Puerto Rico, on September 30.
1963	Moves to New York City in search of fame and fortune.
1966	Forms groundbreaking partnership with Willie Colon.
1975	Begins solo career and rise to stardom.
1993	Dies in New York City on June 29.

▲ ***Hector Lavoe was the greatest salsa singer of his generation but his career was ended by drug abuse.***

Decline

From the 1980s to his death in 1993, Lavoe's life was tinged with tragedy. The popularity of salsa music was on the decline, and Lavoe suffered from a series of personal problems, including the death of his 17-year-old son, and his own abuse of drugs. As a result, Lavoe's music suffered as did his mental and physical condition. In 1988 Lavoe canceled a comeback concert in Puerto Rico and later attempted suicide by jumping from the 10th floor of a hotel. He never fully recovered from his injuries. Lavoe died in obscurity in 1993.

See also: Colón, Willie

Further reading: Pérez, José, and Mejías, Antonio. *The Hector Lavoe Story: 1946–1993*. New York, NY: Lavoe and Infante, 1997.
www.musicofpuertorico.com/en/hector_lavoe.html (Biography).

LEAL, Luis

Academic

A prolific scholar of Mexican, Latin American, and Chicano literature, Luis Leal has achieved international recognition through six decades of academic research, teaching, and writing.

Leal was born in 1907, the eldest child of affluent ranchers in northern Mexico. He graduated from Northwestern University, Evanston, Illinois, in 1940, and received a master's degree in Spanish from the University of Chicago in 1941. His doctoral studies were postponed from 1943 to 1945, when he saw active duty in World War II (1939–1945). Leal then completed his graduate work and received a PhD from the University of Chicago in 1950.

KEY DATES

1907 Born in Linares, Nuevo León, on September 17.

1955 Publishes *México: Civilizaciones y Culturas.*

1973 Publishes *Mexican-American Literature: A Historical Perspective.*

1991 Awarded the Orden Mexicana del Aguila Azteca, in Mexico City, Mexico.

1997 Awarded the National Humanities Medal, in Washington, D.C.

A dedicated scholar

Leal's doctoral thesis demonstrated how fictional elements within Spanish colonial chronicles constitute the origins of the Mexican short story form. He continued to investigate the relationship between history and literature throughout his career as a university professor. Between 1951 and 1976, Leal held teaching and research positions at the University of Chicago, the University of Mississippi, Emory University in Atlanta, Georgia, and the University of Illinois, where he mentored more than 50 doctoral students. Leal became a highly regarded scholar of the Mexican short story with the publication of *Breve Historia del Cuento Mexicano* in 1956. He contributed to the formation and development of Chicano literary criticism with the publication of his seminal study *Mexican-American Literature: A Historical Perspective* in 1973.

After retirement from the University of Illinois in 1976, Leal relocated to California, where he began to teach courses in the Department of Chicano Studies at the University of California, Berkeley. In the early 1980s Leal was named a senior research fellow in the Center for Chicano Studies at the University of California, Santa Barbara (UCSB).

▼ ***Luis Leal is one of the most respected scholars of Hispanic American literature.***

Leal's legacy

In recognition of his academic achievements and leadership, Leal received the Orden Mexicana del Aguila Azteca (Order of the Aztec Eagle), Mexico's highest honor for a foreign national, in 1991. President Bill Clinton honored Leal by awarding him the National Humanities Medal in 1997. Leal's legacy continues through the Luis Leal Endowed Chair at UCSB, which was inaugurated in 1995. In 1998 Leal was elected to the National Academy of Spanish Language. Still working at the age of 95, Leal published *Myths and Legends of Mexico* in 2002.

Further reading: García, Mario T. *Luis Leal: An Autobiography.* Austin, TX: University of Texas Press, 2000.
http://www.chicst.ucsb.edu/chair (Luis Leal Endowed Chair Web site).

LEAÑOS, John Jota
Artist

John Jota Leaños is one of the United States's leading multimedia and digital artists. His challenging and often controversial artworks—encompassing performance pieces, Internet works, and digital murals—address contemporary issues, such as war, technology, torture, and terrorism. He often works in collaboration with other Hispanic American artists, notably in the collective Los Cybrids: La Raza Techno-Crítica.

Cutting edge

John Jota Leaños was born in Pomona, California, in 1969, the son of Mexican American and Italian American parents. After high school, he went to San Francisco State University, where he graduated with a bachelor's degree in humanities in 1993. He later returned to the university to take a master's in photography, graduating in 2000. From 2002 to 2003, he was a fellow of the Center for Arts in Society at Carnegie Mellon University in Pittsburgh, Pennsylvania, and subsequently became assistant professor of Chicana/o Studies, Arizona State University, in Tempe.

During this short time, Leaños has gained a nationwide reputation—even notoriety—for his cutting-edge work. In 2002, he was featured in the Whitney Museum Biennial, one of the most prestigious showcases for contemporary U.S. art. A series of high-profile pieces, including the digital mural *Humaquina: Manifest Tech-Destiny* (2001) and the poster campaign *Public Memorial of Pat Tillman*, have bought him wider media attention. In 2005 Leaños was appointed artist-in-residence at the University of California's Center for Chicano Studies in Santa Barbara.

Art

In his work, Leaños often reflects and draws upon Mexican culture. For instance, in the piece *Los ABCs: ¡Que Vivan los Muertos* (2005), screened at the 2006 Sundance Film Festival, he uses the bold, colorful imagery of the Mexican Day of the Dead to create a darkly humorous attack on war and militarism. His use of public art, from the traditional poster to digital mural and Internet artwork, as a means of making a political comment, stands him in a long tradition in Mexican art, most notably with the work of the muralist Diego Rivera (1886–1957).

More recently, Leaños's strong opposition to U.S. military campaigns overseas has often drawn him into controversy. His manipulation of the disturbing images of torture at the Army internment facility at Abu Ghraib Prison in Baghdad, Iraq, and of a photograph of the former NFL football player and U.S. Ranger Pat Tillman, who was killed by friendly fire in Afghanistan in 2003, have been considered by some as courageous, timely attacks on U.S. militarism and the media's glorification of war. For others, however, such works are lurid and unpatriotic.

▲ A self-portrait of John Jota Leaños. An American of Mexican and Italian ancestry, Leaños says that he belongs to a tribe called Los Mixtupos.

KEY DATES

1969 Born in Pomona, California, around this time.

2003 Appointed assistant professor of Chicana/o Studies, Arizona State University, Tempe.

2004 Produces the poster campaign *Public Memorial of Pat Tillman*, in honor of a former professional football player killed by friendly fire in Afghanistan.

Further reading: www.leanos.net (Leanos's Web site). http://www.cybrids.com/core.html (Los Cybrids collective).

LEBRÓN, Lolita
Political Activist

Lolita Lebrón is one of the best-known and possibly one of the most controversial Puerto Rican nationalists. She was jailed for life in 1954 for opening fire on more than 200 U.S. congressmen in the House of Representatives. She was released from prison in 1979. Lebrón continues to campaign for Puerto Rican independence in her native country.

Early life

Born in 1919 in Lares, Puerto Rico, Dolores Lebrón Sotomayor was the daughter of a coffee plantation foreman and a housewife. Born into very poor circumstances, Lebrón drew attention from a young age because of her remarkable good looks. As a teenager, Lebrón was crowned "Queen of the Flowers of May" in an annual beauty contest held in Lares. Lebrón also had a good brain, however, and was a vehement supporter of Puerto Rican independence from the United States.

Moving to America

In the 1940s Lebrón had a daughter out of wedlock. She moved to the United States, leaving her daughter, Gladys, behind with her family. Expecting a better life with greater opportunities, Lebrón was greeted instead with signs stating: "No blacks, no dogs, no Puerto Ricans." Lebrón worked as a seamstress during the day and went to school at night.

In New York Lebrón became influenced by Dr. Pedro Albizu Campos, leader of the Puerto Rican Nationalist Party (*see box on page 24*). Lebrón attended many Nationalist Party meetings in the city. After Albizu Campos's arrest in 1950 for sedition and conspiracy to assassinate U.S. president Harry S. Truman, Lebrón and Albizu Campos's other supporters continued to campaign for their country's freedom. When the governor of Puerto Rico, Luis Muñoz Marín, signed the Commonwealth Pact in 1952, they felt a great sense of betrayal and decided to show the U.S. government how far they would go to achieve their aims.

Terrorist or activist?

On March 1, 1954, Lebrón, along with Andrés Figueroa Cordero and Irving Flores Rodrigues, bought single tickets and traveled to the U.S. House of Representatives. Making

▲ ***In 1954 former beauty queen and Puerto Rican activist Lolita Lebrón was sentenced to life imprisonment for shooting U.S. politicians in the House of Representatives; she served 25 years.***

their way to the visitors' gallery, they opened fire on the representatives gathered there to debate an immigration bill. In the ensuing gunfire, five congressmen were injured, one of them seriously. Lebrón shouted "Viva Puerto Rico libre" (Long live free Puerto Rico), and unfurled a Puerto Rican flag. She was arrested, and the police later found a note in her purse stating: "The United States of America are betraying the sacred principles of mankind in their continuous subjugation of my country."

Lebrón was initially sentenced to death, although this was commuted to life imprisonment. She was sent to Alderson, West Virginia, to serve her sentence. Lebrón's actions and her glamorous appearance made her a popular figure with Puerto Rican nationalists, who hailed her as a

INFLUENCES AND INSPIRATION

Lolita Lebrón grew up believing that Puerto Rico should be independent. In the 1940s, she moved to the United States; like many Puerto Ricans, Lebrón experienced discrimination there. She said that she arrived in America expecting paradise, but the reality was very different: Puerto Ricans were treated little better than dogs. In New York she corresponded with Pedro Albizu Campos, the nationalist leader, also known as "El Maestro."

As a student at Harvard University, Albizu Campos had become interested in the Indian and Irish independence movements. After he graduated, Albizu Campos returned to Puerto Rico, where he joined the newly formed Puerto Rican Nationalist Party in 1924, rising to become its president in 1930. Albizu Campos's commitment to his country's independence made him enemies, and the San Juan Federal Court ordered his and other nationalist leaders' arrests for "seditious conspiracy to overthrow the U.S. government in Puerto Rico." Although a jury of seven Puerto Ricans and five Americans found the activists not guilty, the judge ordered a new jury to be chosen. Made up of 10 Americans and two Puerto Ricans, it subsequently found the nationalist leader guilty. In 1937, the Boston court of appeals upheld the verdict, and Albizu Campos and other leading nationalists were sent to the federal penitentiary in Atlanta, Georgia. The activist returned to Puerto Rico in 1947, but was jailed again after the 1950 Jayuya Uprising and attempted assassination of President Truman by nationalists Oscar Collazo and Griselio Torresola. In 1951 Albizu Campos was sentenced to 72 years in prison. Although the Puerto Rican governor, Luis Muñoz Marín, pardoned him in 1953, the pardon was revoked following Lebrón's shooting of politicians in the U.S. House of Representatives. Albizu Campos later claimed that radiation experiments had been carried out on him in prison. He was pardoned again by Marín in 1964, but died in 1965.

hero. However, critics called Lebrón's actions cowardly and labeled her a terrorist. In prison Lebrón found religion, and claimed that God spoke to her regularly, leading some people to claim that she was insane. In 1977 Lebrón was allowed to attend the funeral of her 36-year-old daughter, Gladys, who had thrown herself from a moving car while her own young daughter, Irene, watched. Two years later, under international pressure, President Jimmy Carter ordered the release of Lebrón, Cordero, and Rodrigues: Cordero died of cancer before leaving jail, however.

Returning to Puerto Rico, Lebrón was greeted by many nationalists as a hero. She continued to campaign for independence and made several visits to Cuba, where she became friends with Fidel Castro. Eight years after her release, Lebrón married Sergio Irizarry, a doctor who had visited her in prison: The couple live in Puerto Rico. Lebrón's granddaughter, Irene Vilar, wrote *A Message from God in the Atomic Age*, a book about Lebrón and the history of her family.

In 2000, Lebrón participated in protests against the U.S. Navy's use of the island of Vieques for bombing practice. On June 26, 2001, Lebrón was arrested for trespassing on Vieques; she was sentenced to 60 days in prison. On May 1, 2003, the U.S. Navy moved out of Vieques and turned over its facilities to the local government of Puerto Rico.

KEY DATES

1919 Born in Lares, Puerto Rico.

1940s Moves to New York with her family.

1950 Albizu Campos jailed for conspiring to assassinate President Harry Truman.

1952 Luis Muñoz Marín signs the Commonwealth Pact.

1954 With Andrés Figueroa Cordero and Irving Flores Rodrigues, Lebrón opens fire on congressmen in the House of Representatives, injuring five people; sentenced to death but sentence changed to life imprisonment.

1979 Granted clemency by President Jimmy Carter; released from prison and begins campaigning.

2001 Sentenced to 60 days in prison for protests against U.S. bombing on the island of Vieques.

See also: Albizu Campos, Pedro; Muñoz Marín, Luis

Further reading: Vilar, Irene. *A Message from God in the Atomic Age.* New York, NY: Pantheon Books, 1992.
http://www.yasminhernandez.com/lolitastory.html (article).

LEGUIZAMO, John

Actor, Comedian

John Leguizamo has combined comedy and drama throughout his career. He works in film, theater, and television at a steady pace, sometimes appearing in four to five motion pictures a year. Leguizamo's wide acting range is best exemplified by his roles in Baz Luhrmann's *Romeo + Juliet* (1996), in which he played Juliet's hot-blooded cousin Tybalt, and *Moulin Rouge!* (2001). Leguizamo was nominated for a Screen Actors Guild award for his role as French painter Henri Toulouse-Lautrec in *Moulin Rouge!*

Early life

Leguizamo was born in 1964 in Bogotá, the capital city of Colombia. His father was Puerto Rican and his mother a Colombian. When he was four, the family moved to Jackson Heights, a Hispanic American neighborhood in Queens, New York.

As a high-school student Leguizamo wrote comedy material and tried it out before his classmates. Voted as "Most Talkative" student, Leguizamo graduated and then attended New York University, majoring in theater. He was the only Latino in his drama class. Leguizamo also attended Lee Strasberg's Actors' Studio for one day. The following day Strasberg died. Leguizamo saw the funny side, quipping, "I have that effect on people."

KEY DATES

1964	Born in Bogotá, Colombia, on July 22.
1968	Moves to Queens, New York.
1984	Debuts in *Miami Vice*.
2001	Stars in *Moulin Rouge!*

Performing well

Leguizamo started working the comedy club circuit in New York City. Although he was concentrating on stage work, his television debut came in 1984 with a small part in *Miami Vice*. A series of minor roles followed, in films such as *Casualties of War* (1989), *Die Hard 2: Die Harder* (1990), and *Regarding Henry* (1991).

In 1991 Leguizamo's off-Broadway show *Mambo Mouth* was broadcast by HBO. He earned an Obie and an Outer Critics Circle award as well as a Cable ACE citation. In 1993 *Spic-O-Rama*, a follow-up show in which he poked fun at Hispanic American stereotypes, was almost as successful, playing in New York and Chicago and winning a Drama Desk Award and four Cable ACEs. Two years later, a brief stint in the Emmy-nominated television series *House of Buggin* led to more positive reviews.

Award winner

In 1998 Leguizamo debuted on Broadway with *Freak*, a one-man show turned into an HBO film by Spike Lee. His performance brought him an Emmy award in 1999. Subsequently Leguizamo has combined his stage work with a steady string of films, gaining a reputation as a solid performer. In 1999 he embraced a new role, serving as executive producer for *Joe the King*, which won the screenwriting award at the Sundance Film Festival. Leguizamo has also done voice work for film, as in the animated feature *Ice Age* (2002), in which he played Sid, a wise-cracking sloth.

Further reading: Allison, Amy. *John Leguizamo*. Philadelphia, PA: Chelsea House Publishers, 2002.

◀ ***John Leguizamo performs his one-man show in Seattle, Washington, in 2001.***

LEÓN, Tania
Composer

▲ ***Tania León has conducted the music for several television shows and theater productions, including* The Wiz, *an urban version of* The Wizard of Oz.**

Cuban-born Tania León is an internationally respected composer, conductor, and professor of music. León is of mixed African, Spanish, French, and Chinese heritage and arrived in the United States in 1967. She has said that although she is proud of her ethnic background, she considers herself to be an American composer, saying that "the Americas encompass North America, Central America, South America, and the Caribbean."

Early life

Born in Havana, Cuba, in 1943, León was the daughter of Oscar León Mederos and Dora Ferran. From the age of four, León studied music and dreamed of becoming a concert pianist. She went to the Carlos Alfredo Peyrellado Conservatory, where she was taught the music of such Cuban composers as Ignacio Cervantes (1847–1905) and Ernesto Lecuona (1896–1963), as well as that of classical European masters. León was also exposed to the popular Cuban music of Arsenio Rodríguez and Pérez Prado at local dance halls. During this time she began to compose her own music, producing bossa novas and boleros. In 1960, after graduating from the conservatory, León began working in Havana as a pianist. In 1964 she was appointed musical director of a Havana television station.

The pursuit of music

In 1967 León moved to the United States, initially taking an accounting job in New York while she continued to play and compose music. In 1969 she met Arthur Mitchell, the founder of the Dance Theater of Harlem. Mitchell invited León to become the theater's musical accompanist. Greatly impressed by León's musical skill, Mitchell made her musical director. He also encouraged León to write original music scores. In 1973 she wrote *Tones*, her first ballet for Mitchell. León traveled extensively with the dance company; she was also given the opportunity to conduct orchestras both at home and abroad.

KEY DATES

1943 Born in Havana, Cuba, on May 14.

1967 Immigrates to the United States.

1969 Becomes musical director of the Dance Theater of Harlem.

1973 Writes first ballet, *Tones*.

1994 Made full professor at Brooklyn College Conservatory.

Academic career

While working with Mitchell, León continued her studies, first at the Juilliard School of Music in New York and then at New York University from which she gained a BA and then an MA in composition.

During the following decades, León cemented her reputation as a conductor and innovative composer. She was guest conductor with several prestigious orchestras, including the National Symphony Orchestra of South Africa, Johannesburg, and the New York Philharmonic.

A talented teacher, León has taught composition at the Brooklyn College Conservatory since the mid-1980s. She became a professor there in 1994 and was named Tow Distinguished Professor in 2000.

See also: Prado, Pérez; Rodríguez, Arsenio

Further reading: *The Norton/Grove Dictionary of Women Composers*. New York, NY: W.W. Norton, 1995.
http://www.tanialeon.com (León's Web site).

LEVINS MORALES, Aurora

Writer, Academic

Puerto Rican-born activist Aurora Levins Morales is a radical revolutionary poet and feminist thinker. She writes about the contemporary state of the world from a crosscultural perspective that is Puerto Rican, Jewish, and American. Her powerful poetry is broadcast regularly on Pacifica Radio on the program *Flashpoints*.

Early life

Born in Indiera, Puerto Rico, in 1954, Levins Morales is the daughter of the Puerto Rican writer Rosario Morales and Jewish American Richard Levins. Levins Morales was brought up in an intellectual environment. Her parents were communist activists who taught her to question the status quo. Levins Morales began writing poetry at an early age and became fascinated with translating foreign authors into Spanish and English. She later declared that she could not abide bad translations of literary work, even as a child. In 1967 Levins Morales's family moved to the United States; they lived in Chicago and New Hampshire. Levins Morales attended Franconia College in New Hampshire in 1972, after which she moved to Oakland, California, to take a degree in creative writing and ethnic studies. She went on to gain an MA and a PhD from the Union Institute in Cincinnati, Ohio.

A woman of distinction

Levins Morales's work has been published in a number of newspapers, journals, collections, and anthologies. Most notably, Levins Morales was one of several leading authors included in the groundbreaking collection *This Bridge Called My Back: Writings by Radical Women of Color* (1981), the first anthology of Latina female writers in the United States.

Possibly one of Levins Morales's most important books, however, is the eclectic 1986 memoir *Coming Home Alive.* Cowritten with her mother, the book is considered to be one of the most important pieces of work of the Puerto Rican diaspora. The celebrated work is of hybrid literary form that cannot be categorized into one style: It is a collection of short stories, poems, dialogues, journals, and personal recollections written mainly in English, but with occasional words and phrases in Spanish. *Coming Home Alive* shows that "home" can be more than just one place as well as the origin of contradictions and ambiguities.

KEY DATES

1954	Born in Indiera, Puerto Rico.
1967	Family moves to the United States.
1986	Publishes *Coming Home Alive.*
1998	Publishes *Medicine Stories: History, Culture, and Politics.*
2000	Publishes *The History of Latinos in Oakland: Community Narratives.*
2001	Publishes *Remedios: Stories of Earth and Iron from the History of Puertorriqueñas* and *Telling to Live: Latina Feminist Testimonios.*

"Child of the Americas"

One of Levins Morales's most celebrated poems is "Child of the Americas." In it, the writer explores her identity not only as a Puerto Rican, Jew, or American, but also as the product of the complex interconnected history of North, Central, and South America. In "Child of the Americas," Levins Morales views herself as a "crossroads," that is, a true "child of the Americas," as a person who is "Caribbean," "U.S. Puerto Rican Jew," bilingual "Latinoamericana," and "Caribeña."

Levins Morales's other works include the collection of essays *Medicine Stories: History, Culture, and Politics* (1998) and *The History of Latinos in Oakland: Community Narratives* (2000). In 2001, she also wrote *Remedios: Stories of Earth and Iron from the History of Puertorriqueñas* (2001), in which, in poetic prose, she retells Puerto Rican history through the lives of Puerto Rican women and their kin. Levins Morales is also a member of the Latina Feminist Group, made up of leading feminist scholars; the group collectively wrote and edited the volume *Telling to Live: Latina Feminist Testimonios* (2001). Levins Morales's poem "Shema," written after the terrorist attacks of September 11, 2001, was also widely acclaimed.

Further reading: Horno-Delgado, Asunción, and others (eds.). *Breaking Boundaries: Latina Writing and Critical Reading.* Amherst, MA: University of Massachusetts Press, 1989.
http://www.speakersandartists.org/People/AuroraLevinsMorales.html (short biography).

LIFSHITZ, Aliza

Physician, Broadcaster

Celebrity physician and author Aliza Lifshitz is best known for her medical commentary on Radio Unica and the Univision television network. Lifshitz is a four-time president of the California Hispanic American Medical Association, and has served in various capacities for medical associations, including the American Medical Association (AMA). She is also a charter board member of the National Association of Physician Broadcasters.

Media doctor

Born in Mexico City, Mexico, of Russian and German parentage, Lifshitz attended the National Autonomous University of Mexico Medical School. In 1976 she moved to New Orleans, Louisiana, to specialize in internal medicine and clinical pharmacology at Tulane University. She did further postgraduate work in endocrinology at the University of California, San Diego.

In 1988 Lifshitz made her television debut as a health reporter for the United States's leading Spanish-speaking media company, Univision. She was soon one of the network's most popular presenters. Owing to her reputation, Lifshitz was selected by the AMA to launch its 1992 medical ethics consumer information campaign.

In 1997 Lifshitz was elected to the board of directors of Blue Shield of California, a health care organization that serves California consumers. In a winning decade for Lifshitz, she was named "Woman of the 90s" by the *Los Angeles Times* and "Physician of the Year" by the Multicultural Area Health Education Center. In 1999 Lifshitz received the C. Everett Koop Media Award for a series on heart disease written for *La Opinión*, one of the largest Hispanic American newspapers. She was also named as one of the 100 most influential Hispanics of the year by *Hispanic Business Magazine*.

KEY DATES

1950s Born in Mexico City, Mexico, about this time.

1988 Debuts as a medical correspondent on Univision.

1992 Launches AMA's medical ethics consumer information campaign.

1999 Publishes *Mamá Sana, Bebé Sano: Healthy Mother, Healthy Baby*, the first Spanish–English bilingual medical guide for expectant mothers.

▲ ***Aliza Lifshitz is known as "La Doctora Aliza" by her many readers and listeners.***

Business star

Lifshitz is married to Carl J. Kravetz, CEO of a firm specializing in multicultural marketing for the pharmaceutical and health care industries. Within this partnership, Lifshitz has become a powerful Hispanic American brand, lending her star status to public service and product marketing campaigns.

Lifshitz is the medical editor of *Primer Impacto*, a Spanish-language television news magazine, the author of the first bilingual medical guide for expectant mothers, and the host of a one-hour weekly health broadcast, *Consulting with Dr. Aliza*, on Univision Radio. In 2003 Univision invited Lifshitz to help launch a five-year health education campaign targeting the Hispanic community. More recently, Lifshitz has become the spokesperson for the "Got Milk?" campaign targeted at Hispanic Americans and has been appointed executive publisher of Prevention en Español.

Further reading: Lifshitz, A. Aliza, *Mamá Sana, Bebé Sano: Healthy Mother, Healthy Baby.* New York, NY: Rayo, 2002. http://www.ctaf.org/about/members/aliza.ctaf (biography).

LIMÓN, José

Dancer, Choreographer

José Limón was one of the great pioneering figures in American modern dance. As a dancer, he was acclaimed for his powerful, muscular technique and charismatic stage presence. As a choreographer, Limón made his name for the dignity and humanity he brought to his works. Some critics have seen his work as making a peculiarly Hispanic American contribution to dance through his dance troupe. He founded the troupe in 1946 and it still flourishes today as the New York City–based Limón Dance Company.

Early life

José Arcadío Limón was born in Culiacán in Sinaloa, Mexico, on January 12, 1908. He was the eldest of the 11 children of Florencío Limón, the director of the State Academy of Music.

In 1915 the Limón family fled the widespread unrest that followed the Mexican Revolution of 1910, and settled first in Tucson, Arizona, and later in Los Angeles, California. There Limón's father was able to support his growing family by working as a private music tutor.

After high school, Limón enrolled at the University of California, Los Angeles, as an arts major. However, he abandoned his studies when his mother died.

A new ambition

In 1929 Limón went to New York City. The following year he attended a performance by the German modern dancer and mime artist Harald Kreutzberg (1902–1968), and was inspired to become a dancer himself. At the time innovators like Kreutzberg and, in the United States, Martha Graham (1894–1991), Charles Weidman (1901–1975), and Doris Humphrey (1895–1958) were revolutionizing classical ballet. They were creating dances that emphasized human expressiveness and emotion rather than rules and tradition.

In pursuit of his new ambition, Limón enrolled at the New York dance school of Humphrey and Weidman. Despite his late start, he rapidly emerged as one of the most gifted male dancers of his generation.

Throughout the 1930s, Limón performed to great acclaim with the Humphrey-Weidman Company and was heralded by the *New York Times* as the finest male dancer of his time. In 1941 Limón married Pauline Lawrence, the accompanist at the Humphrey-Weidman Company and a costume designer.

Dance and the human spirit

In 1943 Limón was drafted into the U.S. Army to serve in World War II (1939–1945). At first he worked as a truck driver but was later transferred to the Special Services Division, where he performed in shows to entertain the troops. After his discharge in 1945, Limón returned to New

◀ ***José Limón dances on New Year's Day in 1950. He received a* Dance Magazine *Award in that year.***

INFLUENCES AND INSPIRATION

José Limón was inspired to become a dancer by watching a performance by the great German dancer Harald Kreutzberg (1902–1968). Kreutzberg was born in Bohemia, now the western half of the Czech Republic. He trained as a dancer at the Dresden Ballet School and was quickly an international success.

Limón watched Kreutzberg perform in 1929, while the German was performing in a play directed by the experimental Austrian theatrical director Max Reinhardt. At this stage in his career, Kreutzberg was still developing his trademark style.

By the 1930s he had become known for his choreography as well as his performances, and was best known for solos that combined dance with mime. Kreutzberg's routines included free dance with theatrical mimes. He made use of flamboyant costuming to add a new dimension to a dance move. For example, one of the few surviving film clips of his performances shows Kreutzberg appearing to melt into the floor beneath a cape. Kreutzberg's most famous works are the allegory *Der Engel Luzifer* (The Angel Lucifer) and the comic grotesque *Der Hochzeitsstrauss* (The Wedding Bouquet). In 1955 Kreutzberg founded his own dance school in Bern, Switzerland.

York and formed his own company, with Humphrey as the company's artistic director. On January 5, 1947, the José Limón Dance Company made its acclaimed debut in New York City's famous Belasco Theater.

During the 1930s, under Humphrey's guidance, Limón had already made his first tentative steps in choreography, notably with *Danzas Mexicanas* (1937). In the postwar period, however, he emerged as one of the finest U.S. choreographers of the age, although his work always bore the unmistakable mark of his teacher, Humphrey.

Limón's undoubted masterpiece was *The Moor's Pavane* (1949). He distilled the emotional drama of Shakespeare's tragedy *Othello* into a mere 20 minutes, setting the characters' overwhelming passions against the courtly, formal music of the English Renaissance composer Henry Purcell (1659–1695).

In his work, Limón often turned to the Mexican myths and historical stories he had loved as a child. In *La Malinche* (1949), for instance, he retold the story of the Spanish conquistador Hernán Cortés (1485–1547) and his Indian mistress, Marina, while in *Los Cuatro Soles* (1952), he drew upon the famous Aztec myth of the Four Suns. Roman Catholicism, too, played a powerful role in many pieces, notably in *Missa Brevis* (1958), which was inspired by the story of a group of people struggling to rebuild their lives in the aftermath of World War II. For Limón, dance and the human experience were always closely entwined: "I try," he once wrote, "to compose works that are involved with man's basic tragedy and the grandeur of his spirit."

KEY DATES

1908 Born in Culiacán, Sinaloa, Mexico, on January 12.

1915 The Limón family settles in the United States, eventually settling in Los Angeles.

1946 Founds the José Limón Dance Company.

1949 Premiere of *The Moor's Pavane*.

1969 Makes final performance.

1972 Dies in Flemington, New Jersey, on December 2.

Company success

The José Limón Dance Company, meanwhile, went from strength to strength. In 1948 it took part in the Connecticut College Dance Festival, where it subsequently performed every summer until 1973. In 1954 it became the first dance company to embark on an international tour on behalf of the U.S. government. Limón himself received many honors and awards, including two prestigious *Dance Magazine* Awards (1950 and 1957) and a Capezio Dance Award (1964).

Toward the end of his life, Limón was diagnosed with cancer, and while struggling with his own illness he cared for his dying wife. In 1969 he made his final appearance on stage at the Brooklyn Academy of Music, where he danced the role of the Moor in *The Moor's Pavane*. Limón died on December 2, 1972, in Flemington, New Jersey. However, his dance troupe continues to flourish, and his works are regularly performed around the world.

Further reading: Lynn Garafola, ed. *José Limón: An Unfinished Memoir*. Middletown, CT: Wesleyan University Press, 1999.
www.limon.org (Web site of the Limón Dance Company).

LISA, Manuel
Explorer, Trader

Colonial entrepreneur Manuel Lisa outfitted the landmark Lewis and Clark Expedition of 1803. After Lewis and Clark explored and mapped the vast frontier region west of the Mississippi River, Lisa pioneered trading expeditions along the Missouri River and on the Great Plains.

Budding merchant

Manuel Lisa was born in New Orleans, Louisiana, in 1772. Lisa's father, Christopher de Lisa, settled in Louisiana from Murcia, Spain. His mother, Maria Ignacia Rodriguez, was a native of St. Augustine, Florida, the center of the Spanish colony in the region.

By 1796 Lisa was operating a trading vessel along the Mississippi River. He relocated to St. Louis, Missouri, after acquiring substantial property there in 1799. At the time, St. Louis was in French-controlled territory.

Lisa opened a thriving frontier store, but was often unsuccessful in collecting payment on purchases made through credit. Although Lisa enthusiastically advocated free trade, he himself profited mainly through a lucrative monopoly agreement with the Osage people. This government-granted agreement ensured that only he could trade with the group.

Trading places

When Meriwether Lewis and William Clark were sponsored by Congress to explore the route from the Mississippi River to the Pacific Ocean in 1803, the pair prepared for the venture at St. Louis. Lisa provided many of their supplies.

The expedition's return in 1806 inspired Lisa to pursue trading opportunities in the Northwest. Lisa organized a trading group to go up the Missouri River. He set out in 1807 with 42 men to establish trading posts. Lisa founded Fort Manuel at the mouth of the Big Horn River in what is now Montana. In 1809 he founded the St. Louis Fur Company, later renamed the Missouri Fur Company, serving as its president throughout his life.

Lisa founded Fort Lisa in 1812, near present-day Omaha, Nebraska. As such, he is known as the first white settler in Nebraska, despite frequent descriptions of him as the "Black Spaniard" because of his dark skin.

Despite Lisa's status as the era's preeminent fur trader, traveling 26,000 miles (42,000km) in multiple river expeditions, his estate had no value after his death because of the many unpaid debts owed to him.

KEY DATES

1772	Born in New Orleans, Louisiana, on September 8.
1803	Helps to outfit the Lewis and Clark expedition.
1807	Pioneers first trade expedition along upper Missouri River and founds Fort Manuel.
1809	Founds Missouri Fur Company.
1820	Dies in St. Louis, Missouri, on August 12.

▲ ***Manuel Lisa was the first European settler to found a successful trading operation in the Louisiana Territory.***

Further reading: Oglesby, Richard E. *Manuel Lisa and the Opening of the Missouri Fur Trade*. Norman, OK: University of Oklahoma Press, 1963.
http://www.nebraskastudies.org/0400/frameset.html (history of the colonization of the Great Plains).

LOMAS GARZA, Carmen

Artist

Carmen Lomas Garza is a leading Chicana artist based in San Francisco, California. Her artistic focus has been to celebrate and take pride in Hispanic American communities, families, history, and culture. She is also inspired by the feminist movement.

Radicalized childhood

Lomas Garza was born in Kingsville, Texas, in 1948, the second of five children. As a young teenager, Carmen decided to become an artist. She was following in the footsteps of her mother, who was also an artist. Carmen taught herself to draw when art classes were not offered in school. Lomas Garza's schooling also had other, more serious limitations. Students heard speaking in Spanish, for example, were physically punished by teachers and verbally abused by their Anglo classmates.

Such blatant mistreatment of children led Lomas Garza's parents to join the American GI Forum, a World War II veterans' organization for Mexican Americans. The GI Forum was one of the chief advocates for the civil rights of Hispanic Americans.

This activism inspired Lomas Garza to join the Chicano movement, the 1960s struggle for civil rights. Carmen first became aware of the United Farm Workers Union when they marched in Kingsville in 1965 to protest poor wages for farmworkers in the fields of southern Texas.

Carmen was attending Texas A & M University at Kingsville at the time, and there she began to formulate her philosophy and ideas about art. She strove to express Mexican American culture and history through her art, and so inspire other young Mexican Americans to find out more about their ethnic identity and heritage.

Professional artist

After graduating in 1972, Lomas Garza earned a master of education degree from Juarez-Lincoln/Antioch Graduate School in Austin, Texas, in 1973. In the mid-1970s, she moved to San Francisco to work at Galeria de la Raza, and in 1981 earned a master's degree from San Francisco State University. Lomas Garza has since lived in San Francisco, and has become a prominent artist in the city.

She has had solo exhibitions at San Francisco's Mexican Museum; the Laguna Gloria Art Museum in Austin, Texas; the Hirshhorn Museum and Sculpture Garden, Smithsonian Institution, Washington, D.C.; and the Whitney Museum of American Art, New York. Her work is widely collected. In 2000, she was commissioned to make *Baile/Dance*, a large-scale copper cutout for the new international passenger terminal at San Francisco International Airport.

KEY DATES

1948	Born in Kingsville, Texas.
1972	Graduates with a bachelor of science degree.
1981	Earns a master of fine arts degree.
2001	Retrospective exhibition held at San Jose Museum of Art, San Jose, California.

Inspiration

"A little piece of my heart" is how Lomas Garza characterizes her work, in which she depicts personal memories and experiences of her childhood in rural Texas. Her art is rendered in a naive style for simplicity and clarity. The paintings, dating from the mid-1970s to the present, picture everyday activities and long-standing traditions of her Mexican American community.

Lomas Garza also works in the areas of installation and cut paper. She has refined and expanded the art form to create fascinating and complex compositions magically sliced from a single sheet of paper.

The culmination of Lomas Garza's cut-paper work has been a large-scale steel cutout titled *Ofrenda para Antonio Lomas* (1996; Offering for Antonio Lomas), which was the the centerpiece of a dramatic homage to her grandfather.

Lomas Garza herself explains, "Every time I paint, it serves a purpose—to bring about pride in our Mexican American culture. When I was growing up we were punished for being who we were, and we were made to feel ashamed of our culture. My art is a way of healing these wounds, like aloe vera heals burns and scrapes when applied by a loving parent or grandparent."

Further reading: Lomas Garza, Carmen. *Family Pictures/ Paintings by Carmen Lomas Garza.* San Francisco, CA: Children's Books Press, 2005.
http://www.carmenlomasgarza.com/biography.html (Lomas Garza's Web site).

LONGORIA, Felix
Soldier

Felix Longoria led an unremarkable life, but his death in combat during World War II (1939–1945) was to highlight the racial divisions in the U.S. Army and his home state of Texas.

Early life

Felix Z. Longoria was born in Three Rivers, Texas, on April 16, 1919. Three Rivers was a segregated community, located at the confluence of three rivers between San Antonio and Corpus Christi. Hispanic Americans (of Mexican descent) lived on one side of town. The Anglo-Saxon community occupied the other. Schools were segregated, as were the cemeteries and churches.

Longoria began his working life at the age of eight to help support his family during the Great Depression of the 1930s. Longoria managed to finish the third grade, but that was the end of his formal education. A tall child, Felix soon joined his older brother working as a roughneck (a worker on an oil-drilling crew). He gradually moved up the employment ladder and became a truck driver.

Army career

In his late teens, Longoria married his childhood sweetheart Beatriz Moreno, and they lived across the street from his parent's home. The couple struggled when Longoria's job was terminated. They moved in with Beatriz's parents in Corpus Christi, Texas, to save money. However, Longoria could not find a job well-paid enough to support his wife. The couple moved back to Three Rivers. Despite their financial difficulties, the couple soon had a baby girl in 1941, whom they named Adelita.

On November 11, 1944, Longoria joined the U.S. Army. He hoped it would be a means of supporting his family and looked forward to getting veteran's benefits. The war was nearing its conclusion in Europe. However, after basic and advanced infantry training, Longoria was shipped overseas to the Pacific theater where the action against Japanese forces was still intense.

While on routine patrol in the jungles of the island of Luzon in the Philippines in 1945, Longoria was killed by a sniper. Longoria had barely been in the Philippines a month before being killed. Beatriz was notified of his death and that he had been temporarily buried in the Philippines until his body could be shipped to the United States for burial according to the family's wishes.

▲ ***Private Felix Longoria became famous after his death in World War II, when the funeral director in his hometown refused to accept his body for burial.***

Refusal of burial service

Three years later Beatriz received word from the military that her husband's body would arrive in San Francisco, California, in late November 1948. She was shocked at the news. She and Adelita had moved on with their lives and were now living back in Corpus Christi.

The Army asked her to make arrangements for reburial and information on where to transport the body. The widow thought it was best for Felix to rest in his hometown, even if it was in the segregated Hispanic American cemetery. She took the bus from Corpus Christi to Three Rivers and went to the Manon Rice Funeral Home to make arrangements. Both Tom W. Kennedy, Jr., the funeral director, and Manon Rice, the owner, refused to

INFLUENCES AND INSPIRATION

A pivotal figure in the scandal over Felix Longoria's burial was the future U.S. president Lyndon B. Johnson (1908–1973).

Johnson had been elected as a Texas senator the year before. He was one of several public figures petitioned by Hector García. Johnson's response was to arrange for Longoria to be interred in the national cemetery outside Washington, D.C. His views on the matter were expressed in a public statement: "I deeply regret to learn that the prejudice of some individuals extends even beyond this life. I have no authority over civilian funeral homes. Nor does the federal government. However, I have today made arrangements to have Felix Longoria buried with full military honors in Arlington National Cemetery here in Washington where the honored dead of our nation's wars rest ... This injustice and prejudice is deplorable. I am happy to have a part seeing that this Texas hero is laid to rest with the honor and dignity his service deserves."

When Johnson became president in 1963, he continued to tackle racial discrimination. He introduced the Civil Rights Act in 1964, which outlawed segregation.

let her use the chapel for the wake because the white people in town might not like it. Instead they suggested she hold her husband's wake at his parents' home. They would then be happy to bury him in the Mexican cemetery.

The funeral directors could not be swayed, despite Beatriz arguing that her husband had died for his country. For the funeral home, it was a simple commercial decision. If Longoria was laid to rest in the chapel, whites in Three Rivers—the home's main customers—would be offended.

Reluctantly Beatriz agreed to hold the wake in the home the family had abandoned when they moved to Corpus Christi following Longoria's death. It was small, decrepit, dirty, and without utilities. Once back home in Corpus Christi, Beatriz informed her family that her only choice was to hold the wake in their old house. Her sister, Sara Moreno, was outraged. She called the only person then campaigning for Hispanic American veterans, the local doctor, Hector Perez Garcia.

A national scandal

García had formed the American GI Forum in 1948 to advocate for returning Hispanic American war veterans. When Moreno explained the situation, he was appaled. He promptly took action, but not before verifying the facts of the incident. Satisfied this was an act of blatant racism, he called media contacts across the country with the story. He also fired off telegrams demanding an investigation to as many influential people as he could, including the state governor and the new senator for Texas, the Democrat Lyndon B. Johnson. García personally offered Beatriz and the family the financial help of his organization to bury Longoria in Corpus Christi after a proper wake and service.

A hero honored

The syndicated radio broadcaster Walter Winchell caught wind of the news and broke the story to Americans the next day. "The state of Texas, which looms so large on the map, looks mighty small tonight," he began. Winchell proceeded to relate the story of how a war hero was refused a proper burial in his hometown. Most Americans, and practically all Hispanic Americans, were indignant at the offense.

Senator Johnson offered Longaria burial at Arlington National Cemetery in Virginia. Cash donations poured in from across the country to help the family. The Longoria family finally opted for a burial at Arlington. Felix Longoria was buried with full military honors. He has remained a hero to many, and the incident helped build the American GI Forum into the second largest civil rights organization for Hispanic Americans.

KEY DATES

1919 Born in Three Rivers, Texas, on April 16.

1944 Enlists in the U.S. Army.

1945 Killed in action on Luzon, Philippines, on July 15.

1949 Buried as a hero in Arlington National Cemetery on February 16.

See also: García, Hector P.

Further reading: Carroll, Patrick James. *Felix Longoria's Wake: Bereavement, Racism, and the Rise of Mexican American Activism.* Austin, TX: University of Texas Press, 2003.
http://www.arlingtoncemetery.net/longoria.htm (collection of articles commemorating Longoria).

LOPEZ, Al
Baseball Player, Manager

Known for his hands-off managerial style, Al Lopez was one of the most consistent players and managers in major league (ML) baseball history. As a player, Lopez caught 1,918 games from 1928 to 1947, which stood as a major league record for 40 years. In 17 years as a major league manager, Lopez won the 1954 American League (AL) pennant with the Cleveland Indians and repeated the feat five years later in 1959 with the Chicago White Sox. Lopez's teams were the only ones to beat the mighty New York Yankees in competition for the AL pennant between 1949 and 1964. His managerial record of 1,422–1,026 (.581) ranks eighth all-time. A popular manager, Lopez was called "the Friendly Senor" or the "Happy Hildalgo" by sportswriters.

A successful career

Born in the predominantly Spanish-speaking Ybor section of Tampa, Florida, on August 20, 1908, Alfonso Ramon Lopez was the son of a Cuban American cigar-factory worker. In 1925, Lopez earned $45 a week to catch spring-training batting practice for the Washington Senators. He was soon playing in the big leagues himself.

Lopez made his major league debut with the Brooklyn Dodgers in September 1928. Within two years, Lopez was the Dodgers' starting catcher. Lopez played a total of 19 seasons with five different teams. He was with the Dodgers in 1928 and 1930–1935, the Boston Bees (who became the Atlanta Braves) from 1936–1940, the Pittsburgh Pirates from 1940–1946, and played his final season with the Indians in 1947. He had a career batting average of .261, hit 51 home runs, and drove in 652 runs.

KEY DATES

1908	Born in Tampa, Florida, on August 20.
1951	Manages first major league season with the Cleveland Indians.
1954	Leads the Cleveland Indians to the AL pennant.
1957	Becomes manager of the Chicago White Sox.
1959	Leads the Chicago White Sox to the AL pennant
1977	Inducted into the National Baseball Hall of Fame.
2005	Dies on October 30.

▲ ***Former* Chicago Tribune *columnist Jerome Holtzman said that Lopez was the best baseball manager that he had ever met.***

In 1951, Lopez moved on to become Cleveland Indians manager. Three years later, Lopez led the Indians to a then-ML record of 111 wins and the AL pennant. In that year, *Life* magazine said Lopez "seldom leaves the dugout." In 1957, Lopez became White Sox manager, leading the team to the pennant in 1959. In the World Series, they fell to his first ML team, the newly relocated LA Dodgers, in six games. In 1965, Lopez had his last full season with the Sox, but he returned to coach the team for 47 games in 1968 and 17 games in 1969 before he retired.

In 1977 Lopez was inducted into the National Baseball Hall of Fame. He died on October 30, 2005, two days after he suffered a heart attack and just four days after the White Sox won the World Series for the first time in 88 years. The White Sox had not appeared in the World Series since Lopez had led the team to the pennant in 1959.

Further reading: Singletary, Wes, and Jerome Holtzman. *Al Lopez: The Life of Baseball's El Senor*. Jefferson, NC: McFarland & Company, 1999.
http://www.baseballhalloffame.org/hofers_and_honorees/hofer_bios/lopez_al.htm (Baseball Hall of Fame site).

LOPEZ, George
Comedian, Entertainer

Following in the footsteps of his heroes Desi Arnaz and Freddie Prinze, comedian George Lopez is best known for the hugely successful television situation comedy that bears his name. *George Lopez* focuses on a man who works at an airplane factory in Los Angeles, and his family, which includes two children, his mother, father-in-law, and best friend. The sitcom shows a healthy Mexican American family, and its characters stand in opposition to the drug-dealing gangster, illegal alien stereotypes that are often seen in Hollywood's depiction of Mexican Americans. Lopez is also an accomplished movie actor, writer, and producer. In 2005 *Time* magazine named Lopez one of the 25 most influential Hispanics in America.

Early life

Born on April 23, 1961, in Mission Hills, California, Lopez was abandoned by his parents and raised by his grandmother. Lopez's sense of humor developed as a defense mechanism against his grandmother's abusive and belittling behavior. His early familial experience shaped his later relationships with his wife, Ann Serrano, and their daughter; Lopez has also used episodes from his own childhood in his show.

Influence

Lopez has achieved several firsts during his career. In 2001 Lopez was the first Latino to host a morning radio program for Clear Channel in Los Angeles. He came to the notice of actor Sandra Bullock, whose production company was pitching ideas for a Latino TV sitcom. Bullock enjoyed Lopez's work so much that she completely revised her initial plan of a teen-based sitcom, and in 2002 she helped Lopez get his own show on ABC.

KEY DATES

1961	Born in Mission Hills, California, on April 23.
2001	Becomes the first Latino host of a morning radio program on Clear Channel, Los Angeles.
2002	*George Lopez* television series begins.
2004	Releases autobiography *Why You Crying?*
2005	Named as one of the 25 Most Influential Hispanics by *Time* magazine; wife Ann donates a kidney to save his life.

▲ ***George Lopez counts many Hollywood A-list stars among his friends, including Sandra Bullock (left), who is executive producer of Lopez's successful TV show.***

Lopez's CD *Team Leader* was released in 2004 and nominated for a Grammy award for best comedy album. In that same year, Lopez's autobiography, *Why You Crying?: My Long Hard Look at Life, Love, and Laughter*, became a *New York Times* best-seller. In December 2005 Lopez set an attendance record at the Universal Amphitheater in Los Angeles, with 42,000 people attending his seven sold-out shows.

Lopez is also a prominent Latino philanthropist. He has received several awards for his positive contribution to the Chicano community. He has his own charity, the George & Ann Lopez-Richie Alarcon CARE Foundation, focusing on arts and education for children. In 2005 Lopez suffered renal failure; his wife donated a kidney to save his life.

See also: Arnaz, Desi; Prinze, Freddie

Further reading: Lopez, George. *Why You Crying?: My Long Hard Look at Life, Love, and Laughter*. Carmichael, CA: Touchstone Books, 2005.
http://www.imdb.com/name/nm0520064 (biography and work).

LOPEZ, Israel "Cachao"

Musician

Virtuoso Cuban bassist Israel "Cachao" Lopez is best known to audiences as the father of mambo. It is a style of music that draws on both African influences and European dances and was popularized by Pérez Prado.

In the 1950s, Lopez was also credited with revolutionizing Cuban music by introducing "descargas," improvised Latin jazz sessions. In 1962 Lopez fled his native country to escape the rule of Fidel Castro. Lopez worked with many leading Hispanic musicians in the United States, including Tito Rodriguez (1923–1973) and Gloria Estefan, but some music critics claim that it was not until Hollywood actor Andy Garcia produced a 1993 documentary about Lopez that his contribution to 20th-century music was properly appreciated.

Early life

Born in Havana, Cuba, on September 14, 1918, Lopez grew up in a musical extended family that boasted more than 36 double bassists. He began playing the bass at age nine and quickly showed an aptitude for the instrument. By the age of 13 he was playing with the Havana Philharmonic Orchestra, with which he performed for 30 years.

▼ ***Cachao Lopez has played on the albums of several Hispanic American singers, including Gloria Estefan's award winning 1993 album* Mia Tierra.**

KEY DATES

1918 Born in Havana, Cuba, on September 14.

1931 Begins playing with the Havana Philharmonic Orchestra.

1938 Produces *Mambo* with his brother Orestes.

1957 Releases the album *Descargas en Miniature* (Jam Sessions in Miniature).

1962 Leaves Cuba, first for Europe and then America.

1994 Wins Grammy for Best Tropical Latin Album for *Master Sessions, Volume I.*

A revolutionary man

Lopez played with other bands and wrote more than 2,500 *danzóns* with his brother Orestes Lopez (1908–). The two men experimented with music, trying to create something new for their audiences: In 1938 they wrote a *danzón* called the mambo. It revolutionized Cuban music and created a new dance craze. Lopez played in theaters and nightclubs in Havana. He continued to experiment with other musicians during impromptu sessions. Lopez released some of these sessions as the 1957 album *Descargas en Miniature*.

Another life

In 1962, shortly after Castro came to power, Lopez left Cuba, moving to Spain before settling in the United States. He worked with some of the leading Hispanic musicians of the time, including Charlie Palmieri, performing in clubs and doing session work on albums. In the 1980s Lopez moved to Miami, where he played with the Miami Symphony Orchestra and worked as a session musician.

In 1993 Lopez came to international prominence when Andy Garcia's documentary *Cachao: Como Su Ritmo No Hay Dos* (Like His Rhythm There Is No Other) was released. In 1995 Lopez's album *Master Sessions, Volume 1*, won the Grammy for Best Tropical Latin Album in 1995.

See also: Estafan, Gloria; Garcia, Andy; Palmieri, Charlie; Prado, Pérez.

Further reading: http://www.musicweb-international.com/encyclopaedia/l/L106.HTM (biography).

LOPEZ, Jennifer
Singer, Actress

As a singer and actress, Jennifer Lopez was arguably the most successful Latina in the world at the start of the 21st century. She boasts a number of firsts: She was the first Hispanic American actress to be paid $1 million for a movie, *Selena*, in 1997. In 2001 her role in *The Wedding Planner* earned her $13 million, the first eight-figure paycheck in Hollywood history for a nonwhite actress. The same year she became the first actress to have a movie (*The Wedding Planner)* and a music album (*J. Lo*) hit number one in the same week. Despite limited success in the music charts and box office in later years, Lopez remained the highest paid Hispanic American actress in Hollywood, far outpacing all her other counterparts, and commanding a record $14 million for *Monster-in-Law*, in which she starred alongside Jane Fonda in 2005.

Lopez has used her show-business brand to launch a range of products, such as fashion lines, perfumes, and television and movie production. Her business activity has earned Lopez a place on the Forbes 2005 list of top 100 celebrities. She was ranked at number 24 with estimated earnings of $17 million in the movie business alone, and an estimated overall income of more than $35 million a year.

▲ ***Singer and actress Jennifer Lopez earned a spot on the Forbes 2005 list of top 100 celebrities.***

Early life

Born Jennifer Lynn Lopez in 1969 in the Bronx, New York, of Puerto Rican-born parents, Lopez was brought up in a strict Catholic household. She took singing and dancing lessons from the age of five. Following high school, she took a day job, but continued to hone her dancing skills at night hoping to land a job in show business.

Her first break came when she became one of the dancing Fly Girls in the Wayans brothers television show *In Living Color* (1990). Lopez hoped to follow in the footsteps of fellow Nuyorican star Rosie Perez, a former dancer who had made the leap into Hollywood films in 1989 when she starred in Spike Lee's masterpiece *Do the Right Thing.* Perez was the choreographer for *In Living Color,* while Lopez was a dancer in the show.

Lopez eventually left the show to become a back-up dancer for Janet Jackson, and she appeared in music videos for Jackson and Sean "Puff Daddy" Combs (now known as Diddy). However, Lopez aimed to become an actress as well as a singer and used her dancing success to propel herself into those two areas of showbusiness.

Movie career

Lopez initially got roles in short-lived television serials such as *Second Chances* (1993), *South Central* (1994), and *Hotel Malibu* (1994). Her break into Hollywood film came with a small part in Gregory Nava's *My Family* (1995). However, her big break was earning the title role in Nava's *Selena* (1997), which reportedly had the largest casting call in Hollywood history. Lopez's performance as the singer and dancer Selena was the perfect showcase for her talents. (Selena was a successful Tejana—Texan of Mexican heritage—singer who was murdered in 1995 at the age of 23.)

Following the movie, Lopez was given the opportunity to appear opposite some of Hollywoods top leading men. She had roles in *U-Turn* in 1997 with Sean Penn; *Out of Sight* in 2000, opposite George Clooney; *The Wedding Planner* in 2001, with Matthew McConaughey; and *Maid in*

INFLUENCES AND INSPIRATION

During her career, Jennifer Lopez has been linked to many of the largest names in show business. When she first came to the attention of the public (as an actress) in the late 1990s, Lopez's celebrity was further enhanced by her relationship with New York rapper and music mogul Sean Combs, variously known as Puff Daddy, P. Diddy, and later as Diddy. Lopez broke off the relationship after she became embroiled in a criminal investigation after a shooting in a New York nightclub.

In 2004 Lopez married the successful Latino singer Marc Anthony, with whom she first collaborated on her first album, *On the 6*. Lopez's voice has also appeared on one of Anthony's Spanish-language albums, *Amar Sin Mentiras*.

Manhattan (2002) with Ralph Fiennes. She also took top billing in *The Cell* in 2000.

Music career

Lopez released her first album, *On the 6,* in 1999, which went platinum (sold more than a million copies) six times over. As her film career progressed, Lopez released more albums such as *J. Lo* in 2001 and *This Is Me ... Then* in 2002. Both of these albums spawned a string of successful singles around the world.

Lopez also debuted a fashion line in 2001 to make the most of her worldwide appeal. JLo by Jennifer Lopez grossed $130 million by 2004, the most successful line by an actress. Lopez introduced a second fashion line named Sweetface in 2003, and launched a series of fragrances, such as Glow by JLo in 2001, followed by Still in 2003.

Private life in public

During her meteoric rise as a young and multitalented beauty, Lopez's private life came under minute scrutiny. It hinged on her relationships with famous and infamous figures. Her first marriage to Ojani Noa (1997–1998) preceded her superstar status and lasted only months. A relationship with Sean Combs followed and lasted nearly four years.

In 2001 Lopez married her former backing dancer Chris Judd. By 2002 she was engaged to Oscar-winning actor Ben Affleck, and her marriage to Judd was dissolved in 2003. The relationship with Affleck became a global talking point and was nicknamed "Bennifer." Dogged by rumors and last-minute changes of heart, the couple eventually broke up in 2004. Nevertheless, Lopez soon found love again and married singer Marc Anthony in the same year.

KEY DATES

1969	Born in the Bronx, New York, on July 24.
1990	Makes first television appearance as a dancer in the comedy *In Living Color*.
1997	Lands title role in the movie, *Selena*.
1999	Releases first album, *On the 6*.
2001	Launches JLo fashion label.
2002	Begins much celebrated engagement with actor Ben Affleck.
2004	Marries second husband, musician Marc Anthony.
2006	Releases *Bordertown,* produced by her film company, Nuyorican Films.

Maturing star

Lopez's recent career has met with mixed success. Two film roles alongside Affleck were released on the back of the gossip surrounding the pair's relationship. *Gigli* (2003) and *Jersey Girl* (2004) were both flops. Her fourth album, *Rebirth* (2005), was also poorly received. Nonetheless Lopez continued to command top movie roles.

Lopez has also become a film producer through her enterprise Nuyorican Films. One of her first feature films will be *Bordertown* (2006), costarring Antonio Banderas, a film based on the Ciudad Juarez murders: 340 women have been killed in the Mexican border town since 1993. Another release was *El Cantante* (2006), a biopic about the life of Hector Lavoe. Nuyorican Films is also producing the UPN television series *South Beach*. Other ventures include restaurant ownership, more fragrances, and an expanding fashion line.

See also: Lavoe, Hector; Marc Anthony; Nava, Gregory; Perez, Rosie; Selena

Further reading: Furman, Leah. *Jennifer Lopez*. Philadelphia, PA: Chelsea House Publishers, 2001.
http://www.jenniferlopez.com (Lopez's Web site).

LÓPEZ, José M.
Soldier

José López fought during the battle for Normandy that followed the D-Day landings in France in 1944. He was also caught up several months later in the German counterattack against Allied troops in Belgium that became known as the Battle of the Bulge. His heroic actions during this battle earned López the Medal of Honor.

Tough start

Even though his place of birth is often indicated as Mission, Texas, José Mendoza López was actually born in Veracruz, Mexico, in 1910. He never knew his father and was an orphan by the age of eight. With no one to care for him, López migrated north, settling down in the Texas border town of Mission.

From a young age, López was an adventurous person, holding a number of jobs. He loved the sea but was a far from lucky sailor. On one occasion he was stranded at sea for weeks on a cargo boat with nothing to eat but a bunch of bananas. Despite his short stature, López was a successful boxer.

Military hero

In 1936 López joined the Merchant Marine. However, by the time the United States had been drawn into World War II (1939–1945), López was in a U.S. Army unit. He landed at Normandy, France, on the second day of the Allied invasion. Six months later, on December 17, 1944, his unit was near Krinkelt, in the wooded Ardennes region of Belgium, when it came under attack from German tanks. The Germans attacked the Ardennes because it was lightly defended. They forced the Allies to retreat, making a huge bulging dent in the front line. The fighting was thus named the Battle of the Bulge. Although the German attack was eventually halted, more than 77,000 Allied soldiers were killed or injured.

KEY DATES

1910	Born in Veracruz, Mexico, on July 10.
1918	Becomes an orphan.
1945	Wins Medal of Honor for action during the Battle of the Bulge in Belgium.
2005	Dies in San Antonio, Texas, on May 18.

▲ ***José M. López (left) is honored along with two other Medal of Honor recipients during half-time at a San Antonio Spurs game in 2000.***

López was in charge of carrying a machine gun. He was forced to engage an approaching German tank with a large unit of enemy soldiers around it. López killed ten Germans and drew the tank away from his own unit. Despite suffering a concussion from the tank's shell blasts, López repositioned himself and eliminated 25 more enemy soldiers, allowing his fellow soldiers the opportunity to retreat. The series of heroic actions earned López the Medal of Honor.

Old soldier

Lopez remained in the military after World War II, serving in the Korean War (1950–1953). He became a recruiter and then a sergeant in charge of a motor pool. López died in 2005 at his daughter's house in San Antonio, Texas. He had been suffering from cancer.

Further reading: Lemon, Peter C. *Beyond the Medal*. Golden, CO: Fulcrum Publishing, 1997.
http://www.military.com/NewContent/0,13190,MoH_Jose_Lopez,00.html (Medal of Honor citation).

LOPEZ, Nancy
Golfer

Nancy Lopez was born to play golf. By the age of eight, she had her own set of golf clubs. From the age of only nine, Lopez began winning championships. Her first win was a Pee Wee tournament. Lopez won the USGA Junior Girls Championship in both 1972 and 1974. Her winning streak culminated in taking the Ladies Pro Golf Association (LPGA) Championship when she was just 21.

▲ ***Nancy Lopez lines up a putt at the Weetabix Women's British Open Golf Championship in 1995.***

Winning ways

Lopez was born in Torrence, California, in 1957. She began working against the restrictions on female golfers at an early age. When she entered Goddard High School, it had no girls' golf team. Lopez therefore became a member of the boys' team.

When she was 12 years old, Nancy Lopez also broke the age barrier by beating all comers in the New Mexico Women's Amateur Championship. She won her first national competition at the age of 17, when she became the Mexican Amateur champion.

In her first U.S. Women's Open in 1975, Lopez appeared as an amateur and tied for second place. In 1976 she won the AIAW (Association for Intercollegiate Athletics for Women) National Championship and became a member on the World Amateur team. In her freshman year at the University of Tulsa, Oklahoma, Lopez made All-American and was named Female Athlete of the Year.

Professional career

In 1977 Lopez entered the ranks of the professionals. She finished her first three tournaments in second place. She went on to win nine tournaments and was named the LPGA Rookie of the Year. Lopez's second year as a professional golfer began with five tournament wins.

Lopez scored her biggest success by winning the 1978 LPGA Championship. Lopez repeated the feat in 1985 and 1989. Lopez won 48 tournaments in her professional career and was named Player of the Year three times.

In 1989 Lopez was officially inducted into the LPGA Hall of Fame. In 1997, at the age of 40, Lopez won her last tournament. Health problems then curtailed her golf career, but in 2002 Lopez competed in 14 events and scored the third hole-in-one of her career. 2005 saw her named captain of the U.S. Solheim Cup Team. Lopez has been married to baseball player Ray Knight since 1982.

KEY DATES

1957 Born in Torrence, California, on January 6.

1969 Wins the New Mexico Women's Amateur Championships.

1978 Winner of the Ladies Pro Golf Association Championship.

1989 Inducted into the LPGA Hall of Fame.

1998 Winner of the Bob Jones Award for Distinguished Sportsmanship.

Further reading: Lopez, Nancy. *The Education of a Woman Golfer*. New York, NY: Simon and Schuster, 1979. http://www.nancylopezgolf.com/nl/index.cfm (Lopez's official Web site).

LOPEZ, Trini
Musician

With his unique style of folk music, Trini Lopez became a popular figure in the 1960s as one of the first Hispanic American pop music stars.

Early life

Trinidad Lopez, III, the son of Mexican immigrants, was born in Dallas, Texas, in 1937. His father bought him a guitar when he was about 12 years old and taught him to play. Soon Lopez was playing Mexican and American pop songs on street corners for change, and then in Mexican restaurants around town. As one of six children growing up in a barrio—a Hispanic American neighborhood—money was often short, and Lopez dropped out of high school to perform music full time to help support his family.

Lopez recorded a single for a Dallas record company in 1958 and then moved up to King Records in Cincinnati, Ohio, a major rhythm-and-blues label. Lopez had a minor hit in Dallas, but he wanted to play a different kind of music and moved to Los Angeles, California, in 1960.

Stardom

Lopez began performing at PJ's, a popular Los Angeles nightclub. One night a record producer saw Lopez's show and introduced the young singer to Frank Sinatra. Sinatra offered him a record deal, and in 1963 Lopez made a live album called *Trini Lopez at PJ's*. The songs ranged from Mexican standards like "Cielito Lindo," to up-tempo versions of American folk music. Lopez gave his songs a danceable Latin flavor, and his music would regularly induce often jaded nightclub crowds to sing along.

"If I Had a Hammer," a cover of a Pete Seeger protest song, became Lopez's first hit single, rising to number three on the music charts. The song was also a hit in Europe and South America. Sinatra's company, Reprise Records, rushed out another album and produced another U.S. hit, this time a cover of the blues song "Kansas City." Lopez also had more international successes with renditions of "La Bamba," "Am-er-i-ca," and "This Land Is Your Land."

▲ ***Trini Lopez was the first Latino pop star, blending a Latin style into folk and blues music.***

KEY DATES

1937 Born in Dallas, Texas, on May 15.

1958 Records first single.

1963 Records first album, *Trini Lopez at PJ's*, and has hit single with "If I Had a Hammer."

1967 Plays Pedro Jimenez in the movie *The Dirty Dozen*.

2003 March 21 is declared Trini Lopez Day in Los Angeles, California.

Acting talent

Lopez recorded nearly two dozen albums, but only hit the American charts twice more. His innocent songs no longer matched the mood of a country in the depths of the Vietnam War. Lopez tried his hand at acting, most famously playing a Puerto Rican soldier in *The Dirty Dozen*. While he crossed over ethnic boundaries with his music, Lopez's acting career saw him in stereotypical Hispanic American roles. Lopez continues to play music, and was inducted into the International Latin Music Hall of Fame in 2003.

Further reading: http:www.trinilopez.com (Lopez's Web site).

LÓPEZ, Yolanda
Artist

Yolanda M. López is one of the most prominent contemporary Latina artists. As a leading Chicana artist and activist, López paved the way for future generations of artists to express cultural pride. López's work examines such themes as Mexican popular and religious traditions, working-class experiences, and Hispanic women's lives.

Early life

Born on November 1, 1942, in National City, just outside of San Diego, California, López was one of three children. She was raised in Logan Heights in central San Diego by her mother and her grandparents. Her family had migrated to the United States from Mexico in the early 20th century. López found her calling as an artist at a young age, and was encouraged by her uncle, Miguel, who gave her the art supplies that she needed.

Activism

Aware of political issues from an early age, López worked for John F. Kennedy's presidential campaign while still at school. After graduating, López moved to San Francisco, California, where she spent several years working as an artist. López became involved with the Student Nonviolent Coordinating Committee (SNCC), which used peaceful tactics such as sit-ins and demonstrations to challenge racial inequality.

In the mid-1960s López went to study art at San Francisco State University, where she took part in student strikes in support of immigrants from third world countries, including those coming from Central America. López created artwork to promote the cause of Los Siete de la Raza, seven Hispanic American immigrants accused of killing a white police officer in San Francisco's Mission district in 1968. She eventually dropped out of college.

After holding her first exhibition at the Galleria de la Raza in 1970, López returned to her studies. She earned a BA degree in painting and drawing from San Diego State University in 1975. Three years later she received an MFA in visual arts from the University of California, San Diego.

Challenging perceptions

Among López's most recognized work are three paintings, all produced in 1978, which represent her grandmother, mother, and López herself. *Portrait of the Artist as the Virgin of Guadalupe,* possibly López's most recognizable work, portrays the artist as an energetic runner, with a mantle of stars billowing behind her. *Margaret F. Stewart: Our Lady of Guadalupe* (1978) shows López's mother creating a mantle of stars. *Victoria F. Franco: Our Lady of Guadalupe* shows López's grandmother skinning a snake. Although the original Virgin of Guadalupe is passive, López's "Guadalupes" are mobile and hardworking, reflecting a positive representation of the Latina. The paintings met with a mixed response, however: The artist was criticized by some commentators for using such a revered religious icon in Mexican culture in paintings portraying her mother, grandmother, and herself.

Much of López's other work is aimed at increasing awareness of the social injustice experienced by Hispanic American women: the series *Woman's Work Is Never Done,* for example, includes a series of prints, as well as the installation *The Nanny*, which explores the invisibility of immigrant women as domestic workers.

López produced the video "When You Think of Mexico" to challenge cultural stereotypes in print and electronic media. She said that it is important to explore the "cultural mis-definition of Mexicans and Latin Americans that is presented in the media." López has taught modern Chicano art at the University of California at Berkeley and San Diego. She has received several awards, including the Chicanos in Arts Award from the National Association for Chicano Studies (1993).

KEY DATES

1942	Born in National City, California, on November 1.
1968	Takes part in San Francisco State University's Third World Strike for Ethnic Studies.
1970	First exhibit at San Francisco's Galleria de la Raza.
1978	Earns MFA in Visual Arts from the University of California, San Diego.
1978	Creates *Portrait of the Artist as the Virgin of Guadalupe*.
1993	Receives the Chicanos in Arts Award from the National Association for Chicano Studies.

Further reading: http://www.yolandalopez.net (López's official Web site).
http://cemaweb.library.ucsb.edu/lopez_bio.html (biography).

LORENZO, Frank
Airline Entrepreneur

The son of Spanish immigrants, airline entrepreneur Frank Lorenzo became infamous in the 1980s for his harsh business practices. He was once described as the "most hated man in America."

Born in Queens, New York, in 1940, Lorenzo grew up with an interest in aviation. He attended public schools before going to Columbia University. Lorenzo then went on to study at Harvard Business School, graduating in 1963.

The making of the "most hated"

After college Lorenzo went to work for Trans World Airlines and Eastern Airlines. In 1969 he co-founded Jet Capital Corporation, an aircraft leasing company. In 1971 the company acquired the Houston-based Texas International Airlines, after it filed for bankruptcy. Lorenzo set out to turn the business around. He undercut the fares of competitors and radically reduced labor costs by laying off workers and offering the remaining staff lower wages. The strategy paid off and the airline began to thrive.

The Airline Deregulation Act of 1978 ended government control over airline routes and pricing and allowed nonunionized airlines. This gave Lorenzo the opportunity to expand his business empire. Throughout the 1980s he acquired ailing airlines.

Many critics found Lorenzo's business tactics questionable, particularly his employees, who were paid less than union rates. Pilots and crew protested Lorenzo's harsh methods and promoted a boycott of the newly formed New York Air, a nonunion business.

Lorenzo refused to back down, and continued to clash with the unions. Following his 1982 takeover of Continental Airlines, Lorenzo forced the company into the bankruptcy courts, enabling him to fire union members. He then restarted the company, hiring nonunion labor at less than half the pay of the old staff. The new employees also worked longer hours with shorter breaks. Lorenzo's business reputation suffered as customers complained of poor service, and Lorenzo's critics accused him of taking over troubled airlines in order to strip them of their assets. He subsequently sold his interests in Continental.

KEY DATES	
1940	Born in Queens, New York, on May 19.
1971	Takes over Texas International Airlines.
1978	Deregulation Act allows Lorenzo to expand his business.
1991	Files for bankruptcy.

▲ ***After 20 years running airlines, Frank Lorenzo's business collapsed and a court ruled he was unfit to run another company. Despite his business failures, Lorenzo acquired a substantial personal fortune.***

Business failure

In 1986 Lorenzo bought Eastern Airlines for $615 million. He immediately began to reorganize the company, transferring many of the airline's assets to his holding company and firing union staff. In 1989 he came up against the powerful International Association of Machinists (IAM) union. After Lorenzo asked the machinists to take a pay cut, the IAM called a strike that was supported by pilots and flight attendants. The airline was eventually forced into bankruptcy court, which ruled that Lorenzo's practices were questionable and that he was unfit to run the airline. A year later Lorenzo disposed of his airline interests. In 1993 he attempted to start Friendship Airline, but was prevented from doing so by the U.S. Transportation Department.

Further reading: Bernstein, Aaron. *Grounded: Frank Lorenzo and the Destruction of Eastern Airlines*. New York, NY: Simon and Schuster, 1990.
http://www.pbs.org/kcet/chasingthesun/innovators/florenzo.html (article on Lorenzo).

LOS LOBOS

Musicians

Los Lobos is a successful, world-famous band. In its 30-year career the band has had numerous worldwide hit singles and played alongside many legends of popular music. The band's members are highly acclaimed for their skills as performers, especially for their traditional Mexican music.

The Wolves of East Los Angeles

Formed in East Los Angeles, California, in 1974, Los Lobos quickly became a highly respected band with original and wide-ranging musical interests. Its members drew inspiration from their Chicano heritages. Los Lobos, which means "The Wolves" in Spanish, is a shortened version of the band's original name, Los Lobos del este de Los Angeles (The Wolves of East Los Angeles).

David Hidalgo, Conrad Lozano, Louie Perez, and Cesar Rosas, the four founding members of the band, were friends in high school. They started out together playing Mexican music at parties and weddings, and in restaurants in their East Los Angeles neighborhoods. The band developed a style uniquely its own, drawing on a range of influences, and the ambitions of its members soon began to outgrow the scale of their early gigs.

As well as being interested in music, Los Lobos were also involved in local Hispanic American politics. In 1976 they released *Sí Se Puede*, a benefit album for the United Farm Workers (UFW). The labor union, formed by César Chávez, was fighting for the rights of the many Hispanic Americans working on the farms of southern California.

Recording career

In 1978 Los Lobos recorded their first commercial album: *Los Lobos Del Este de Los Angeles (Just Another Band from East L.A.)* on the independent label New Vista Records. They sold most copies at their by now very popular live shows. Early Los Lobos music is often described as "roots rock," a folk-inspired rock and roll. The band's popularity

▼ ***Los Lobos have been performing for more than 30 years and have fans around the world.***

INFLUENCES AND INSPIRATION

The output of Los Lobos has been influenced not only by its members' various cultural heritages but also by their home in East Los Angeles. One of the band's earliest recordings was in support of the injustices experienced by local Hispanic American workers.

Musically, Los Lobos has drawn from a range of eclectic influences, including American rock and roll, Tex-Mex, country, folk, rhythm and blues, blues, and more traditional Spanish and Mexican music. Some of those influences are hybrid forms themselves. Tex-Mex, for example, is a blend of Mexican and Southwestern musical elements. Norteño music is another influence. This genre is related to the polka, and has its roots in northern Mexico.

In 2004 Los Lobos recorded *The Ride* with some of the artists who have inspired the group. Among others, the album featured Elvis Costello.

Los Lobos members have developed several side projects, which have become popular in their own right. David Hidalgo and Louie Perez, for example, founded The Latin Playboys, which has its own loyal following.

in and around the vibrant Los Angeles music scene drew the attention of other groups. One of them, a rockabilly band named The Blasters, booked Los Lobos as its warm-up act. As a result Los Lobos secured a recording contract and found a new member—saxophonist Steve Berlin, who joined from The Blasters.

With Berlin onboard Los Lobos went on to record *...And a Time to Dance* in 1983. One of the tracks, "Anselma," won a Grammy the following year for Best Mexican American Performance.

Critical acclaim

In 1987 the band made a mainstream commercial breakthrough with *La Bamba*, the original soundtrack to the movie of the same name that told the story of Latino singer Ritchie Valens. The album earned the group a second Grammy, for Best Rock Performance by a Duo or Group. Los Lobos consolidated its success later the same year with *By the Light of the Moon*, a rock-based studio recording.

In 1988 Los Lobos veered away from pop and rock and produced *La Pistola y el Corazon*, an acoustic recording of traditional folk songs that won another Grammy for Best Mexican American Performance. In 1992 Los Lobos returned to experimentation with the album *Kiko*, which contained a wide range of musical styles and became the *Los Angeles Times'* Album of the Year. The group also won a MTV video award in 1992 for "Kiko and the Lavender Moon."

KEY DATES

1974	Formed in East Los Angeles, California.
1976	Release benefit album for the United Farm Workers labor union.
1983	"Anselma" wins Grammy award.
1987	Record soundtrack for *La Bamba* motion picture.
2005	Make live recordings to celebrate 30th anniversary.

Different directions

Los Lobos diversified further in 1995, bringing out an album for children, *Papa's Dream: Music for Little People*, with the East Los Angeles musician Lalo Guerrero. One track—"Mariachi Suite"—won a fourth Grammy for Best Pop Instrumental.

In 2002 Los Lobos produced *Good Morning Aztlán*. The album combined a return to the rock-inspired energy of earlier work with an exploration of Mexican mythology. (Aztlán is the mythical homeland of the Aztecs.) In 2005 the band celebrated its 30th anniversary with a live retrospective album recorded over two days at the Filmore in San Francisco, California.

Los Lobos have been highly influential. They illustrated how musical cultures and styles could be blended in commercially successful ways. By combining musical instruments commonly found in Norteño and other traditional styles of Mexican music with U.S. rock and roll, the band was able to develop a unique musical sound. Consequently members of Los Lobos have not had to downplay their cultural backgrounds in order to reach mainstream audiences.

See also: Chávez, César; Guerrero, Lalo; Valens, Ritchie

Further reading: http://hollywoodrecords.go.com/LosLobos (Web site maintained by Los Lobos's record company).

LUJAN, Manuel Luis

Politician

Manuel Luis Lujan was a politician who served as a cabinet member in the administration of President George H. W. Bush. As secretary of the interior, Lujan was responsible for public land, including mines, Native American reservations, and national parks. While in office he worked to cut down on air and water pollution, protected wetlands, and oversaw the clean-up operation after the *Exxon Valdez* oil spill in Alaska in 1989.

Early life

Lujan was born in San Ildefonso, New Mexico, in 1928. San Ildefonso is a tiny Native American pueblo beside the Rio Grande. Lujan grew up on a farm on the outskirts of the ancient settlement. Lujan went to grade school and high school at Our Lady of Guadalupe. He graduated from St. Michael's High School in Santa Fe in 1946. After a brief spell at a college in California, Lujan earned a BA from the College of Santa Fe in 1950. He joined the National Guard Reserve and served as vice chairman of the New Mexico Republican Party.

Political career

Lujan's father had been mayor of Santa Fe and had also run for the state governorship and for Congress. However, it was the younger Lujan who was the first to win a state election. On January 3, 1969, Lujan was elected to Congress as a Republican. He served in this capacity for the next 20 years.

On January 26, 1989, Lujan was nominated by President George H. W. Bush to be secretary of the interior. He served in the post for almost four years. On February 8, 1989, at Lujan's swearing-in ceremony, President Bush commented that Lujan had experience in dealing with the issues of the department. The president mentioned Lujan's duties as a member of the House Committee on Interior and Insular Affairs. He noted that in 20 years of service in Congress, Lujan had kept in touch with the people who were affected by government policies. (Lujan was well known for celebrating his Hispanic American roots by wearing a bolo tie while in office.)

Despite many successes, Lujan's term of office was not smooth. He was prone to making gaffes in public, once admitting in a press conference on mining rights, "I don't know what I'm talking about." Nevertheless, Lujan served for a full four-year term. Lujan lives in Albuquerque, New Mexico, and launched the think-tank Hispanic Alliance for Progress Institute in 2004.

▲ ***Manuel Lujan was the first Hispanic American to be appointed secretary of the interior.***

KEY DATES

1928 Born in San Ildefonso, New Mexico, on May 12.

1950 Graduated from the College of Santa Fe in Santa Fe, New Mexico.

1969 Elected to Congress.

1989 Nominated as secretary of the interior of the United States on January 26.

Further reading: Enciso, Carmen. *Hispanic Americans in Congress, 1882–1995.* Washington, D.C.: Government Printing Office, 1995.

LUJÁN, Tony
Musician

Tony Luján is a jazz trumpeter who is unafraid to venture into uncharted musical territory. His unique style of jazz fuses Latin jazz with mainstream influences, in what one critic has described as an "historic and revolutionary creativity."

Early life

Born Saul Antonio Luján, III, in 1956 in Albuquerque, New Mexico, Luján soon showed a gift for music. His early musical training came from his father, a self-taught musician who sang, played the trumpet, the button accordion, and the guitar in church and in local mariachi bands. Luján began playing the trumpet at the age of nine, encouraged by his father to play by ear and without sheet music. "You have to have an ear first," Luján recalls his father telling him. It was after he developed this ability that Luján began studying musical theory in a more formal way. Like many jazz musicians, Luján's first public performances were in church.

Luján's talent was recognized early and nurtured through private lessons that helped put him on to musical success. Luján's high-school band director introduced him to jazz trumpet legend Clark Terry (1920–) in 1971. Luján so impressed the jazz master that they formed a life-long friendship. Luján called Terry his "musical father."

Luján won many awards while in high school. He performed with the Albuquerque Youth Symphony, and was named to the All-City and New Mexico All-State jazz bands. While still in high school, Luján was also a member of the University of New Mexico (UNM) Honor Band. After high school, Luján attended UNM for two years before transferring to the University of Nevada in Las Vegas, where he played music "24-hours a day." After school Luján washed dishes by day and played his trumpet by night in Las Vegas hotel bands. There he accompanied some of the greatest entertainers in the world, and his career began to take off. In 1981 Luján got his break when he was invited to join Clark Terry on a world tour.

KEY DATES	
1956	Born in Albuquerque, New Mexico, on October 3.
1981	Tours the world with jazz legend Clark Terry.
2003	Releases *Tribute*.

▲ ***Jazz trumpeter Tony Luján was responsible for developing the Bop Latino style.***

Latin influences

In the 1980s Tito Puente hired Luján and introduced him to Latin jazz. He went on to play with every major Latin jazz name, including Eddie Palmieri, Carlos Santana, Poncho Sanchez, and many others.

During the 1980s and 1990s, Luján played on hundreds of records and television and movie soundtracks. He also toured with Ray Charles, Vikki Carr, Luis Miguel, Frank Sinatra, Gerald Wilson, Bob Florence, and others. Luján was also lead trumpet for the international tour of the Broadway musical *A Chorus Line*.

The 21st century has seen Luján mature into a leading jazz innovator. His 2003 recording, *Tribute*, is an homage to his trumpet heroes and is dedicated to mentor Clark Terry. Luján is an active composer, leads his own ensembles, and teaches the trumpet through clinics and master classes throughout the United States and abroad.

See also: Carr, Vicki; Miguel, Luis; Palmieri, Eddie; Puente, Tito; Sanchez, Poncho; Santana, Carlos

Further reading: Fernandez, Raul A. *From Afro-Cuban Rhythms to Latin Jazz*. Berkeley, CA: University of California Press, 2006.
http://www.tonylujan.com/TonyLujanMain.html (Luján's Web site).

LUNA, Solomon
Politician

Solomon Luna was a leading businessman and politician in the transitional period of New Mexico from a United States territory to statehood. He was a Hispano—a Mexican living in New Mexico—and a member of the upper classes. As such Luna represented the interests of wealthier people in New Mexico.

Family ties

Solomon Luna was born in New Mexico in 1858. He was descended from Spanish nobleman Domingo de Luna, the first European to settle in the area on land that eventually became Los Lunas in Valencia County, New Mexico. Luna was also related by marriage to the Otero family, another powerful New Mexico family with links to Spanish nobility. Luna married Adelaida Otero, and Manuel A. Otero married Luna's sister Eloisa.

Luna was a graduate of St. Louis University, Missouri, and was president of the Albuquerque Bank of Commerce. With his brother Tranquilino, he established a financial network in Valencia County that lasted well into the 20th century. He served as president of the Sheep Growers' Association and president of the Sheep Sanitary Board.

▼ ***Solomon Luna was a member of a wealthy New Mexico family. Unlike many of his relatives at the time, he was remembered for his honesty.***

KEY DATES

1858	Born in New Mexico about this time.
1892	Elected sheriff.
1894	Becomes treasurer of Valencia County, New Mexico.
1912	Dies in Horse Springs, New Mexico, about this time.

Luna monument

New Mexico politics and business were intricately linked. The Otero and Luna families prospered while many smaller farms were going out of business. In 1880 the Atchison-Topeka-Santa Fe Railway wanted to pass through Luna property and paid a high price for the land. Don Antonio José Luna, the head of the family, also had the railroad build him a new house, which became the Luna-Otero Mansion, a New Mexico landmark. When Don Antonio José died, the house was passed on to Tranquilino Luna; at his death, the house went to Solomon Luna.

Political career

Luna began his career in public service in 1885, when he was elected to be probate clerk in Valencia County. He was later elected sheriff and the county treasurer and tax collector. In 1896 he was elected to the National Republican Committee from New Mexico, but declined the Republican nomination to run for Congress in 1900. However, he did accept a delegate seat at the 1910 Constitutional Convention of New Mexico, leading a delegation of 35 Hispanic Americans.

Luna had a significant impact on New Mexico's constitution, ensuring the equality of the English and Spanish languages and enforcing the rights of Mexicans enshrined in the Treaty of Guadalupe Hidalgo (1848). For his hard work, Luna County, New Mexico, was named for him. Luna died under mysterious circumstances in 1912 while overseeing the dipping of his sheep. His body was found in a vat of acid and soap. Murder and suicide were both considered, but his death was ruled an accident.

See also: Otero Family

Further reading: http://elibrary.unm.edu/oanm/NmU/nmu1%23mss102bc (biography).

MACHITO

Musician

Machito is universally recognized as the godfather of Latin jazz, one of New York City's three original mambo kings, and a major inspiration for the later birth of salsa music. Between 1940 and his death, Machito led one of the best, most authentic, and influential Cuban bands in the United States: Machito and His Afro-Cubans.

KEY DATES	
1912	Born in Tampa, Florida, on February 16, 1912.
1928	Begins playing with big bands in Havana.
1937	Moves to New York City.
1940	Co-founds Machito and His Afro-Cubans with Mario Bauzá.
1975	Bauzá leaves the band after 35 years.
1982	Machito wins a Grammy for the album *Machito and His Salsa Big Band*.
1984	Dies while on tour in London, England, on April 16.

Early life

Machito was born Francisco Raúl Gutiérrez Grillo in Tampa, Florida, in 1912, where his Cuban father was a migrant tobacco worker. Machito moved to Havana, Cuba, with his family as a small child. (Some sources have Machito being born in Havana itself between 1908 and 1915.)

The innovative career of Machito cannot be separated from that of his brother-in-law Mario Bauzá. The pair cofounded the Afro-Cubans. Machito played the role of the charismatic front man with the voice and maracas, while Bauzá was the behind-the-scenes innovator skillfully balancing complex Cuban rhythms with jazz influences. Together, Machito and Bauzá practically invented the musical genre Latin jazz in the 1940s; it is even called Afro-Cuban jazz largely because of their group.

Moving to New York

Machito and Bauzá began their musical career in the big bands of 1930s Havana. They both moved independently to New York in the later part of that decade, just two members of the huge Hispanic immigration to the city that had begun in the 1920s. As a result of the influx of immigrants, mainly from Puerto Rico, East Harlem was being transformed into El Barrio. East Harlem was near Harlem, the most important African American community in the United States at the time and a world capital of jazz. The musicians began assimilating Cuban rhythms and black American jazz with their own homegrown musical

▼ ***Machito plays the maracas as he leads his band, The Afro-Cubans, in 1940s New York. Mario Bauzá is the trumpet player left of the drum set.***

INFLUENCES AND INSPIRATION

The irony of both Machito and Bauzá's musical careers lies in the fact that they became permanently estranged from their homeland after the Cuban revolution in 1959. Neither man performed in Cuba after 1957, nor did either ever become famous in Cuba. Despite this fact, Machito's long musical career benefited from a solid grounding in Cuban big bands during the 1930s.

After arriving in New York City, but before joining Bauzá in 1940 to form the Afro-Cubans, Machito recorded with Puerto Rican pianist Noro Morales (1911–1964), as well as with Xavier Cugat's famous orchestra.

Machito's success in the United States playing a hybrid musical style also made him a major influence on a wide range of U.S. musicians and musical styles from jazz and rhythm and blues to salsa. At Bauzá's urging, many leading jazz musicians collaborated with Machito's band in the 1940s and 1950s, including Dizzy Gillespie and Charlie Parker.

Machito's pianist and musical arranger, Rene Hernandez, was especially influential. He developed a signature piano style that was also a major influence on jazz musicians.

Finally, Machito inspired the likes of Willie Colon and Johnny Pacheco, who pumped new life into Latin music in the 1970s under the label "salsa." When asked in the 1980s about modern Latin music, Machito said, "Salsa is a replica of what we have been doing for the past fifty years."

styles. On top of all this was the fact that between exclusive, high society downtown, and the liberal and exciting uptown, New York City provided an incomparable mixture of musical venues, tastes, and ethnicities that included African Americans, Cubans, Puerto Ricans, Jews, and Italians.

The Afro-Cubans were formed in 1940, when Bauzá left Cab Calloway's jazz band to work with Dizzy Gillespie and Machito himself, who had just arrived in New York in 1937. The band was formed with the express purpose of creating a fusion between the popular Afro-Cuban music the pair had grown up with and the African American jazz they were surrounded by in New York.

Afro-Cuban jazz is born

The fruit of this creative fusion was evident soon after the band began performing in December 1940, with hit songs such as "La Paella" and "Sopa de Pichon" written by Machito, "Nagüe" by Chano Pozo, and "La Rumba Soy Yo" by the group's sometime vocalist Miguelito Valdés. Until 1942 the group's repertoire was strictly Cuban. However, their unique talent at combining Cuban music with U.S. jazz became evident when they debuted Bauzá's "Tanga," considered the first Afro-Cuban jazz piece, at New York's La Conga cabaret in 1943.

Machito and Bauzá were hugely successful with the Afro-Cubans. Also, given the band's mixed racial ancestry they were instrumental in breaking down the racial barriers that had previously prevented "black" orchestras from playing on Broadway. They also succeeded in coming up with an original yet authentic sound that could appeal both to blacks and whites, Latinos and Anglos, and hard-to-please jazz afficionados, as well as the most demanding mambo dancers.

Competition

Afro-Cuban jazz was a musician's music played more for listening to than for dancing. By the late 1940s, a new, high-energy style of Cuban music began to compete and sometimes combine with Machito's jazz in New York. Spreading rapidly from Cuba to Mexico to New York and then across the world, the new style was called mambo.

Machito and his band were soon incorporating mambo into their performances. From 1947 to 1966, the Afro-Cubans performed at the nonstop dance competitions taking place at New York's Palladium Ballroom on Broadway. Machito alternated with two other "mambo kings" (and sometime collaborators), the Puerto Rican bandleaders Tito Puente and Tito Rodríguez (1923–1973).

Two years after winning a Grammy in 1982 for one of his last albums, *Machito and His Salsa Big Band*, Machito died of a heart attack and brain hemorrhage just before taking the stage at Ronny Scott's jazz club in London.

See also: Bauzá, Mario; Colón, Willie; Cugat, Xavier; Pacheco, Johnny; Prado, Perez; Pozo, Chano; Puente, Tito

Further reading: Acosta, Leonardo. *Cubano Be, Cubano Bop: One Hundred Years of Jazz in Cuba*. Washington, DC: Smithsonian Books, 2003.
http://www.gale.com/free_resources/chh/bio/machito.htm (biography).

MACHUCA, Esther N.

Activist

Mexican American Esther Machuca was an important figure in the early history of the League of United Latin American Citizens (LULAC). LULAC is the oldest surviving Hispanic American civil rights organization in the United States. During the 1930s, Machuca was instrumental in developing the women's counterpart to the male-dominated LULAC—Ladies LULAC. By challenging the male domination of the league, alongside other pioneering Latinas such as Alice Dickerson Montemayor (1902–1989), Machuca helped alter its male-centered ideology.

Early life

Esther Nieto was born in 1895, in Ojinaga, a border town in the Mexican state of Chihuahua. Her parents were well off and middle class, and she received a good education.

In 1915, Machuca married Juan C. Machuca, and the couple settled in El Paso, Texas. During the 1920s, Mexican Americans living in Texas were subjected to discrimination and kept segregated from other citizens. In response, Juan Machuca, like a number of middle-class Tejanos (Mexican Americans living in Texas), became involved in civil rights activity. This culminated in the foundation of LULAC in Corpus Christi, Texas, in 1929.

Feminist activism

Hispanic American women, however, were barred from becoming LULAC members. In addition female activists, generally the wives and daughters of male LULAC members, were usually confined to auxiliary roles, helping out with administrative tasks or acting as hostesses at meetings.

By 1932, women activists were growing frustrated with their secondary role and were beginning to organize themselves independently of the men. The following year saw the foundation of Ladies LULAC, a sister organization to the male-only league.

Local councils, or chapters, of Ladies LULAC began to appear across Texas. In 1934, Machuca became a founding member of the ninth Ladies LULAC council in El Paso. She was also the council's first treasurer. At first the female "LULACers" were not always welcomed by their male colleagues, many of whom considered activism to be the preserve of men. Many male LULAC members chose to ignore the activities of the sister councils. Several national leaders of LULAC refused even to accept the existence of Ladies LULAC. In protest, Machuca and the rest of the El Paso Ladies council briefly disbanded in 1936. In the following year, however, the group reorganized with a renewed vigor, and Machuca began to establish more councils across the Southwest.

In charge

Between 1938 and 1939, Machuca served as the organizer general of Ladies LULAC. During her tenure she helped set up new chapters in Las Vegas, New Mexico, and Dallas, Texas, as well as in Arizona and California.

Machuca also used her position to heighten awareness of women's issues across the whole civil rights movement. In 1939, she edited an edition of *LULAC News* that contained stories and articles by LULAC women about Ladies LULAC activities. These encompassed everything from fundraising to the setting up of care programs for the sick and the elderly and voter-registration schemes.

Ladies LULAC continued to flourish for several decades. By the 1970s, LULAC councils were fully integrated, and Ladies LULAC councils had all but disappeared. Machuca remained an active LULAC member until her death in January 1980.

KEY DATES

1895 Born in Ojinaga, Mexico, on October 10.

1915 Moves to El Paso, Texas.

1934 Helps found El Paso council of Ladies LULAC (League of United Latin American Citizens).

1937 Establishes 15th Ladies LULAC council in Laredo, Texas.

1938 Becomes organizer general of Ladies LULAC.

1939 Edits women's edition of *LULAC News*, the monthly newspaper of LULAC.

1980 Dies in El Paso, Texas, on January 26.

Further reading: Kaplowitz, Craig Allan. *LULAC, Mexican Americans, and National Policy*. College Station, TX: Texas A&M University Press, 2005.
http://www.tsha.utexas.edu/handbook/online/articles/MM/fmadb.html (biography).

MANZANO, Sonia
Actor

Sonia Manzano played the role of Maria Rodriguez on the long-running children's television series *Sesame Street* for more than 30 years. One of the first Hispanic American actors to appear regularly on television, Manzano has been a positive role model for millions of young viewers, playing a key part in educating children about diversity. She has received numerous honors for her work, including two nominations for an Emmy Award for her performance in the show, and 15 shared awards with her *Sesame Street* cowriters.

Early life
Sonia Manzano was born in 1950 on the Lower East Side of Manhattan, New York City, to Puerto Rican parents who later moved the family to the South Bronx area. A talented performer, Manzano studied acting at the High School of the Performing Arts in New York City. She went on to win a scholarship to Carnegie-Mellon University in Pittsburgh, Pennsylvania, but left in her junior year to star in the Broadway musical *Godspell*.

▼ ***Sonia Manzano joins the* Sesame Street *character Grover in 2002 to celebrate the 4,000th episode of the children's show.***

KEY DATES

1950	Born in New York City, New York.
1973	Begins the role of Maria on *Sesame Street*.
2003	Wins Hispanic Heritage Award for Education.

The way to *Sesame Street*
In 1969 Manzano was cast as the voice of Smart Tina, a muppet character on *Sesame Street*. However, in 1973 she was cast as the human resident Maria Rodriguez. The role brought Manzano lasting fame. After 10 years as Maria, Manzano also began cowriting *Sesame Street's* scripts. She has since written Nickelodeon's award-winning series *Little Bill* and the critically acclaimed children's book *No Dogs Allowed!* (2004).

Manzano has had a few small roles in feature films, including *Death Wish* (1974), *Firepower* (1979), and *Night Flowers* (1979). Her film career has otherwise been dominated by feature-length *Sesame Street* productions, including *Elmo Saves Christmas* (1996) and *The Adventures of Elmo in Grouchland* (1999). On stage Manzano has starred in several plays, including *The Vagina Monologues* (2002) and *The Exonerated* (2003).

Wider recognition
Manzano has shared several prestigious awards with her *Sesame Street* cowriters, including numerous Emmy Awards. She has been nominated twice for the Emmy for the Outstanding Performer in a Children's Series. Manzano won the Hispanic Heritage Award for Education in 2003. She has also been honored by the Congressional Hispanic Caucus, the Association of Hispanic Arts, the National Hispanic Media Coalition, and the Committee for Hispanic Children and Families.

Manzano has worked for the March of Dimes charity and currently serves on the board of the New York arts center Symphony Space. She lives in New York City with her husband and daughter.

Further reading: Borgenicht, David. *Sesame Street Unpaved: Scripts, Stories, Secrets and Songs.* New York, NY: Hyperion Books, 1998.
http://www.soniamanzano.com (Manzano's Web site).

MARC ANTHONY

Singer

Marc Anthony was the top-selling salsa singer of the 1990s. Born Marco Antonio Muñiz in 1969 in New York City, he later changed his name to avoid confusion with the Mexican singer (born 1933) for whom he had been named. His parents, Felipe and Guillermina Muñiz, were Puerto Ricans. He was introduced to Latin rhythms by his father, and grew up listening to music by Rubén Blades, Héctor Lavoe, Willie Colón, and José Feliciano. At age seven he enrolled at the East Harlem Music School. Five years later commercial producer David Harris heard him performing a Mickey Mouse tune, and hired him as a backing singer. Before long Marc Anthony was singing and even writing material for artists such as Safire, The Latin Rascals, and Menudo.

Hitting the charts

Marc Anthony's professional career began in 1991 when "Little" Louie Vega invited him to be his singer. Later that year Anthony released a single of his own, "Ride on the Rhythm," which spent 11 weeks in the *Billboard* Top 10 and a further eight weeks on the top 40 radio, dance, and music lists.

In 1992 Latin bandleader Tito Puente asked Anthony and Vega to open his show at Madison Square Garden. The following year Anthony released his debut album, *Otra Nota*, featuring the track "Hasta que te conocí," which became his first salsa hit.

Anthony was first nominated for a Grammy in 1995 for his Spanish collection *Todo a su tiempo*, and won the award three years later for the album *Contra la corriente*. He has since received further Grammys, as well as numerous awards from the Recording Industry Association of America (RIAA), including 12 Latin and standard gold and platinum certifications.

KEY DATES

1969	Born in New York City, New York, on September 16.
1991	Has first solo hit single with "Ride on the Rhythm."
1992	Releases debut album, *Otra Nota*.
2000	Marries Dayanara Torres, a former Miss Universe.
2004	Marries Jennifer Lopez; appears in *Man on Fire*, a movie with Denzel Washington.

▲ ***Marc Anthony has recorded in both Spanish and English to help bring salsa to a wider audience.***

Anthony's success has not been limited to music. He has also acted in numerous movies, most notably *Hackers* (1995), *Big Night* (1996), *Bringing Out the Dead* (1999), *The Substitute* (1999), *In the Time of the Butterflies* (2002), and *Man on Fire* (2004), with Denzel Washington. He has also featured in *New York Magazine*'s top 10 list of influential New Yorkers.

Personal life

In his youth Marc Anthony had a daughter, Ariana, by a woman in New York. In May 2000 he married Dayanara Torres, a former Miss Universe. The couple had two children, Cristian and Ryan, before divorcing in June 2004. Later that year Anthony married the singer Jennifer Lopez.

See also: Blades, Rubén; Colón, Willie; Feliciano, José; Lavoe, Héctor; Lopez, Jennifer; Menudo; Puente, Tito; Vega, "Little" Louie

Further reading: Benson, Sonia B. *The Hispanic American Almanac. A Reference Work on Hispanics in the United States.* Detroit, MI: Gale, 2003.

MARGIL DE JÉSUS, Antonio
Missionary

Antonio Margil de Jésus stands out as one of Texas's most celebrated missionaries. Margil wrote that he evangelized Native Americans for "the good of their souls." Margil lobbied strongly against the enslavement of native people by colonial landowners, and helped Indians become accustomed to farming and ranching near the missions. He is also associated with a miracle called "The Eyes of Father Margil": During a time of extreme drought, Margil was reported to have struck a rock twice into the bed of a dry creek, after which water poured from the place that he had hit until the rains came to restore the creek's water level.

Early life

Born in Valencia, Spain, in 1657, Margil was the son of Juan Margil and Esperanza Ros. From an early age, he described himself as *"la misma nada,"* translated as "nothingness itself." At age 15, Margil entered the Franciscan religious order, and it is thought that he added "de Jesús" to his name at about this time.

From Spain to the New World

Margil excelled in the study of philosophy and theology. Ordained as a priest in 1682, in the following year Margil set sail for the New World. He first served at the Franciscan College of Querétaro, outside Mexico City. Margil preached in the nearby mountains to Native American tribes such as the Talamancas and Lacandóns.

From 1697 to 1701 Margil supervised the Franciscan College of Santa Cruz, Mexico. Through 1706, he preached in Central and South America. In 1707 Margil founded the College of Our Lady of Guadalupe in Zacatecas, Mexico, which served as a resource for missionaries who preached and established missions throughout the countryside.

KEY DATES

1657	Born in Valencia, Spain, on August 18.
1683	Sets sail for America on March 4.
1716	Directs East Texas missions.
1720	Founds the famous San Antonio mission.
1726	Dies in Mexico City, Mexico.

▲ ***Antonio Margil de Jésus was a devoted missionary who traveled across East Texas in his bare feet to found his missions.***

Margil joined an expedition bound for Texas in 1716. He founded four missions, including Our Lady of Guadalupe in present-day Nacogdoches, Texas, and Our Lady of the Immaculate Conception in present-day San Antonio: Conception (named Conception of Ágreda after the Spanish mystic María de Ágreda) is considered Texas's best preserved Spanish mission. Margil founded two additional missions, and served as president of all of the Texas missions founded by Zacatecas missionaries. In 1720 he founded the noted San Antonio mission, St. Joseph and St. Michael of Aguayo. He supervised the College of Zacatecas for three years, after which he resumed missionary work in Mexico until his death in 1726.

Further reading: Chipman, Donald E. *Explorers and Settlers of Spanish Texas*. Austin, TX: University of Texas Press, 2001. http://www.tsha.utexas.edu/handbook/online/articles/MM/fma45.html (biography).

MARICHAL, Juan
Baseball Player

Juan Marichal was a major-league baseball pitcher for 14 years. He was known for his energetic pitching style and a high kick. His style earned him the nickname "The Dominican Dandy." Marichal was also highly aggressive, and often attempted to intimidate opposing batters by aiming to hit their helmets.

Early career

Juan Antonio Marichal Sanchez was born on October 20, 1937, in Laguna Verde, Dominican Republic. He left school in the 11th grade and became a pitcher for a number of local teams. His amateur career was impressive enough that he was signed by the Santo Domingo team Escogido Leones, who scouted the pitcher for the San Francisco Giants.

On July 19, 1960, Marichal was called up to the majors and became the starting pitcher for the Giants against the Philadelphia Phillies. He struck out the first two batters he faced, ending the game with a 2–0 win. Marichal spent the next several years building up an impressive record. 1963 was a banner year for him, with 25 wins and eight losses. On June 15, 1963, Marichal pitched a perfect no-hitter against the Houston Colt 45s.

▲ ***Juan Marichal poses at his locker after winning his 200th game as a pitcher for the San Francisco Giants in 1970.***

Dominant figure

While pitching for the Giants during the 1960s, Marichal won more than 190 games, leading the National League with most games won. Marichal was an All-Star player nine times, pitching in eight of the games. His career spanned a decade and a half, during which time he was known for his high leg kick while pitching and his domination on the mound.

It was this tendency toward intimidating players that caused some problems for Marichal. Batting in a game against the Los Angeles Dodgers in 1965, Marichal got angry at the tactics of Dodger catcher John Roseboro and hit him on the head with his bat. Marichal was fined by the baseball commission, and sued by Roseboro.

KEY DATES

1937 Born in Laguna Verde, Dominican Republic, on October 20.

1960 Makes his major league debut against the Philadelphia Phillies on July 19.

1965 Named All-Star Game Most Valuable Player.

1983 Inducted into the Baseball Hall of Fame.

Other setbacks

Marichal suffered from several injuries. In 1962, when appearing in his only World Series game, he fractured his index finger trying to bunt. He suffered from several more minor injuries, but continued to play. However, Marichal's career was badly affected by back problems from 1972, which forced him to retire a few years later. He retired with a 243-142 record. Marichal later became the minister of sports for the Dominican Republic.

Further reading: Devaney, John. *Juan Marichal: Mister Strike.* New York: Putnam, 1970.
http://www.baseballhalloffame.org/hofers_and_honorees/hofer_bios/marichal_juan.htm (biography).

MARIN, Cheech

Actor

Along with Canadian actor Tommy Chong (1938–), Richard "Cheech" Marin was half of the iconic counter-culture comedy partnership Cheech and Chong. Popular in the 1970s and early 1980s, the duo starred in six Cheech and Chong films. They also made six gold-disk comedy recordings, winning a Grammy for one of them.

Marin's solo career has spanned four decades and includes directing, television roles, and voiceover work for animated films. Marin has championed Chicano art to a wider American audience, and is known for his charitable contributions to the Hispanic American community.

KEY DATES

1946 Born in Los Angeles, California, on July 13.

1973 Wins Grammy for Best Comedy Recording.

1978 *Up in Smoke* grosses $100 million.

1999 ALMA Community Service Award for work on behalf of the Latino community.

2005 Directs *Latinologues* on Broadway.

Early life

Richard Anthony Marin was born on July 13, 1946, in South Central Los Angeles, California, to second-generation Mexican American parents. His father, Oscar Marin, was a Los Angeles police officer, and his mother, Elsa Meza, raised seven other children. The nickname "Cheech" came from his fondness for chicharrónnes, deep-fried pork rinds.

When Marin was 10, his family moved to the Granada Hills suburb in the San Fernando Valley, Los Angeles. A musical child who sang and played the guitar, Marin performed with neighborhood rock bands at high school. He graduated with straight A grades and enrolled at California State University, in part to avoid the draft. Majoring in English, Marin dropped out in 1968 just eight credits short of getting his degree, again to avoid the draft. He moved to Canada, settling in Vancouver.

Marin met Tommy Chong in a Vancouver comedy club owned by Chong's brother. He approached Chong asking for the opportunity to perform in the club. Eventually the

▼ ***Cheech Marin (sitting) appears with musician Bob Dylan in the 2003 comedy* Masked and Anonymous.**

INFLUENCES AND INSPIRATION

Marin cites Mexican American culture as his inspiration, and throughout his career he has frequently drawn on his ethnic heritage for his characterizations and other creative work. Marin is also passionate about introducing Chicano (Mexican American) art to a wider audience and educating Americans about the contribution of Chicanos to U.S. culture. Marin has said that he values work that talks about the experience of being Chicano. A self-taught art appreciator, Marin began collecting art when he became wealthy during his early movie career. His private collection of Chicano art is now the world's largest. He has shared it with the public through the exhibition "Chicano Visions: American Painters on the Verge," and his accompanying book. In doing so, he has also helped establish the Chicano school of painting.

pair combined their talents in the improvisational comedy and music group City Works. This evolved into the double act Cheech and Chong, in which the two men played hippies searching for marijuana. Marin returned to Los Angeles with Chong, and the duo began opening for rock bands including The Rolling Stones.

The golden years

Cheech and Chong's first comedy recording, *Cheech & Chong* (1971), went gold, a title awarded to albums that sell over 500,000 copies. Their next album, *Big Bambu* (1972), became the best selling comedy record of all time. In 1973 the pair won a Grammy for their *Los Cochinos* album, which featured the novelty hit record "Basketball Jones." This was followed by *Cheech & Chong's Wedding Album* and *Sleeping Beauty*.

As a result of their popular success, Cheech and Chong were invited by Warner Brothers to make *Up in Smoke* (1978). It became one of the company's highest-grossing films, taking more than $100 million worldwide. The pair made a further five Cheech & Chong films, which they cowrote, with scores by Marin: *Cheech & Chong's Next Movie* (1980), *Nice Dreams* (1981), *Things Are Tough All Over* (1982), and *Still Smokin'* (1983).

The duo also made guest appearances in *Yellowbeard* (1983) and Martin Scorcese's *After Hours* (1985). *Cheech & Chong's The Corsican Brothers* (1984) was considerably less successful than their earlier films. The Cheech and Chong partnership ended in the mid 1980s as attitudes toward drug use made their act outdated. The last Cheech and Chong film was the mock documentary *Get Out of My Room* (1985).

Solo career

Marin directed *Get Out of My Room*. However, his breakthrough as a film director came with the immigration movie *Born In East L.A.* (1985), which he wrote, directed, and starred in as a third-generation Mexican American. Acting roles followed in *Fatal Beauty* (1987), *Ghostbusters II* (1989), and *Shrimp on the Barbie* (1990). Marin has undertaken many popular voiceover roles, including playing the dog Tito in Disney's *Oliver and Company* (1988) and the hyena Banzai in *The Lion King* (1994). In 1992 he was reunited with Tommy Chong as the Beetle Boys in *FernGully: The Last Rainforest* (1992). Marin's television appearances have included the sitcom *The Golden Palace* (1992), *Judging Amy* (1999 to the present), and *Resurrection Blvd* (between 2000 and 2002). Marin joined the police drama *Nash Bridges* in 1996 as Don Johnson's partner, Inspector Joe Dominguez.

Marin has worked with Mexican American filmmaker Robert Rodríguez six times, in *Desperado* (1995), *From Dusk till Dawn* (1996), *Spy Kids* (2001), *Spy Kids 2: Island of Lost Dreams* (2002), *Spy Kids 3-D: Game Over* (2003), and *Once upon a Time in Mexico* (2003). Marin's later film roles include *Christmas with the Kranks* (2004), *The Underclassman* (2004), the first Hispanic-American produced animated film *Sian Ka'an* (2005), and Disney's *Cars* (2006).

Chicano work

Marin has released bilingual albums for children, including *My Name Is Cheech the School Bus Driver* (1997). Committed to supporting community programs, Marin earned the ALMA Community Service Award in 1999. In 2005 he directed *Latinologues*, a collection of monologues about the Hispanic American experience in America. Marin is married with three children and lives in San Francisco.

See also: Rodríguez, Robert

Further reading: Menard, Valerie. *Cheech Marin*. Bear, DE: M. Lane, 2002.
http://www.chicano-art-life.com/cheech.html (biography).

MARIN, Rosario
Politician

Rosario Marin's life story is proof of the power of the American dream. She began as a young Mexican immigrant unable to speak English and ultimately reached the highest levels of U.S. government. At all levels of political office, from mayor to treasurer of the United States, Marin has worked across party lines to form a consensus. Moreover, she successfully fulfilled her public duties while raising a family.

Born in Mexico

Rosario Marin was born in Mexico City, Mexico, in 1958. She was raised by her parents, Mariano and Carmen Spindola, a janitor and a seamstress. When Marin was 14, her family moved to Huntington Park, California. There she confronted the first of her life's many great challenges when she applied to the local public school.

Marin failed the school's standardized assessment tests because she could not read or speak English. Consequently, the school diagnosed her as mentally disabled. Nevertheless, through grit—and a lot of study—she graduated from high school with honors. Marin has shown similar levels of determination throughout her public and private life.

Multitasker

Marin had learned the hard way that education is essential for success. She had to work her way through college because her family was far from wealthy. Consequently it took her four years to complete a two-year degree at East Los Angeles College. For the next three years Marin juggled a day job at City National Bank while she earned her bachelor of science degree by attending night classes at California State University in Los Angeles.

On September 19, 1981, Marin married Alex Marin. When their first child, Eric, was diagnosed in 1985 with Down syndrome, Marin quit her job to care for him. The couple later had two more children, Carmen and Alex.

▲ ***While serving as U.S. treasurer between 2001 and 2003, Rosario Marin was the highest ranking Hispanic American woman in George W. Bush's first-term administration.***

KEY DATES

1958	Born in Mexico City, Mexico, on August 4.
1983	Graduates with bachelor's degree from California State University, Los Angeles.
1985	Advocates for the disabled when son Eric is diagnosed with Down syndrome.
1994	Elected as mayor of Huntington Park, California.
1995	Awarded Rose Fitzgerald Kennedy Prize.
2000	Appointed U.S. treasurer until 2003.
2004	Chairs California Integrated Waste Management Board.

Launches political career

Initially, Marin anguished over her son's disability. She felt it to be a tragedy. She abandoned her ambitions of eventually owning a bank. However, in 1992 Marin

INFLUENCES AND INSPIRATION

Marin attributes her strong work ethic to her father, Mariano, who never lost a day's work through illness. She also says her mother, Carmen, gave her an unshakable faith in God, herself, and her family as a whole. These influences helped her immeasurably as she faced a new school environment when she first arrived in California, and when her first son, Eric, was unexpectedly born with an incurable disorder.

Outside the family, Marin sums up her parents' legacy by revealing that she sees herself as an "obrera de la communidad," a "worker on behalf of the community." This is apparent in many of Marin's life's undertakings: championing the rights of the disabled, leading efforts to bring literacy programs to Hispanic Americans, promoting financial literacy to the poor, and promoting diversity.

founded FUERZA, Inc., the country's first Spanish-speaking support group for parents of children with Down syndrome. Marin worked tirelessly assisting families, and became a forceful advocate of their needs at the California state legislature.

Marin's political skills drew the attention of then California governor Pete Wilson, who asked her to serve as chief of legislative affairs for the Department of Development Services. During Marin's service, Wilson (a Republican) signed into state law the most comprehensive reforms in aid of disabled persons for more than 20 years.

While successfully serving in a variety of posts in the Wilson administration, Marin won election in 1994 to the city council of Huntington Park, California, as a Republican. Huntington Park is a predominantly Hispanic American and Democratic suburb of Los Angeles of about 85,000 residents. The city council elected Marin the city's mayor. Her success in the post ensured that she was reelected in 1999.

In the late 1990s, Marin was also appointed public relations manager for AT&T's Hispanic customers in Southern California. She still found time to graduate from Harvard University's John F. Kennedy School for Senior Executives in State and Local Government.

Marin for U.S. treasurer

Marin's political activities had made her a well-known figure throughout California. She had become the vice president of the California Republican National Hispanic Assembly. During the 2000 Bush-Cheney presidential campaign, Marin leaped onto the national scene. She proved herself an effective Spanish-speaking advocate for Bush, and she became better known among Hispanic Americans outside of California, too. Once Bush had been installed as president, he nominated Marin to the post of treasurer of the United States in recognition of her important help during the election campaign.

Marin was sworn in as the 41st treasurer on August 16, 2001, becoming the highest-ranking Latina in President Bush's administration. As treasurer, Marin's official duties included overseeing the Bureau of Engraving and Printing and all matters relating to U.S. coinage and currency. The treasurer's signature also appears on all new U.S. paper currency produced while he or she is in office. In addition to her official duties, Marin traveled widely to promote financial literacy among Hispanic Americans and other people whose poor credit history excludes them from the mainstream banking system.

Out of office

In 2003 Marin resigned from her Washington post, saying she wanted to return to California and spend more time with her family. However, her political ambitions were not yet fulfilled. She attempted to win the Republican nomination for California for the 2004 U.S. Senate race. However, she lost out to Bill Jones.

In the same year, Governor Arnold Schwarzenegger appointed Marin as a full-time member of the state's Integrated Waste Management Board. She was elected the chair of the board later that year. Marin's main mission is now to partner with the state's 500 local governments to reduce the amount of resources that end up in landfill sites and recycle them into marketable materials.

Marin has been honored for her work in and out of politics. She received the Rose Fitzgerald Kennedy prize from the United Nations in 1995 for her work on behalf of the disabled. Marin was also awarded an honorary Doctor of Laws degree from California State University.

Further reading: Han, Lori Cox. *Women and American Politics: The Challenges of Political Leadership*. New York, NY: McGraw-Hill, 2007.

http://www.treas.gov/organization/bios/marin-e.html (U.S. Treasury biography).

MARISOL

Artist

Marisol is a sculptor born in France of Venezuelan parents who has lived in the United States since 1950. After studying painting in Paris and New York, she turned to sculpture as her main art form. Her work has been categorized as pop art, but her work also relates a social commentary that places her apart from this movement.

Early life and influences

Marisol Escobar was born in Paris in 1930, and grew up in Europe, the United States, and Caracas, Venezuela, as her wealthy family moved residence. Marisol became interested in art after the death of her mother in 1941. In 1949 she began to study painting at the École des Beaux Arts, Paris. Moving to New York the following year, she studied first at the Art Students League and then, between 1951 and 1954, at the progressive New School for Social Research and at the Hans Hofmann School of Fine Arts, which is considered her most important artistic influence.

Marisol mingled in New York artistic circles at the height of abstract expressionism and as pop art appeared. On top of these influences she also began to explore Hispanic American roots and became interested in native and pre-Columbian art. This led her to switch from painting to sculpture.

Works

Marisol approached sculpture as a three-dimensional collage, and combined woodcarving and plaster casts with drawn and painted surfaces and, at times, added found objects. While Marisol shared pop art's fascination with celebrity, her work emphasized the emptiness of glamour and fame.

In the 1960s she depicted life-size figures of women, both wealthy and poor, in everyday situations; in the 1970s she produced a series of small carved wood fishes with colorful bodies and her own likeness for a head; in the 1980s she returned to life-size figures and produced a series of homages to artists and world personalities.

Marisol has had numerous solo exhibitions and has enjoyed critical success. She established herself in 1958 with a solo exhibition at the Leo Castelli Gallery in New York and has more recently been included in major retrospectives of American art. Marisol's work can be seen in several national museums including the Museum of Modern Art, New York, and the National Portrait Gallery, Washington, D.C.

▲ ***Marisol poses with her sculptures in 1957. Her work generally contains images of people.***

KEY DATES	
1930	Born Paris, France, on May 22.
1950	Moves to New York.
1958	First solo exhibition.
2001	Retrospective exhibition held at New York's Neuberger Museum of Art in Purchase, New York.

Further reading: Rivera, José. *Marisol*. New York, NY: Dramatists Play Service, 1999.
http://www.tfaoi.com/aa/2aa/2aa661.htm (biography and examples of Marisol's work).

MARQUÉS, René

Writer

One of the leading figures of the Puerto Rican intellectual movement known as the "The Generation of the 40s," René Marqués was a prolific and many-sided author and playwright. His literary, linguistic, and political ideas have influenced following generations of Puerto Rican thinkers and artists.

Becoming a writer

Born in Arecibo, Puerto Rico, into a middle-class family, Marqués's early literary inclinations did not begin to materialize until the 1940s. In 1942, Marqués became an agronomist. However, he also founded a drama circle and an artistic society in Arecibo.

In 1946, after a few years of working for Puerto Rico's Department of Agriculture, Marqués moved to Spain to study literature at the Universidad de Madrid. He was particularly interested to learn more about classical and modern Spanish theater.

In 1949, with a grant from the Rockefeller Foundation, Marqués began to study theater at Columbia University in New York City. He also began to attend German theatrical director Erwin Piscator's (1893–1966) famous dramatic workshop in the city.

By the end of the 1940s, Marqués had established himself as a literary journalist, producing features and reviews for several major Puerto Rican newspapers. He had also published one book of poetry and two plays, *El Sol y Los MacDonald* (The Sun and the MacDonalds) and *Palm Sunday*.

The Oxcart

During the 1950s Marqués's literary reputation skyrocketed, mainly as a playwright but also as a short story writer. He began working as a writer in the Department of Education, Division of Community Education. By 1953, he was head of its editorial division. Between 1951 and 1952, Marqués published his most important play, *La Carreta* (The Oxcart), presented in New York in 1953 and in San Juan, Puerto Rico, in 1954. *La Carreta* is a drama about Puerto Rican industrialization and its detrimental consequences. It characters are poor peasants who move to San Juan and then to New York City, and finally back to the countryside of Puerto Rico. This play left Marqués's mark in the history of Puerto Rican and Hispanic American theater.

KEY DATES

1919 Born in Arecibo, Puerto Rico, in October 4.

1942 Qualifies as agronomist.

1946 Studies literature at Universidad de Madrid, Spain.

1949 Studies theater at Columbia University in New York City with a grant from the Rockefeller Foundation.

1952 Publishes *La Carreta* (The Oxcart).

1953 Becomes chief editor of Puerto Rico's Department of Education.

1957 Receives a grant from the Guggenheim Foundation.

1958 Receives four awards from the Puerto Rican Athenaeum for his work in theater, short story, essay, and novel.

1963 Receives an award from the William Faulkner Foundation at the University of Virginia, Charlottesville, for his novel, *La Víspera del Hombre* (The Eve of the Man).

1979 Dies in San Juan, Puerto Rico, on March 22.

In 1957, on a fellowship from the Guggenheim Foundation, Marqués wrote a novel, *La Víspera del Hombre* (The Eve of the Man). In 1958 the Puerto Rican Athenaeum honored his work in four literary genres: theater, short story, novel, and essay. In 1963 he received an award from the William Faulkner Foundation of the University of Virginia, Charlottesville, for *La Víspera del Hombre*.

The intellectual

From the 1950s to his death in 1979, Marqués stood as one of the leading voices in Puerto Rican intellectual life, along with other artists, such as Lorenzo Homar. Marqués published a second novel, *La Mirada* (The Gaze), in 1976. His work had a political dimension. He helped promote the Spanish language as a way of advocating independence from the United States, and in so doing maintained Hispanic American cultural identity.

See also: Homar, Lorenzo

Further reading: Reynolds, Bonnie Hildebrand. *Space, Time, and Crisis: The Theatre of René Marqués*. York, SC: Spanish Literature Publishing Company, 1988.

MARTÍ, José
Activist, Writer

José Martí is one of Cuba's greatest heroes. He was a founder of the Cuban Revolutionary Party, and dedicated his life to his country's struggle for independence from Spain. Martí was also a professor and writer: He is viewed by many literary commentators as one of the greatest Hispanic writers. Martí published poems, stories, philosophical writings, and political essays that reflected his beliefs in freedom, liberty, and democracy.

Early life

Born in Havana, Cuba, on January 28, 1853, Martí was the son of impoverished Spanish parents. His father had been a soldier, but retired to become a watchman. Martí was one of eight children. In 1866 the educator and reformer Rafael María Mendive (1821–1886) persuaded Martí's father to allow his son to study at the Instituto de Havana. Martí's opposition to Spain's repressive rule began early, and he began to work on the underground periodicals *El Diablo Cojuelo* and *La Patria Libre*. He also published his first play, a patriotic drama written in verse called *Abdala,* when he was just 15.

Arrest and exile

Arrested at age 15 for his subversive views, Martí was sentenced to six years hard labor. Martí's legs became severely lacerated from wearing chains. A year into his sentence, Martí was deported to Spain in 1871. In that year he published *El Presidio de Cuba*.

Martí's life changed drastically in Spain. He studied law and philosophy at the universities of Madrid and Zaragoza. During this time he published attacks on Spanish colonial rule and the practice of political imprisonment in Cuba.

Love affair with Cuba

Martí faithfully loved his country until his death. During his lifetime Martí returned to Cuba three times, but his political views and activities made him so unpopular with authorities that he was forced to live abroad in exile for most of his adult life.

He moved to Mexico in 1875, where he took a job as a journalist in the capital and was reunited with his family. He then moved to Guatemala City in 1877, where he accepted a position as a professor of history and literature; he also married Carmen Zayas Bazán, with whom he had a son, José; the couple later separated.

▲ ***José Martí's work is known to millions of people around the world, particularly through the popular song "Guantanamera," which is based on one of his poems, and was made famous by the composer Joseíto Fernández.***

In 1878, Martí was allowed back into his beloved Cuba, but within a year his political work had upset the authorities. He was arrested for conspiring against the government and again deported. After a brief period in the United States, he moved to Venezuela, working again as a professor of literature.

In New York

In 1880 Martí returned to the United States, where he made New York his home for the next 15 years. Martí reported on life in the United States for various Latin American newspapers. He also produced a magazine for children called *Edad de Oro*, wrote many political essays, and published a volume of poetry, *Versos Sencillos*, in 1891.

Martí worked as an official representative of Uruguay, Paraguay, and Argentina for several years. He wanted to protect Latin America from domination by the United

INFLUENCES AND INSPIRATION

More than a century after his death, José Martí is still highly regarded in both Cuba and the United States.

The airport in Havana, Cuba, is named after Martí, and there is a monument to him in the Plaza de la Revolución. Cuban children read Martí's work in school.

The Cuban president, Fidel Castro, has paid tribute to Martí as a revolutionary hero. Castro claims that Martí's assertion that Cuba would never be truly free without economic, racial, and sexual equality, is true and that communism is the way to achieve all those objectives. Critics argue that Martí was a lifelong supporter of individual freedom and the upholding of human rights; he would therefore, they claim, have strongly disapproved of Castro's dictatorship.

The Cuban community living in exile in the United States strongly opposes Castro's regime. Many of its most vocal advocates emphasize the liberal aspects of Martí's literature and teaching. The U.S. government has created radio and television channels named after Martí to broadcast anti-Castro messages to people still living in Cuba. Since Martí found much to fault in the political system of the United States, some commentators find this situation somewhat ironic.

States. He also believed that Latin American security depended on political freedom for the Caribbean.

Martí's feelings toward the United States were complex. He admired the U.S. Constitution, and was attracted by the United States's image as the land of opportunity. Martí also had great respect for Ralph Waldo Emerson and Walt Whitman, and deep admiration for the great antislavery campaigner Wendell Phillips. However, Martí also believed that the United States was deeply flawed. He wrote that "Democracy has been corrupted and undermined and has given birth to menacing poverty and hatred." Martí was deeply concerned by the oppression of racial minorities and the treatment of the lowest-paid workers in America. Above all, Martí was extremely critical of the U.S. government's wish to exert influence over other countries, particularly in Latin America.

Revolution

In 1892, Martí helped to found the Cuban Revolutionary Party and the newspaper *Patria*. He dedicated his time to the cause of liberating Cuba, bringing together several important and influential individuals, such as Calixto García, Antonio Maceo, and the military leader Máximo Gómez. Martí got considerable support from the Cuban American community. They helped Martí raise the money required to fund an invasion of Cuba.

Martí was convinced that the best hope for Cuban liberation from the Spanish was to mobilize the working classes; he spent much of his time talking to the black Cuban tobacco workers who had come to Tampa and Key West, Florida, in search of work. He also made detailed plans for a new political structure in Cuba after the overthrow of Spanish authority.

KEY DATES

1853	Born in Havana, Cuba, on January 28.
1869	Imprisoned in Cuba for his political beliefs.
1871	Exiled to Spain.
1878	Returns briefly to Cuba.
1892	Helps to found the Cuban Revolutionary Party.
1895	Arrives in Cuba with revolutionary expedition on April 11, but dies in battle against Spanish forces on May 19.

Death

When senior U.S. politicians started to talk of annexing Cuba, Martí was horrified, however. His plans for Cuba's liberation accelerated rapidly. In January 1895, Martí's force set sail from Florida to Cuba, but it was intercepted by the U.S. Navy, which confiscated three ships loaded with weaponry. The Navy alerted the Spanish authorities accordingly. Despite that, Martí arrived on Cuba's eastern shores on April 11, 1895, with a group of supporters; they made for the mountains to join the Revolutionary Army. On May 19, 1895, Martí rode into his first and only battle; he was shot and killed. For three years, the revolutionary forces battled against the Spanish. In 1898, the United States joined Cuban forces against Spain, and Cuba finally gained independence from the European nation. It subsequently became subject to U.S. influence.

Further reading: Martí, José. *Selected Writings*. New York, NY: Penguin Classics, 2002.
http://www.fiu.edu/~fcf/jmarti.html (short biographical sketch of Martí).

MARTIN, Ricky
Singer

Initially known as a member of the Puerto Rican boy band Menudo, Ricky Martin has since become a star in his own right. His smash hit "Livin' La Vida Loca" brought him worldwide fame and positioned him as one of the most popular Latino performers.

Child performer

Martin was born Enrique José Martin Morales, IV, in Hato Rey, Puerto Rico, in 1971. As a child he was called Kiki (short for Enrique). His father, Enrique Morales, III, was a psychologist; his mother, Nereida Morales, was an accountant. His parents divorced when Ricky was only two, and he lived with his mother. He grew up listening to rock bands like Journey, Cheap Trick, and Boston, although his mother took him to concerts by Celia Cruz and Tito Puente so he could appreciate Latin music. When he was six, Ricky began acting in TV commercials.

At the age of 12, Martin first auditioned for Menudo, but was rejected because he was too short. He was eventually accepted on his third try. After the customary Menudo training in Miami, Florida, Martin toured around the world

KEY DATES

1971 Born in Hato Rey, Puerto Rico, on December 24.

1984 After a third audition, Martin joins Menudo.

1991 Releases his first Spanish-language album, *Ricky Martin*.

1994 Stars as Marius in the Broadway show *Les Miserables*.

1998 Releases *Vuelve*, featuring "La Copa de la Vida."

1999 Releases first English-language album, also titled *Ricky Martin*, featuring "Livin' La Vida Loca."

2000 Releases *Sound Loaded*, featuring "She Bangs."

2004 Receives a lifetime achievement award at the Premios Lo Nuestro.

▼ ***Ricky Martin performs in the gardens of Buckingham Palace, London, in a concert to celebrate the 50-year reign of Queen Elizabeth II in 2003.***

INFLUENCES AND INSPIRATION

Ricky Martin's early musical career bears the imprint of Menudo, and his later recordings have been influenced by the talent of former Menudo bandmate Robi Rosa, who wrote many of Martin's solo hits.

Martin has worked with producers such as Jon Secada, Emilio Estefan, and Walter Afanasieff, each of whom left a strong impression on the Latin rhythms and pop-oriented melodies of the artist's work.

Martin has a reputation as a fashionable dresser, and his stylish performances on stage and his personal appearance off it reflect the influence of performers such as the Spanish star Miguel Bosé, a multitalented singer and actor who has appeared occasionally in the movies of his compatriot, the director Pedro Almodóvar.

During the Menudo years, Ricky Martin learned that a punishing recording and performing schedule requires firm self-discipine. In order to stay fit, the singer practices yoga, adheres to a strictly controlled diet, and spends several hours every day training in a gym.

with the band for five years. Despite its fun-loving image, and the young age of its members, Menudo was an act run by strict schedules and guidelines. As a result, Martin was away from home for long periods of time. During this time, his relationship with his parents suffered.

Going it alone

In 1989 Martin left the band and returned home to San Juan, Puerto Rico, to graduate from high school. A year later he moved to New York, where he stayed with friends and lived on the money saved during his Menudo years. In 1991 he moved to Mexico City, Mexico. He worked on the soap opera *Alcanzar una Estrella* and recorded his first Spanish solo album, *Ricky Martin*, assisted by ex-Menudo member Robi Rosa (1969–). In 1993 Martin released a second album, *Me Amarás*. Both albums sold well and established him as a solo singer.

In 1994 Martin got the part of Miguel Morez in the soap opera *General Hospital*. A year later he played the part of Marius in the Broadway musical *Les Miserables*. Simultaneously, he released a third, more rock-oriented Spanish album, *A Medio Vivir*, which went gold, selling half a million copies.

In 1997, after working on Disney's soundtrack for the animated feature *Hercules*, Martin recorded *Vuelve*, his fourth album. Released in 1998, the album went gold in six months. To promote the album, Martin toured heavily. At the 1998 soccer World Cup Finals in France, he performed "La Copa de la Vida," the tournament's official song. The appearance brought him before an audience of two billion. The event granted him instant fame and recognition around the world—except in the United States. Martin began to concentrate his efforts on the English-language market in order to confirm his status as a world-class musical act.

Big break

Martin's big break in the United States came during the 1999 Grammy Awards, where he won the award for Best Latin Pop Performance and dazzled the audience with his performance. The response was so enthusiastic that singers like Madonna offered to record duets with him. In May 1999, riding this wave of popularity, Martin released his first English-language album, also titled *Ricky Martin*. Its first single, "Livin' La Vida Loca," hit the number one spot on the charts immediately and became 1999's smash hit. The album was a number-one in dozens of countries around the world, establishing Martin as an international superstar.

Martin has continued recording albums at a steady pace, alternating between English and Spanish productions. In 2000, still benefiting from his popularity boom, he released a second English album, *Sound Loaded*, which sold seven million copies. *La Historia* followed in 2001, as well as a compilation of his hits, beginning a transition to the Hispanic American market. In 2003 *Almas del Silencio*, an album for Martin's Hispanic fans, sold four million copies.

In 2004 Martin received a lifetime achievement award at the Hispanic American award show Premios Lo Nuestro in Miami. His charitable foundation sponsors People for Children, a program aiming to eliminate worldwide trafficking and sexual exploitation of children. By the fall of 2005, Martin was promoting a new album titled *Life*.

See also: Cruz, Celia; Estefan, Emilio; Menudo; Puente, Tito; Secada, Jon

Further reading: Parker, Judy. *Ricky Martin*. New York, NY: Children's Press, 2001.
http://www.rickymartin.com (Martin's official Web site).

MARTINEZ, A.
Actor

An actor of Mexican descent with a lengthy film and television career, A. Martinez is most remembered for his roles in soap operas. He also appeared in feature films like *The Cowboys* (1972), an award-winning movie also starring John Wayne. In it, Martinez played the role of Cimmarón, a Hispanic American cowhand. He played the same character in a 1973 television spin-off.

Early life

Martinez was born Adolfo Larrue Martinez, III, in 1948 in Glendale, California. At the age of 12, he made his singing debut winning a talent competition at the Hollywood Bowl. Before becoming a professional actor, Martinez also played on a semiprofessional baseball team.

While attending the University of California, Los Angeles (UCLA), Martinez was spotted by casting director Fred Roos, who encouraged him to pursue an acting career. At first Martinez tried to combine his acting career with his commitment to music but, as roles followed, he focused on film and television.

Popular performer

His film debut was in *The Young Animal* in 1968. This was soon followed by a string of roles in popular television shows, such as *Mission: Impossible*, *Ironside*, *Bonanza*, *The Streets of San Francisco*, *Hawaii Five-O*, *Kung Fu*, *Petrocelli*, *The Hardy Boys*, *Baretta*, *Quincy, M.E.*, *ChiPs*, *Fantasy Island*, *Falcon Crest*, and *Remington Steele*.

By appearing in many of the most important television shows of the 1970s and 1980s, Martinez became one of the best known Latino faces of his generation. His longest running television role was eight years as Cruz Castillo in *Santa Barbara*, from 1984 to 1992. The role earned Martinez an Emmy in 1990.

For three years (1999–2002), Martinez was Roy DiLucca in *General Hospital*; for two years (1992–1994) he played Daniel Morales in *L.A. Law.* More recently he has acted in shows such as *JAG* and *Profiler*.

KEY DATES

1948	Born in Glendale, California, in September 27.
1971	Debuts in *Born Wild*.
1990	Wins an Emmy for his role in *Santa Barbara*.

▲ ***A. Martinez poses as the* Santa Barbara *character Cruz Castillo, whom he played for eight years.***

Martinez's feature films are just as varied. They include *Change of Habit* (1969), with Elvis Presley; *Shoot the Sun Down* (1981), with Christopher Walken; *Beyond the Limit* (1983), with Michael Caine, Richard Gere, and Elpidia Carrillo; and *She-Devil* (1989), with Meryl Streep.

In 1995, Martinez returned to his musical efforts, releasing an album titled *Fragrance and Thorn*. He is married and has two daughters and a son.

See also: Carrillo, Elpidia

Further reading: Keller, Gary D. *A Biographical Handbook of Hispanics and United States Film*. Tempe, AZ: Bilingual Press/Editorial Bilingüe, 1997.
http://www.amartinez.com (Martinez's official Web site).

MARTÍNEZ, Antonio José

Priest

Parish priest of Taos, New Mexico, Antonio José Martínez is one of the most important figures in the 19th-century history of the region. After his death, Martínez was portrayed by some U.S. historians as corrupt and backward-looking. He was also featured as a villain in the U.S. writer Willa Cather's novel *Death Comes to the Archbishop* (1927). However, Martínez is now widely recognized as a Nuevomexicano patriot, a liberal thinker who defended the rights of the poor and who mediated between the Hispanic population of New Mexico and their new U.S. rulers.

▲ ***Antonio José Martínez was an influential religious figure, progressive thinker, activist, political leader, and defender of local native rights.***

The padre of Taos

Antonio José Martínez was born on January 17, 1793, in Abiquiu, New Mexico, into a wealthy Spanish colonial family. In 1804 his family moved to Taos, where he grew up in the large hacienda built by his father, Severino Martínez. In 1813 the young Martínez married Maria de la Luz, but she died a year later. Martínez decided to become a Roman Catholic priest; in 1826 he became parish priest of Taos. He soon established himself as one of the most popular spiritual and political leaders of the region.

Martínez helped transform Taos into an important center for learning and culture. He established a school, and in 1835 set up the Southwest's first printing press. He used the press to print school textbooks and also to set up the region's first newspaper, *El Crepusculo de Libertad* (The Dawn of Liberty).

Far from opposing U.S. rule in New Mexico, Martínez played an active part in the new government. In 1850, when New Mexico officially became a U.S. territory, Martínez was given the honor of becoming its first American citizen. He went on to serve as a deputy in the the first General Territorial Assembly at Santa Fe.

KEY DATES

1793	Born in Abiquiu, New Mexico, New Spain, on January 17.
1826	Becomes the parish priest of Taos, New Mexico.
1835	Sets up the first printing press in the Southwest.
1857	Excommunicated by Bishop Jean Baptiste Lamy.
1867	Dies on July 27 in Taos.

In the 1850s, Martínez came into increasing conflict with the French-born bishop of Santa Fe, Jean Baptiste Lamy (1814–88). Lamy tried to force Martínez to raise taxes among his parishioners in order to fund the building of a lavish new cathedral. When Martínez resisted, Lamy excommunicated him from the Roman Catholic church in 1857. Martínez continued to act as parish priest until his death in 1867, however.

Martínez was buried in the cemetery of Taos, currently the Kit Carson Memorial State Park Cemetery. On his tombstone, he was commended with "La Honra de su País" ("the Honor of his Homeland"). In 2006, a 6-foot (1.8m) bronze sculpture was raised in his memory in Taos.

See also: Religion

Further reading: March, John, et al. "Antonio José Martínez," in *A Reader's Companion to the Fiction of Willa Cather*. Westport, CT: Greenwood Press, 1993.

MARTÍNEZ, Betita
Activist, Author

Elizabeth "Betita" Martínez is a prominent Chicana activist who has dedicated her life to fighting discrimination. She has written and taught about the effects of colonialism and oppression based on race, gender, and class. Martínez has published six books and many articles about the struggle for social justice. She is best known for her bilingual book, *500 Years of Chicano History in Pictures*, the basis for a video that Martínez also codirected.

KEY DATES

1946 First Chicana to graduate from Swarthmore College.

1947 Works for seven years for the United Nations as a translator, researcher, and administrator.

1965 Works for three years with the Student Nonviolent Coordinating Committee (SNCC).

1982 Becomes the first Chicana to run for the governorship of California.

1997 Becomes cofounder and director, Institute for MultiRacial Justice.

The road to political consciousness

Martínez grew up in a middle-class suburb of Washington, D.C. Her Mexican father had arrived in the United States after the Mexican Revolution and had worked his way up to become a secretary in the Mexican embassy. Martínez grew up listening to stories of the revolution and U.S. imperialism, and developed a political consciousness as a young girl. As the only nonwhite student at her school, she also experienced racism and discrimination at an early age. After high school, Martínez became the first Chicana to graduate from Swarthmore College.

In 1947 she went to work for the United Nations as a researcher and translator. She worked mainly on decolonization strategies. During the 1950s, Martínez watched several of her colleagues' careers suffer after they were investigated as suspected communists by Senator Joseph McCarthy. In 1959 she went to Cuba to witness first hand the effects of Castro's revolution.

Back in the United States, Martínez became involved in the civil rights movement, working with fellow Latina Maria Varela for the predominantly black Student Nonviolent Coordinating Committee (SNCC). She headed the New York office. In 1968 she moved to New Mexico, where she launched a newspaper called *El Grito del Norte* (The Cry of the North), which reported on civil rights action around the world. Martínez was also a leading Chicana rights activist.

Since the mid 1970s, she has been active in the San Francisco Bay area as a community organizer and teacher of ethnic studies and women's studies at Hayward State University. In 1982 she ran unsuccessfully as the Peace and Freedom Party's candidate for governor of California.

In 1997 Martínez cofounded the Institute for MultiRacial Justice in San Francisco, a resource center whose aim is to build alliances among peoples of color. Martínez is a popular speaker on Chicano studies topics, Latina women's issues, racism, and multiculturalism. Martínez has received more than 20 awards, including the Scholar of the Year in 2000 from the National Association of Chicana and Chicano Studies, and the Movimiento Estudiantil Chicano de Aztlán (MEChA) Lifetime Achievement award.

▼ ***Betita Martínez has been a leading civil rights activist for many years: In the 1960s she was one of only two Latinas to hold a top position in the SNCC.***

Further reading: http://news.eltecolote.org/news/view_article.html?article_id=597c80f5b82ecca9fda9424664cc6862 (interview with Martínez).

MARTINEZ, Bob

Politician

Bob Martinez was the first Hispanic American to be elected as Florida governor. Having started his career as a Democrat, he switched to the Republican Party. President George H. W. Bush later appointed Martinez as the director of the Office of National Drug Control Policy, dubbed the "drug czar."

Early life

Martinez was born in Tampa, Florida, on December 25, 1934, the only son of a waiter. He has some Cuban ancestry, and was the grandson of Spanish immigrants who came to Tampa to work in the cigar industry.

Raised in a Hispanic neighborhood, Martinez attended local public schools, then studied education as a major at the University of Tampa, combining this with a semiprofessional career in baseball. He graduated from Tampa in 1957, after marrying his high-school sweetheart, Mary Jane Marino, three years earlier. Martinez continued his education at the University of Illinois, and received a master of arts in labor and industrial relations in 1964.

Political ambitions

Martinez then returned to Tampa to work as a management consultant, advising firms on labor relations. In 1965 he began a career in teaching, eventually becoming a high-school social studies teacher. This led to involvement in Tampa's teaching union, which he led between 1966 and 1975. There was one strike during his leadership. He first ran for mayor of Tampa in 1974, but lost.

The following year Martinez decided to change career direction again and bought a Spanish restaurant. He was also appointed to the governing board of the Southwest Florida Water Management District by Florida's then governor. Martinez rose to the position of vice-chairman of the organization.

In 1979 Martinez once again ran for mayor of Tampa, and was elected for the first of two consecutive terms. While in office he helped to revitalize the downtown area by encouraging construction and by the restoration of various public buildings. Martinez also reduced the size of city government without decreasing services. In fact the Tampa police department's numbers were increased.

In 1983, while serving as mayor, Martinez became a member of the Republican Party. He resigned from his post to run successfully for governor of Florida three years later.

▲ ***Bob Martinez was the tough-acting "drug czar" who waged President George H. W. Bush's "War on Drugs."***

Governor of Florida

Martinez started his term as Florida's governor in January 1987. As in Tampa, Martinez made tackling wasteful spending by legislators a top priority.

Martinez's environmental protection agenda is often considered his greatest achievement as governor. He oversaw the nation's largest land-purchasing scheme, and helped preserve both wilderness areas and the state's surface waters, including Lake Okeechobe and Tampa Bay.

President George H. W. Bush praised Martinez's drug and crime policies. Martinez refused to commute any death sentences, and signed more than 130 death warrants. He also greatly increased the number of Florida's prison sentences and withdrew driving licenses from drug users. He is credited with creating narcotic-free schools and supporting treatment programs. Martinez also became the National Governors' Association's lead governor on substance abuse and drug trafficking, contributing to the nation's drug control strategy.

Attempts by Martinez to limit abortion rights, however, drew criticism from some quarters. Many people were also unimpressed when he chose to use obscenity laws to arrest members of a rap group.

INFLUENCES AND INSPIRATION

Bob Martinez was just one in a long line of drug czars. The first had been appointed by President Richard Nixon in 1971. By 1998 the czar's role was to head up the Office of National Drug Control Policy (ONDCP), created by outgoing president Ronald Reagan. The first drug czar of the modern age was William Bennett. Bennett was a political conservative and this was reflected in his attitude toward drugs. He once agreed with a radio phone-in caller that drug dealers should be beheaded.

Martinez succeeded Bennett in 1991. In 1993, when Bill Clinton took office, Martinez was replaced by Lee Brown. Brown was the first African American drug czar and was also the first to be elevated to the level of the president's cabinet.

In 1996 Barry McCaffrey took on the job. He was a retired general who had once commanded all U.S. forces in Latin America. His appointment as drug czar reflected how the War on Drugs was being waged.

In 2001 George W. Bush chose a figure from his father's administration to head the ONDCP. John Walters had worked under both William Bennett and Martinez.

Martinez was regarded as an increasingly important member of the Republican Party until he supported an unpopular tax increase opposed by the party as a whole. He eventually changed his mind, but it was too late, and he lost the governorship election in 1991.

Drug czar

In the same year, however, President Bush appointed Martinez to the cabinet, naming him as the nation's drug czar. He was responsible for developing policy to reduce the use and sale of illegal drugs. One of his key strategies was to eradicate heroin production in Mexico and Colombia by destroying the poppies used to make the narcotic. He later acknowledged that this had been only partially successful.

Tackling drug use is a contentious subject, and like his predecessors in the role, Martinez attracted both considerable praise and criticism. The main focus of disagreement is whether it is best to treat drug addiction as a crime or an affliction. Martinez put the emphasis on the former and attempted to attack drug trafficking by sending as many drug offenders to prison as possible. His critics, however, argued that law enforcement fails to diminish the problem. They claimed that users were forced to support their addictions by criminal activity.

Martinez's opposition to needle exchanges was another controversial decision. These are centers where drug users can dispose of syringes safely and collect new ones. Their supporters claim that they reduce the spread of diseases, such as Human Immunodeficiency Virus (HIV), which can be spread by sharing needles, and also encourage addicts to start treatment programs. However, Martinez believed that the exchanges encouraged drug use and, by attracting addicts to an area, increased local crime.

Martinez was the subject of some embarrassing allegations while leading the campaign against drugs. It was claimed that he had received campaign contributions in the 1980s from a drug trafficker subsequently convicted of importing cocaine in 1989.

When Bush lost the presidential election in 1993, Martinez also left the government. He later worked as a government consultant for a law firm and also ran a company in Florida selling satellite systems. He has provided political commentary for television.

Martinez has received various prestigious awards in the course of his career, including the Center of Ethics 1999 award in recognition of his integrity. He continued to live in Tampa in the early 21st century.

KEY DATES

1934 Born in Tampa, Florida, on December 25.

1957 Graduates from the University of Tampa with a bachelor of science degree.

1964 Receives master of arts degree in labor and industrial relations from the University of Illinois.

1979 Elected mayor of Tampa.

1983 Joins Republican Party.

1987 Elected governor of Florida.

1991 Given the position of drug czar in the administration of President George H. W. Bush (until 1993).

Further reading: http://dhr.dos.state.fl.us/museum/collections/governors/about.cfm?id=47 (official portrait and biography of Martinez as Florida governor).

MARTINEZ, Cesar A.
Artist

Cesar A. Martinez is a leading Chicano artist working in Texas. His work has been shown in several retrospective exhibitions around the world.

Early life
Cesar Augusto Martinez was born in the Texas border town of Laredo on June 4, 1944. His father died when he was less than a year old, and Martinez was raised as the only child in a female-dominated household made up of his mother, grandmother, and two aunts. Much of Martinez's extended family lived south of the border in Mexico.

During Martinez's teenage years, he crossed into Nuevo Laredo, Mexico, to attend bullfights and spend time hunting, fishing, and camping outdoors on the family ranch near Monterrey. There, a cousin named Armando introduced Martinez to art, and his Aunt Lydia gave him his first camera.

Martinez also developed a life-long passion for bullfighting during this time. He dreamed of becoming a matador, an ambition he eventually realized. He continues to fight as an amateur today.

▼ ***Cesar Martinez's 1986 portrait* Hombre Que Le Gustan Las Mujeres *(The Man Who Liked Women).***

KEY DATES

1944 Born in Laredo, Texas, on June 4.

1968 Graduates from Texas A & M University-Kingsville with a bachelor of science in art education.

1982 Paints *El Pantalon Rosa* (The Red Trousers). It wins the grand prize of the Canadian Club Hispanic Art Tour.

1997 Records interview for the Archivos Virtuales of the Smithsonian Archives of American Art.

Emerging artist
Martinez struggled at college until he discovered art. He was classmates with other Mexican American artists Amado Peña and Carmen Lomas Garza, and graduated with a degree in art education.

After graduation Martinez was drafted into the U.S Army and served in Korea. He continued his interest in photography during his service and was honorably discharged in 1971. He then settled in San Antonio, Texas, at the suggestion of his college buddies, and began a career as an artist. He taught at Texas Institute for Educational Development (TIED) and later won a grant to photograph Chicano murals across the Southwest. During his travels, he met many Chicano artists, who at the time were forming into art collectives such as Tlacuilo, Pintores de la Nueva Raza, and Con Safos (C/S). Martinez and fellow artist Pedro Rodriguez formed the Instituto Chicano de Artes y Artesanias. Later the pair formed Los Quemados with Carmen Lomas Garza.

Productive artist
Martinez produced his first two series of artwork during the 1970s. Four more followed in the next two decades, establishing him as a national art figure. His work includes paintings, charcoal drawings, pastels, and prints.

See also: Lomas Garza, Carmen; Peña, Amado

Further reading: Martinez, Cesar. *Cesar A. Martinez: A Retrospective*. San Antonio, TX: McNay, Marion Koogler McNay Art Museum, 1999.
http://www.aaa.si.edu/collections/oralhistories/transcripts/martin97.htm (interview with Martinez).

MARTÍNEZ, Félix

Businessman, Publisher, Politician

One of the most prominent Latinos of his day, Félix Martínez was a high-profile businessman and influential politician in El Paso, Texas, at the turn of the 20th century. Martínez owned and published several newspapers, and was appointed to the diplomatic position of president of the Panama–Pacific Commission by President Woodrow Wilson in 1912.

Early life

Born in Penasco, New Mexico, on March 29, 1857, Martínez was academically inclined and business-minded. His formal education began at St. Mary's College in Mora, New Mexico. After five years of study, he moved to Colorado in 1871, where he took a job as a store clerk. He continued his education through private business courses and became a part owner of a mercantile business.

Moving toward politics

In 1886 Martínez turned his attention to politics, publishing, and real estate. Although he lost his first race in a run for San Miguel county treasurer on the 1884 Democratic ticket, his campaign opened a fissure in the county's solid Republican stronghold. Two years later, Martínez won a bid for county assessor and, in 1888, he was elected to the territorial House of Representatives.

Sympathetic to the rising populist movement in San Miguel County, Martínez assumed leadership of El Partido del Pueblo Unido (the United People's Party), and purchased a small Santa Fe newspaper entitled *La Voz del Pueblo* (The People's Voice) in 1890. *La Voz* soon became the foremost Spanish-language paper in New Mexico. From 1893 to 1897 Martínez served as clerk for the U.S. and Territorial Courts for the Fourth Judicial District of New Mexico. Two years later he became the owner and publisher of the *El Paso Daily News*. He went on to found several companies and help with many community projects. He was also director of the National Bank of El Paso, as well as the Dallas District's Federal Reserve Board. Martínez bought the *Tribune-Citizen* in Albuquerque in 1909, but sold it two years later.

In 1912, Martínez became president of the Panama–Pacific Commission and helped facilitate the construction of the Elephant Butte Dam. Finished in 1916, the dam solved the persistent basin-flooding problem for those living near the Rio Grande; it still provides irrigation water for the El Paso and southern New Mexico regions. In 1916, Martínez died of pneumonia.

▲ ***Félix Martínez was a leading businessman and publisher of several important local newspapers.***

KEY DATES

1857	Born in Penasco, New Mexico, on March 29.
1888	Elected to the territorial House of Representatives.
1890	Purchases *La Voz del Pueblo*.
1899	Publishes *El Paso Daily News* for 10 years.
1912	Becomes president of the Panama–Pacific Commission.
1916	Dies of pneumonia.

Further reading: Vigil, Maurilio E. *Los Patrones: Profiles of Hispanic Political Leaders in New Mexico History*. Washington, DC: University Press of America, 1980.
http://www.tsha.utexas.edu/handbook/online/articles/MM/fmadj.html (short biography).

MARTÍNEZ, Manuel Luis

Writer, Academic

Manuel Luis Martínez is widely considered to be one of the finest young Mexican American authors writing today. An associate professor of English at Indiana University, Bloomington, Martínez has written two acclaimed novels, *Crossing* (1998) and *Drift* (2003), together with a handful of short stories. He has forged a reputation for both his literary craftsmanship and powerful, gritty vision of contemporary working-class Chicano life. In 1999, *Crossing* was selected as one of the 10 outstanding books by a writer of color by the PEN American Center.

Early life

The grandson of Mexican migrant workers, Manuel Luis Martínez was born, raised, and educated in San Antonio, Texas. He grew up listening to his grandmother's stories about her life in Mexico and the experience of trying to find a home and a sense of identity in her new country.

Martínez developed a love of literature at an early age. He said that he grew up reading white American literature by such writers as Mark Twain, Joseph Heller, J. D. Salinger, and Kurt Vonnegut. He said: "They are all dark writers whose characters find a way to survive in a hostile world, but lessen the pain of that brutal world through a sardonic, ironic, sense of the absurd."

Finding Chicano literature

It was not until Martínez was studying for a degree at San Antonio's St. Mary's University that he began to read Mexican American writers such as Tomas Rivera, Ernesto Galarza, Oscar Acosta, and Sandra Cisneros. Martínez went on to graduate with a BA in 1988, after which he carried on studying, receiving a master's degree in 1989 from Ohio State University. Martínez was later awarded his doctorate degree from Stanford University in 1997, the same year in which he was appointed associate professor at Indiana University. As an academic, Martínez focused his research on postwar U.S. and Chicano literature. In 1993 he published a groundbreaking study of the U.S. Beat writers, *Countering the Counterculture: Rereading Postwar American Dissent*. In the book Martínez compares and contrasts the iconic counterculture figures of the 1950s, such as the writer Jack Kerouac, with Chicano and nationalist writers such as the Austin Chicano–Native American poet Raul Salinas.

KEY DATES

1960s	Born in San Antonio, Texas.
1997	Appointed an associate professor at Indiana University, Bloomington.
1998	Publishes *Crossing*.
2003	Publishes *Drift*.

Fiction

Although Martínez did not publish his first work of fiction until 1998, he began writing his own work at the age of 20 as a way of communicating his thoughts and feelings to his father, who was dying of cancer. His first published substantial work of fiction was *Crossing*. Martínez wrote the book after reading a newspaper article about 13 undocumented Mexican workers left to suffocate in a boxcar. Critics saw *Crossing* as a bitter attack on the heartlessness and inhumanity that lie behind the American Dream. The book was critically well received, and established Martínez as a serious Latino writer.

Drifting

Martínez has often said that he is an autobiographical writer. He often depicts the effects of the rootless and transitory lifestyles that he believes are pervasive among working-class Mexicanos and Chicanos in the U.S.–Mexican borderlands. Martínez examines this theme in his second novel, *Drift*. The story centers on the protagonist Robert Lomos, a troubled, tough-talking Chicano teenager who is unable to settle at school and whose family has fallen apart. A first-person coming-of-age narrative in the tradition of J. D. Salinger's *Catcher in the Rye* (1951), the novel follows Robert as he journeys from San Antonio to Los Angeles and back again, struggling to recover his roots and his lost sense of community and home.

See also: Acosta, Oscar; Cisneros, Sandra; Galarza, Ernesto; Rivera, Tomas

Further reading: Martínez, Manuel Luis. *Crossing*. Tempe, AZ: Bilingual Review Press, 1998.
www.laprensa-sandiego.org/archieve/april25-03/drift.htm (review of *Drift*).

MARTINEZ, Mel

Politician

Mel Martinez is a prominent Hispanic American politician. He served in the cabinet during President George W. Bush's first-term administration. He then became a Republican senator from Florida, the first Cuban-born American to be elected to the Senate.

Refugee

Born in 1946 in Sagua la Grande, Cuba, Melquiades Rafael Martinez came to the United States from Cuba in 1962 as part of Operation Peter Pan. This was a program that sent 14,000 children from Cuba to the United States between 1960 and 1962, so that they could avoid being sent to schools in the countryside as part of the revolutionary reorganization of education in Cuba. Parents who believed that the family and religion were the foundations of society feared that both would be weakened if their children were sent to state boarding schools. The Catholic church and the U.S. mission in Havana, Cuba, facilitated the exit.

When the Cuban Missile Crisis in October 1962 ended flights to the United States, the "Peter Pans" were left without their parents. Most of them entered orphanages or foster homes, where they lived for years until their family members could come to reclaim them. Mel Martinez lived for four years in a children's camp in South Florida and in two different foster homes. He and his family were reunited in Orlando, Florida, in 1966, when his parents and siblings arrived.

Like all "Peter Pans," Martinez was deeply affected by the experience. Although he missed his family and spoke only a few words of English on arrival, he was lucky to be placed with nurturing foster families. As a result, he felt an abiding obligation to involve himself in public affairs.

Despite being a recipient of several federal welfare programs as a youth, Martinez generally supports the reduction of government-sponsored services to the needy.

KEY DATES

1946	Born in Sagua la Grande, Cuba, on October 23.
1998	Elected mayor of Orange County, Florida.
2000	Appointed secretary of housing and urban development by incoming president George W. Bush.
2005	Sworn in as a U.S. senator for Florida.

In 2001, when he became secretary of housing and urban development in President George W. Bush's cabinet, Martinez said, "I came to this country as a teenage refugee with nothing but faith in God and myself, and the conviction that America, like nowhere else in the world, was a place where hard work and a life of principle would be rewarded."

Entering politics

Martinez's political activism developed after he completed undergraduate and law degrees at Florida State University in Tallahassee between 1967 and 1973. He married his college sweetheart and returned to Orlando to work as a personal injury lawyer. One of the firm's partners was elected as the city's mayor in 1980, and Martinez agreed to serve on the board of the Orlando Housing Authority.

Martinez's role was to tackle the problems caused by rapid development and expanding population in Florida and the resulting lack of affordable housing. Despite reflecting progressive views through this work, Martinez's staunch conservatism began to emerge when he ran for lieutenant governor (deputy to the state governor) in 1994. He lost the election, but succeeded in becoming mayor of Orange County in 1998. His conservatism was tempered as he courted the votes of Orlando's large Puerto Rican community by creating health clinics and state-sponsored after-school programs.

President's man

Martinez's next public office was an appointed one. In 2001 he joined the cabinet of President Bush, for whom he had been a major supporter and fundraiser in the 2000 election campaign. In a Congressional disclosure statement following his appointment, the former penniless refugee declared he had a net worth of $4 million.

After Martinez left his cabinet position at the end of 2003, his political views again came under scrutiny when he stood for the U.S. Senate in 2004. The campaign was one of the most personal and negative of any race that year, as Martinez sought to make a clear distinction between his views and those of his opponent.

During the campaign, Martinez went on record with his views on some controversial issues. For example, he declared his support for the 2003 war in Iraq, public displays of religious devotion by elected officials, a

INFLUENCES AND INSPIRATION

Three factors provide the driving forces in Mel Martinez's life, and all of them stem from loss. The first is the permanent loss of his homeland. As a teenager, Martinez had a strong Cuban identity and, like most Cubans, he had liked all things Cuban. When the Castro government closed private church schools and officially declared Cuba an atheistic state, many parents sent their children away. Martinez remembers leaving with his brother and telling him that they would probably never see Cuba again. Taking part in civic life represents Martinez's efforts to retrieve a civic culture and to exercise his political will.

The second influence is the temporary loss of his family. He found himself alone in a place where he could not communicate because of the language barrier. Martinez became depressed and anxious. While still in full-time education, Martinez worked to save money to buy the family a used car when his parents arrived from Cuba. He found a job for his father, a veterinarian, to ease the way for the whole family. His strong belief in personal self-sufficiency stems from this painful personal experience.

The third factor is his religious faith. Martinez is a practicing Catholic who supports religion in public life because he witnessed the arbitrary destruction of religious institutions by a radical government. By supporting greater fusion of church and state in the United States, Martinez is seeking to actively influence the moral development of his fellow citizens.

▲ ***Mel Martinez faces press questions after being appointed as secretary of housing and urban development by President George W. Bush in 2000.***

reduction of taxes for the wealthy, cuts in federal spending on health care, a termination of amnesty for illegal immigrants, the elimination of the present Social Security system, the continuation of the death penalty, and the revocation of abortion rights for women, including those who become pregnant as a result of rape.

Independent voice

Martinez's apparent swing to the right in the 2004 election caused many opposition politicians to label him "George Bush's lapdog." However, once in the Senate, Martinez began defying that description by modifying his earlier conservative position. He advocated closing the U.S. prison camp at Guantánamo Bay, Cuba, which holds suspected combatants in the "War on Terror" without trial. Martinez also promoted legislation to expand low income home ownership opportunities nationally.

Martinez delivered his first speeches to Congress in both English and Spanish, and criticized Bush for following a policy of neglect in Latin America. On his introduction as a new senator in 2005, Martinez was the only one of seven new Republican members to advocate bipartisan cooperation with the Democrats. Additionally, Martinez has joined liberal Congressional Hispanic organizations, signaling his will to champion Hispanic American issues. He prefers to be known, however, as a U.S. senator who just happens to be Hispanic.

Further reading: http://martinez.senate.gov/public/ (Martinez's Web site).

MARTÍNEZ, Narciso
Musician

Mexican-born accordionist Narciso Martínez is considered by many music commentators to be the father of "conjunto," a style of music today associated with South Texas. Known as "El Huracán del Valle" ("The Hurricane of the Valley") because of his versatility as a musician, Martínez revolutionized conjunto music in the 1930s by popularizing the right-hand, treble-button style of playing the instrument (*see box on page 78*).

Early life
Martínez was born in Reynosa, Tamaulipas, across the Rio Grande from McAllen, Texas, on October 29, 1911. As a baby Martínez moved with his family to La Palma, near Brownsville, Texas, in the Lower Rio Grande Valley. After listening to the music that his brother played on his one-row accordion, Martínez taught himself to play, moving on to play the two-row instrument in the 1930s. He began playing the three-row accordion in the 1950s.

Influenced by the music of regional orchestras (*orquestas tipicas*), which featured a flute, bass, guitar, and violins, and by such accordionists as José "La Bamba" Rodríguez and Alejandro Aguirre, Martínez began to develop his own distinctive style of playing, which emphasized the treble buttons of the accordion.

Making a name
Martínez began playing with the Almeida family orchestra at age 14, and by his late teens he had established a name for himself as a talented accordionist. Performing with Texas-born *baja sexto* (12-string Mexican guitar) player

▼ ***The accordionist Narciso Martínez, shown (right) with his wife, Iduvina, revolutionized conjunto music by virtually ignoring the bass-chord buttons on his accordion and concentrating instead on the right-hand, treble-melody keys.***

LEGACY

Conjunto music (known as "música norteña" outside of Texas) evolved in north and south Texas in the second half of the 19th century, when music businesses began importing the German-made accordion. Local musicians liked the sound that the instrument made and it became very popular at *fandangos* (local working-class dances), especially since one accordionist could play music all night. Many local white Texans disliked the dances because they thought that they promoted idleness among Mexicans. The *San Antonio Express* reported that they were "a curse to the country." Despite this, *fandangos* continued and conjunto music became increasingly popular with Hispanic Texans.

By the early 20th century, conjunto accordionists were often accompanied by musicians playing the *bajo sexto* (Mexican guitar), and the *tambora de rancho* (ranch drum).

In the 1930s Narciso Martínez revolutionized conjunto music by abandoning the traditional way of playing to concentrate on the right-hand, treble/melodic buttons on the two-row accordion. Santiago Almeida (1911–1999), his *bajo sexto* player, picked up the bass and harmony normally provided by the left-hand buttons of the accordion.

Martínez and Almeida created a distinctive, much brighter and cleaner style of conjunto. From the mid-1930s they began recording conjunto songs and their records influenced other musicians, including the accordionist Valerio Longoria.

KEY DATES

1911 Born in Reynosa, Tamaulipas, Mexico, on October 29.

1920s Begins playing with Santiago Almeida, with whom he played until the 1950s.

1936 Records first session for Bluebird records, featuring "La Chicharronera."

1976 Features in the documentary *Chulas Fronteras* (Beautiful Borders).

1983 Inducted into the Conjunto Hall of Fame; awarded the National Heritage Fellowship Award.

1989 Nominated for a Grammy.

1992 Dies in San Benito on June 5.

Santiago Almeida, Martínez played the melody while Almeida supplied the bass, creating the distinctive sound for which they became famous. The two men performed at local farmers' dances, where they came into contact with the Czech, Bohemian, and German music played by local migrants. Martínez and Almeida included in their sets some of the polkas, mazurkas, and waltzes that they heard.

From stardom to obscurity

In 1936 Martínez and Almeida made their first recording for RCA's Bluebird label; the record included the conjunto standard "La Chicharronera." The two men soon became among the most popular and influential dance musicians in South Texas.

In 1946 Martínez was employed as house accordionist for IDEAL records in San Benito, Texas. He was one of the first conjunto musicians to accompany singers, usually duos, on commerical records.

By the 1950s both Martínez and Almeida were forced to take a series of menial jobs in order to survive financially, and they stopped performing together. Almeida moved first to Indiana and then to Washington, earning a living picking apples with his family. Martínez drove trucks and worked as a caretaker, although he continued playing at weddings, parties, and other special occasions on weekends. From 1973 onward he was a caretaker at the Gladys Porter Zoo in Brownsville.

Exposure

In 1976 Martínez came to public attention again, after he was featured in the documentary *Chulas Fronteras* (Beautiful Borders) and received credit for his pioneering role in the development of conjunto music. In 1983 Martínez was inducted into the Conjunto Hall of Fame; he was also awarded the National Heritage Fellowship Award in that year. Martínez began recording again and won critical recognition. In 1989 he received a Grammy nomination for his work. He died in San Benito in 1992.

See also: Music and Hispanic Americans

Further reading: Pena, Manuel. *The Texas–Mexican Conjunto.* Austin, TX: University of Texas Press, 1985.
http://www.pbs.org/accordiondreams/pioneers/index.html (PBS focus site on conjunto and its pioneers, including Martínez).

MARTINEZ, Oscar
Artist

Oscar Martinez's art represents the geographical and cultural shift between Puerto Rico and the United States. It employs a mixture of picturesque, folkloric, and surreal imagery. Martinez's artwork spans three decades. His numerous group and solo exhibits throughout the Caribbean, Mexico, and the southern and midwestern United States have established him as a leading figure in the Hispanic American art community.

KEY DATES

1953 Born in Maragüez, Puerto Rico, in September.

1977 Graduates with degree in medical art.

1990 Founds the Latin American Museum of Art in Chicago, Illinois.

1994 Receives National Trust for Hispanic Preservation Scholarship.

Early career

Born in Maragüez, Puerto Rico, in 1953, Martinez settled in Chicago and emerged in the 1970s as a muralist. His active involvement in this movement resulted in his numerous murals that depicted scenes of prenatal life and birth. Martinez's highly controversial exhibit at the University of Illinois at Chicago in 1977 launched his career as a daring and unique visionary whose artistic evolution has been popular among both critics and general audiences. Concerning his philosophy, Martinez states: "My artwork is about the mysteries of the mind, the revelation found in dreams, and the ever present and elusive perception of what we call reality."

▲ ***Oscar Martinez is pictured in front of his painting* Se Ilumina Mi Ser *(My Being Illuminates Itself).***

Martinez's affections and memories of his hometown continually serve as a strong source of inspiration in his art. Martinez left Maragüez when he was 14, and although the town was later flooded by a broken dam, he continues to evoke in his paintings his childhood memories of his grandmother's singing, his grandfather's violin playing, and his aunts' discussions about spirits and myths.

Career and achievements

Martinez studied science and art at the University of Illinois at Champaign, and received a bachelor of science in medical art from the University of Illinois Medical Center in 1977. He began his career as a medical artist, illustrating scientific journals. His many artistic credits include exhibits in the Museum of Bellas Artes and the National Historical Museum in Mexico, the Desplaines Museum in Illinois, Northern Illinois University Museum's Gallery in Chicago, the Field Museum in Springfield, Illinois, and its gallery in Chicago at the State of Illinois Building.

Some of his awards and recognitions include inclusions in *Who's Who in Hispanic America* and *Who's Who in America*, the McCormick Place Purchase Award, the Evanston Cultural Center Vicinity Award, the Chicago Jaycees Outstanding Citizen Award, and the Aspira Inc. of Illinois Leadership Award.

Martinez also is also the founder and president of the Latin American Museum of Art in Chicago, whose mission is to create a museum and cultural institution that is international in scope, while addressing the needs of the local, regional, and national communities.

Further reading: Lackritz Gray, Mary. *A Guide to Chicago's Murals*. Chicago, IL: University of Chicago Press, 2001. http://www.oscarmartinez.com (Martinez's official site).

MARTINEZ, Pedro
Baseball Player

Pedro Martinez is an award-winning power pitcher. He is known for his fastball and curveball and was one of the pitchers most feared by batters in the late-20th and early-21st centuries.

Break into the big league

Martinez was born in Manoguayabo, Dominican Republic, in 1971. He and his older brother Ramon loved playing baseball as children. Ramon also became a major league pitcher. In 1992 Martinez was signed by the Los Angeles Dodgers, where Ramon had been playing for four years. Martinez made his first professional appearance in that year as a relief pitcher. He managed to pitch only eight innings that year.

In demand

In November 1993, Martinez was traded to the Montreal Expos, despite a 10-5 record and an earned run average (ERA) of 2.61. He quickly became a starter for the Expos, with a sure arm and a solid record. During the next four years with the Expos, Martinez accumulated a 53–33 record of wins and losses. He won the Cy Young Award in 1997. That year also saw Martinez score a 17–8 record, with a 1.90 ERA. He was in such demand that Montreal was unable to keep him for another year.

Martinez was traded in 1997 to the Boston Red Sox. During his first season on the team in 1998, Martinez finished in second place for the Cy Young award. In the course of his pitching career, Martinez faced his brother only once in a game. They reunited on the same team in 1999, when Ramon was also picked up by the Red Sox. In 2004 Martinez signed with the New York Mets, but his pitching record suffered because of multiple injuries.

KEY DATES

1971 Born in Manoguayabo, Dominican Republic, on October 25.

1992 Makes first professional baseball appearance with the Los Angeles Dodgers.

1997 Wins the National League's Cy Young award.

1999 Declared All-Star Most Valuable Player.

2004 Signs a $53 million contract with the New York Mets.

▲ ***Pedro Martinez is known for his low pitching position. At the height of his career, Martinez's fastball traveled at 95 miles per hour (153 km/h).***

All-star player

Martinez holds the single-season strikeout record for both the Boston Red Sox and the Montreal Expos. Martinez was named to the National League All-Star teams of 1996, 1997, and 1998, and started the American League All-Star game in 1999. He struck out five out of six batters he faced from the mound, and was chosen Most Valuable Player.

In 1999 Martinez won the American League's Pitcher of the Month award four times. He also won that year's American League Pitching Triple Crown. He received the Cy Young award again in 2000. Injuries plagued him in the latter part of 2005, but the Mets still saw him as an integral part of their pitching staff going into the 2006 season.

Further reading: Krasner, Stephen. *Pedro Martinez*. Philadelphia, PA: Chelsea House Publishers, 2002.
http://www.baseball-reference.com/m/martipe02.shtml (Martinez's baseball statistics).

MARTINEZ, Tomas Eloy

Writer

The Argentine-born writer Tomas Eloy Martinez is a prolific and accomplished journalist and essay writer who is best known for his fiction. He has written two of the most significant novels based on Argentina's recent history, *The Perón Novel* and *Santa Evita*. He is also a distinguished academic who continues to teach at Rutgers University in New Jersey.

Newspaper career

Tomas Eloy Martinez was born and raised in Tucumán, northern Argentina, the site of the first colonial Spanish capital. From an early age, Martinez was passionate about story telling. He received a bachelor's degree in Spanish and Latin American literature from Tucumán University.

In 1957 Martinez moved to Buenos Aires, Argentina's capital, where he started work as a movie critic for the daily newspaper *La Nación*, and as editor-in-chief of another weekly publication, *Primera Plana*. He also wrote articles for a number of other publications, including *La Opinión*, *Panorama,* and *Abril*.

Between 1969 and 1970, *Abril* sent Martinez to Paris, France. While there he worked as the paper's European correspondent and studied for his master's degree.

Fiction writing

Martinez published his first novel, *Sagrado*, in 1969. His second book, published in 1974, was an account of the massacre of guerrillas as they tried to escape from a prison at Trelew, Argentina. *La Pasión de Trelew* combined various literary genres—prose, drama, poetry, and journalism. Martinez would later use a similar combination of different genres to great effect in *The Perón Novel*.

Back in Argentina, Martinez resumed work as a journalist, first on the weekly publication *Panorama* and then, in 1972, as the editor of the culture supplement of the daily newspaper *La Opinión*. Martinez wrote on numerous subjects but had a particular interest in movies. He even wrote a number of screenplays. His most frequent topic, however, was Argentina's troubled politics. The military was gradually taking control of the country. At the start of the 1970s, the former Argentine president Juan Domingo Perón (1895–1974) returned from exile in Madrid, Spain, to resume the presidency. His last brief period in office heralded the start of a repressive military dictatorship that would last until 1984.

▲ ***Tomas Eloy Martinez makes an acceptance speech after being awarded a Spanish book prize in 2002.***

Exiled

In 1975 Martinez was forced into exile after his writings fell afoul of the military regime. Martinez moved to the Venezuelan capital, Caracas, where he remained until he immigrated to the United States eight years later. In Caracas he edited the literary section of *El Nacional* newspaper between 1975 and 1977. In 1979 Martinez launched *El Diarío de Caracas*, where he worked as editor in chief. In 1978 he published a collection of his essays, *The Witnesses from Outside*, followed by *Picture of the Masked Artist* in 1982. He also started work on the novel that was to make his literary reputation, *The Perón Novel*.

In 1983 Martinez immigrated to the United States. Between 1984 and 1987 he was professor of Latin American literature at the University of Maryland.

INFLUENCES AND INSPIRATION

Juan Perón, with his charismatic second wife Eva Perón (1919–1952) at his side, came to power in 1946 as a hugely popular figure. Perón introduced radical reforms that initially brought financial improvements to Argentina in the late 1940s.

Eva Perón was Argentina's first lady until her premature death in 1952. Although never officially elected to a government position, Evita, as she was affectionately known, was the second most powerful person in Argentina. She championed the poor and the working classes, whom she called *los descamisados* ("the shirtless ones"). They loved her as much as the middle classes hated her.

Evita also fought for women's suffrage. The 1952 election was the first in which Argentine women were able to vote. After Evita's death from cancer at age 33, two million Argentines stood in the streets around the country to mark her funeral.

After a decline in the economic fortunes of Argentina, Perón's own popularity fell and he became increasingly authoritarian. Forced into exile following a military coup d'état in 1955, he stayed away from Argentina until he was invited back in 1973. He was reelected as president but died in office in 1974. The resulting political instability gave rise to a military regime responsible for the bloodiest period in Argentina's history.

The Perón Novel was published in 1985, with its English translation appearing in 1987. It blended fact and fiction as it recounted Argentina's history under Perón.

In the novel, Martinez describes Perón's brief resumption of power between 1973 and 1974 from three different perspectives—the president's own hazy memories, the account of one of his ministers, José Lopez Rega (1916–1989), and a journalist's impressions, based on interviews with Perón. Martinez himself interviewed Perón on numerous occasions while they were both in Caracas and later in Madrid. He concluded that Perón invented much of his own personal history to suit his own needs. In its account of Perón and his legacy, the novel investigates the natures of history and fiction.

Evita and beyond

Martinez followed the success of *The Perón Novel* with an even more successful book, *Santa Evita*, which took as its subject Eva Perón, or more precisely, her body. Published in Spanish in 1995, *Santa Evita* has become the most translated Argentine novel of all time. Using the same literary techniques he used in *The Perón Novel*, Martinez examines Argentina through its reaction to Evita's death and the military's attempts to steal her body for propaganda purposes.

Santa Evita was written while Martinez was also working as an academic. He moved from the University of Maryland in 1987 to Rutgers University in New Jersey, where he continued to teach into the early 21st century. In 1995 he was appointed distinguished professor and director of the Latin American Program, and in 2000, he was appointed director of the Center for Hemispheric Studies and writer in residence. He has also taught at universities in Argentina and Europe, and is the recipient of seven honorary PhDs.

Martinez's career as a journalist has also continued. In 1991 he helped set up a daily newspaper in Guadalajara, México. Since 1996 he has been a regular columnist for *La Nación* in Buenos Aires and a *New York Times* syndicated columnist. His articles are reprinted in about two hundred newspapers across the Americas and Europe.

With the end of the military dictatorship in 1984, Martinez's first three books were reprinted in Argentina. His latest novel, *El Cantor de Tango*, appeared in Spanish in 2004. The English translation, *The Tango Singer*, was published in 2006.

KEY DATES

1934 Born in Tucumán, Argentina, in July.

1975 Goes into exile in Venezuela.

1983 Moves to the United States.

1985 Publishes *The Perón Novel*.

1995 Publishes *Santa Evita*.

2006 Latest novel, *The Tango Singer*, published in English in the United States.

Further reading: Martinez, Tomas Eloy. *The Tango Singer*. New York, NY: Bloomsbury, 2006.
http://www.lettre-ulysses-award.org/jury04/bio_martinez.html (biography).

MARTINEZ, Victor
Writer

As the first Hispanic American to win the coveted National Book Award, Victor Martinez's talent has brought him to a wider audience than most other Chicano authors. Using rich imagery and an elegant narrative style, Martinez weaves a thread of commonality that speaks to people of all races and socioeconomic levels.

Early life

The son of migrant workers, Martinez was born in 1954 and grew up in a Fresno, California, housing project with his 11 siblings. Martinez began working as a farm laborer as a young child, and often worked in the fields after school until the 12th grade. These experiences had a lasting effect on the young Martinez that would later surface in his writing.

As a boy, Martinez read a lot, but did not see himself as a writer. Nor was he a particularly high-achiever. Early in high school a teacher crumpled up the first poem Victor ever wrote and threw it toward a wastebasket. When he missed, the teacher rudely remarked, "It's so bad even the trash can won't take it." Determined to prove him wrong, Victor spent six weeks writing a 27-line poem about his grandmother. He knew his efforts were paying off when another teacher read his commentary on Hawthorne's *The Scarlet Letter* out loud to the entire English class, saying, "For those of you who want to become writers, this paper exemplifies what I think is excellent writing."

By graduation Martinez knew he wanted to become a poet, but he lacked the funds to pursue his ambition. With the assistance of an affirmative action program, Martinez was able to attend California State University at Fresno and later went to Stanford University. Guided by professors who recognized his potential, Martinez cultivated his blossoming talent and entered the literary world.

KEY DATES

1954 Born in Fresno, California.

1996 Publishes his first novel, *Parrot in the Oven: Mi Vida*, which wins the National Book Award for Young People's Literature.

1998 *Parrot in the Oven: Mi Vida* wins the Pura Belpre Award, named after the first Hispanic American librarian at the New York Public Library.

▲ ***Victor Martinez's best-selling novel* Parrot in the Oven: Mi Vida *is a coming-of-age story about a Latino boy growing up in California.***

Professional writer

Martinez's poems, short stories, and essays soon appeared in a number of prestigious journals. However, he could not make a living as a poet or an essayist, so he began writing fiction to supplement his income.

Martinez's debut novel, *Parrot in the Oven: Mi Vida*, was a great success. The book won the National Book Award for Young People's Literature in 1996 and the Pura Belpre Award in 1998. The story painted a portrait of life in a barrio (Hispanic American district). However, Martinez's characters' highs and lows struck a chord with readers from all backgrounds.

Like many Latinos, Martinez regards himself as an "outsider" from mainstream America. He believes that this gives him a unique perspective. "An outsider can tell you a lot," he says. "For a writer, that's advantageous."

Further reading: Martinez, Victor. *Parrot in the Oven: Mi Vida.* New York, NY: Harper Collins, 1996.
http://www.theguardsman.com/20021009/missionscribe.html (interview with Martinez).

MARTÍNEZ, Vilma
Lawyer

A leading Latina attorney in the area of corporate and employment law, Vilma Martínez is best known for her work with the Mexican American Legal Defense and Education Fund (MALDEF), a nonprofit organization that was incorporated in 1967. MALDEF seeks to promote Latino civil rights through advocacy and litigation. As MALDEF's director and general counsel during the 1970s and early 1980s, Martínez led successful legal battles to overturn discriminatory state laws. Her most notable success was in the 1982 Supreme Court case of *Plyler v. Doe*, in which she secured free public education for the children of undocumented migrants.

▲ ***As the most prominent Hispanic American civil rights lawyer, Vilma Martínez has used the law to fight prejudice against Latinos.***

A high-flying career

Vilma Socorro Martínez was born in 1943 in San Antonio, Texas, and grew up at a time when much of her home state was racially segregated. She was the victim of prejudice from an early age. During her education, bilingual Hispanic children were doing less well in school than English speaking students, and many dropped out of school. Martínez was a good student in junior high, yet her counselor proposed she take a place at a nonacademic vocational high school with large numbers of Hispanic students, where she would "be more comfortable."

At the age of 15 Martínez was inspired to become an attorney after working as a volunteer in the office of the prominent lawyer and civil-rights activist Alonso S. Perales (*see box on page 85*). After high school, Martínez went on to study at the University of Texas at Austin, from which she graduated in 1964. She subsequently studied at the prestigious Columbia Law School in New York City, earning a bachelor of law degree in 1967.

Despite facing prejudice as both a woman and Mexican American, Martínez rapidly made her mark in her chosen profession. She initially worked as an attorney for the National Association for the Advancement of Colored People (NAACP), where she took part in cases filed under the 1964 Civil Rights Act. The act had made it illegal for employers to discriminate against employees on grounds of their race, color, religion, sex, or national origin. Martínez subsequently joined the law firm of Cahill, Gordon & Reindel and specialized in employment law.

In 1973, at the age of just 29, Martínez was appointed chief counsel and director of MALDEF. Initially based in San Antonio, Texas, by the time of Martínez's appointment the organization's national office had moved to San Francisco, California. Despite a $2.2 million grant from the Ford Foundation, MALDEF had at first met with little success, but under Martínez's leadership the organization flourished. Over the following decade Martínez worked hard to give MALDEF a national profile, to raise funds, and to direct its energies into cases that she considered would make a lasting difference to Mexican American lives.

INFLUENCES AND INSPIRATION

Martínez's commitment to civil-rights litigation as a means of countering discrimination is part of a strong and ongoing tradition of Latino activism. It can be dated back to the work of the League of United Latin American Citizens (LULAC) in the 1930s and 1940s. Indeed, Martínez had a direct connection to LULAC through her work in the legal practice of Alonso S. Perales (1898–1960), one of the LULAC organization's founders. Perales was a formative influence on Martínez's career.

Perales was a committed member of the Democratic Party and believed passionately in the value of the law in achieving change. Martínez inherited the liberal, assimilationist values of LULAC and Perales. This contrasted with the more militant and confrontational style of activism adopted by many other Mexican Americans of her generation, for whom street protest offered a more powerful challenge to the status quo than court-room advocacy.

Making a difference

Among MALDEF's early successes under Martínez was its joint campaign with the Southwest Voter Registration Education Project to end electoral practices that denied many Mexican Americans the vote. A dogged program of lobbying led to the Voting Rights Act Amendments of 1975, which extended the protection enshrined in the Voting Rights Act of 1965 to people with Hispanic surnames. Another of Martínez's early achievements was setting up the San Antonio–based Chicana Rights Program to combat sex discrimination against Mexican American women.

Perhaps Martínez's best-known and most significant achievement, however, was in the field of education. In the Supreme Court case of *Plyler v. Doe* of 1982, she argued that the state of Texas's refusal to educate the children of undocumented Mexican migrants was a violation of the Equal Protection Clause of the Fourteenth Amendment. The Supreme Court agreed, arguing moreover that children could not be held responsible for their parents' economic and political status and that by denying them their right to education the state was effectively condemning them to a lifetime of illiteracy.

KEY DATES

1943 Born in San Antonio, Texas, on October 17.

1967 Graduates from Columbia Law School, New York City, with an LLB law degree.

1973 Appointed director and chief counsel of the Mexican American Legal Defense and Education Fund (MALDEF).

1982 Leads a successful lawsuit in the Supreme Court case of *Plyler v. Doe*.

1982 Leaves MALDEF to join Los Angeles law firm of Munger, Tolles, and Olson.

1994 Successfully overturns California's Proposition 187, which would have denied free education to undocumented immigrants.

1994 Sits on U.S. president's Advisory Committee on Trade Policy and Negotiations.

The struggle continues

The *Plyler v. Doe* case was a high point of Martínez's leadership of MALDEF as well as a milestone in Chicano history. That same year she left the organization to become a partner in the Los Angeles law firm Munger, Tolles, and Olson. There Martínez continued her career-long struggle against discrimination and prejudice. Most notably in 1994—in a case with clear echoes of *Plyler v. Doe*—she led a successful challenge to California's Proposition 187. This legislation would have denied the children of the state's undocumented migrants access to public-school education.

Martínez's courageous public service has won her many awards, including both a Pioneer Award and LEX Award from the Mexican American Bar Association, a Medal for Excellence from Columbia Law School, and a Valerie Kantor Award for Extraordinary Achievement from MALDEF. Martínez also served as a member of the University of California Board of Regents between 1976 and 1990, as chair of the Pacific Council's study group on Mexico, and on the advisory boards of Columbia Law School and the Asian Pacific American Legal Center of Southern California. From 1994 to 1996, she sat on President Clinton's Advisory Committee on Trade Policy and Negotiations.

Further reading: Rosales, Francisco A. *Chicano! The History of the Mexican American Civil Rights Movement.* 2d rev. ed. Houston, TX: Arte Público Press, 1997.
www.nwhp.org/tlp/biographies/martinez/bio.html (biography).

MARTINEZ, Xavier

Artist

Xavier Martinez was a significant artistic figure at the turn of the 20th century in California. He united a sophisticated European training with his Californian indentity and Mexican heritage to produce his work, primarily landscape paintings. These are now a highly valued part of California's cultural heritage. Martinez was part of the group of artists who were later categorized as the tonalists, a distinctively American development of French Impressionism.

◀ ***Xavier Martinez, pictured here in 1905, was one of California's most admired painters.***

Early career

Born in Guadalajara, Mexico, in 1869, Martinez moved with his family to San Francisco, California, when his stepfather was made consul-general in 1893. There he studied for two years at the Mark Hopkins Institute of Arts under Arthur Mathews (1860–1945). Mathews was one of the leading artists of the San Francisco Bay Area at the end of the 19th century.

In 1895 Martinez won a scholarship to study at the École des Beaux Arts in Paris, France. He stayed in Paris to continue studying at the Académie Carriére between 1897 and 1901. His work was praised by the great American expatriate artist James McNeill Whistler (1834–1903), who was to become his main influence.

Returning to San Francisco, Martinez established a studio. He became a member of the city's exclusive Bohemian Club in 1904. Following the earthquake and fire in 1906 in San Francisco, Martinez, like many other artists, lost most of his work.

Maturing talent

In 1907 Martinez moved to Piedmont, California, where he joined a group of leading artists from San Francisco including William Keith (1838–1911), Arthur Mathews, Eugen Neuhaus (1879–1963), Charles Rollo Peters (1862–1928), Gottardo Piazzoni (1872–1945), and Will Sparks (1862–1937), who turned the ballroom of the Hotel Del Monte in Monterey, California, into an art gallery. This led to the founding of the Del Monte Art Gallery and the beginning of the Monterey Peninsula art colony.

The Monterey area offered the perfect setting for the somber tones of Martinez's landscapes of the coastline, the Carmel Hills, and the ruins of the Spanish missions. Martinez's new paintings were exhibited at the Vickery, Atkins, and Torrey Art Gallery in San Francisco. He also began teaching at the newly founded California College of the Arts in 1908, where he taught until his death in 1943. By 1914 Martinez lived in a house in Alameda County designed by the architect Frederick Meyer, founder of the California College of the Arts; the house was a meeting place for artist and writers of the time.

Legacy

Martinez has been praised as one of the major artists of tonalism. His *Afternoon in Piedmont* (1911) has been hailed as the masterpiece of California tonalism. In the 21st century he has also been credited as a major influence on a contemporary generation of Northern California landscape painters.

Further reading: http://www.tfaoi.com/aa/2aa/2aa594.htm (essay on the California tonalist school of painting).

KEY DATES

1869	Born in Guadalajara, Mexico, on February 7.
1893	Moves to San Francisco, California.
1895	Moves to Paris, France.
1908	Begins teaching at the California College of the Arts.
1943	Dies in Carmel, California, on January 13.

MARTINEZ TUCKER, Sara

Activist

As the president and chief executive of the Hispanic Scholarship Fund (HSF), Sara Martinez Tucker hopes to almost double the rate of Hispanic college college graduates to 18 percent by 2010. She has transformed the organization since joining in 1997, helping thousands more disadvantaged Hispanic Americans.

Martinez Tucker was born in Laredo, Texas, in 1955, the eldest of three children with Mexican American parents. She attended Catholic schools, then became the first in her family to attend college by studying journalism at the University of Texas, followed by a master's degree in business administration.

Following her studies, Martinez Tucker worked for the telecommunications company AT&T for 16 years. She rose to become a regional vice president, the company's first Hispanic American woman to achieve the executive level. At the age of 40, Martinez Tucker left her job in search of greater fulfillment. She joined HSF, then a small not-for-profit organization.

More Hispanic graduates

Hispanic Americans have the highest high-school drop-out rate (48 percent) and the lowest college graduation rate (11 percent) of any ethnic group in the country. Increasingly, well-paid jobs require employees to have degrees, and poverty among Hispanic Americans is growing. Hispanic Americans underachieving in education may also pose dangers to the economy. Between 1990 and 2000, the Hispanic American population grew by 44 percent, making them the nation's largest minority. Martinez Tucker realized that if the group remained undereducated, the country was likely to have an inadequate workforce.

KEY DATES

1955 Born in April, in Laredo, Texas, about this time.

1976 Receives bachelor's degree in journalism from the University of Texas, Laredo.

1979 Receives masters degree in business administration from the University of Texas.

1997 Joins Hispanic Scholarship Fund.

2001 Appointed to the board of directors of the Student Loan Marketing Association. Helps to found the National Center for Educational Accountability.

▲ ***Sara Martinez Tucker gave up a well-paid job to devote herself to getting more Hispanic Americans into higher education.***

Raising money and awareness

Martinez Tucker used her business acumen and marketing strategies to propel the HSF to greater success. In 1996 the charity offered $3 million of funding to students. This had increased to more than $25 million by 2002. HSF then assisted more than 6,000 students annually.

Martinez Tucker has convinced corporations, such as the Ford Motor Co., that to donate is an investment proposition. She has also persuaded the philanthropic foundation the Lilly Endowment to donate $50 million to HSF.

Martinez Tucker has also widened the organization's scope to help graduating high-school seniors, community college students seeking to transfer to universities, and existing college students to complete their degrees.

HSF now has outreach programs called Project LEAD for parents, and hosts workshops around the country to help students apply for college.

Further reading: http://www.hsf.net/about/ceo_msg.php (Martinez Tucker's welcome message to the Hispanic Scholarship Fund Web site).

MAS CANOSA, Jorge

Activist

Following the death of Jorge Mas Canosa in 1997, South Florida's main daily newspaper, the *Miami Herald*, noted, "When the story of the 20th century is written for South Florida, there will surely be page after page on Jorge Mas Canosa. His influence extended far beyond his own community, extending especially to Washington, D.C., and Cuba." Whether Mas Canosa influenced things for better or worse remains a debatable question. That he was a self-made man, a political king-maker, and a man committed to influencing Cuban history is indisputable.

For many U.S. citizens outside South Florida, Mas Canosa's views came to represent those of all Cuban Americans in Miami. The politician's high profile in the national media reinforced this assumption. For many Americans, his was the only Cuban American name they recognized. The Cuban dictator Fidel Castro (1926–) also endorsed this position by vilifying Mas Canosa as a constant violent threat to Cuba and portraying him as the head of a "Miami mafia." Mas Canosa did nothing to alter this view since it increased his influence and appealed to his constituency.

▲ ***Jorge Mas Canosa was a powerful voice for Cuban Americans exiled from Castro's Cuba.***

Cuban exile

Jorge Mas Canosa certainly did not begin life with privilege or prominence. Born in Santiago, Cuba, in 1939, Mas Canosa was the son of a poorly paid army veterinarian. During adolescence Mas Canoas spoke out publicly against the U.S.-sponsored dictator Fulgencio Batista (1901–1973), and was quickly sent by his parents to a strict boarding school in Pennsylvania to avoid retribution.

After Castro's revolutionary army took over Cuba in 1959, Mas Canosa joined anti-Castro forces but was forced to flee to Miami in July 1960 because the government was close to arresting him. In exile, Mas Canosa persisted with his anti-Castro activities, becoming involved in Radio Swan, a CIA-sponsored station that broadcast to Cuba.

Military service

The following year, Mas Canosa participated in the failed Bay of Pigs invasion. This was another CIA-sponsored operation, which saw U.S.-trained Cuban rebels killed and captured as they attempted to storm a beach on the south coast of Cuba. Mas Canosa never made it to land and he returned unharmed. He then joined a special Cuban military outfit trained by the U.S. Army at Fort Benning, Georgia. However, once he realized that the United States was very unlikely to support or fund another military action against Cuba, Mas Canosa left in search of better-paid employment.

Construction business

Throughout the 1960s and 1970s, Mas Canosa continued to believe in armed struggle as the best way to defeat Castro. During this time he supported himself, his wife Irma, and their children first as a milkman and later as a shoe salesman. He also became active in a U.S.-backed coalition of exiled activists called the Cuban Representation in Exile. Simultaneously he began to make his fortune.

Mas Canosa took on work for a Puerto Rico-based construction firm named after its two founders, Iglesias y Torre. He dug holes for phone poles and cable pipes and soon became the manager of the Miami office. In 1971 he bought the business for just $50,000, translating the name of the company into English to establish Church and Tower. Within a year Mas Canosa won a million dollar contract with Southern Bell (now BellSouth) to lay

LEGACY

"Take no comfort in the passing of Jorge Mas Canosa. That is because Jorge's legacy will forever live in the hearts and minds of future generations of Cubans who will fulfill his dream of a nation without bloodshed, with no exile, with no human misery, with no injustice, and with no hate." That was the statement of the board of directors and staff of the Cuban American National Council following Jorge Mas Canosa's death in 1997.

Mas Canosa's legacy includes influencing the direction of U.S. foreign policy toward Cuba, including the stringent economic embargo that can only be lifted by Congress under very specific conditions. Mas Canosa also developed a powerful lobby that represents conservative Cuban interests at all levels of government. He also left his family a corporation that is worth hundreds of millions of dollars.

telecommunication cables. Ditch diggers' salaries were low and the profits were high, making Mas Canosa a wealthy man in a short time. He went on to develop a small family telecommunications firm, MasTec, into a multimillion-dollar public company.

Political activity

In the early 1980s, Mas Canosa turned to politics to influence U.S. policy on Cuba. He was tutored in how to succeed in Washington politics by a Zionist group, the America-Israel Public Affairs Committee. In 1981 he founded the Cuban American National Foundation (CANF). The foundation was established by 24 members who committed themselves to paying at least $10,000 per year. Most contributed more. Mas Canosa was the undisputed leader. The group used pressure tactics and rewards to build one of the most influential lobbying organizations in the United States. Bringing down Fidel Castro was their sole purpose.

KEY DATES

1939 Born in Santiago de Cuba on September 21.

1960 Enters exile on July 15 at age 20.

1961 Joins the Bay of Pigs invasion.

1971 Buys Church and Tower and gains $1 million in business from Southern Bell.

1981 Sets up the Cuba American National Foundation (CANF).

1994 Forms MasTec. Valued at $500 million in 1997, it is the largest Hispanic American-owned corporation in the United States.

1996 Is instrumental in tightening the U.S. trade embargo on Cuba.

1997 Dies of cancer on November 23.

Through CANF, Mas Canosa also built a network of local supporters using the traditional political patronage of old-time bossism. With his network of business connections and personal wealth, he was able to influence newcomers from Cuba, giving them financial assistance and jobs. CANF also administered the relief programs paid by the U.S. government. The first was a program to bring to Miami Cuban exiles living in Latin American countries who were unable to get visas for the United States. The project, called Exodus, was paid for by the U.S. Immigration and Naturalization Service, and critics saw it simply as a way for CANF to build a loyal constituency using public dollars. A second project began with CANF funds in 1994 to help with the resettlement of rafters (those who had tried to flee Cuba for the United States on rafts) who were being held in detention camps at Guantanamo Bay, the U.S. Navy base in southern Cuba. When the government refused to underwrite the costs, Mas Canosa shut the project down the same day.

Lasting impact

Mas Canosa's legacy is maintaining the Cuban trade embargo that created harsher economic conditions for ordinary Cubans. Mas Canosa believed that this hardship would lead to a citizens' revolt against Castro. He also created an anti-Castro broadcasting company that beams propaganda into Cuba. So absolute was Mas Canosa's control on the Cuba issue, that a former U.S. diplomat in Cuba is quoted as saying, "Had it not been for Jorge Mas Canosa, we probably would have had normal relations with Cuba. He has almost single-handedly blocked all that." Mas Canosa did not live to see a Cuba without Castro.

Further reading: Bardach, Ann Louise. *Cuba Confidential: Love and Vengeance in Miami and Havana*. New York, NY: Random House, 2002.
http://www.canf.org/2005/principal-ingles.htm (CANF web site).

MATA, Eduardo
Conductor

Eduardo Mata was an internationally renowned conductor and composer. A Mexican by birth, Mata spent much of his professional career in the United States, first with the Phoenix Symphony Orchestra in Arizona and then with the Dallas Symphony Orchestra in Texas. He was also a guest conductor with many of the world's finest orchestras, including the Berlin Philharmonic.

Early life

Born in Mexico City, Mexico, in 1942, Mata showed musical talent from an early age. He studied the guitar for three years and began to compose his own music. Aged 15, Mata conducted his first orchestra. Three years later he went to study composition at the National Conservatory of Music, where he was taught by the Mexican composer and conductor Carlos Chávez (1899–1978) and the Spanish-born composer Julián Orbón (1925–1991).

In 1964 Mata was awarded a fellowship by the Serge Koussevitzky Music Foundation of the Library of Congress to study conducting and composition at Tanglewood Music Center in Massachussets.

Mata's exceptional musical talent led to his appointment as permanent conductor of the Guadalajara Symphony Orchestra when he was just 23 years old. In 1965 he was also made head of the music department of the National Autonomous University of Mexico (UNAM).

Mata became known for his clean interpretation of a wide range of music. He was particularly interested in the work of Latin American composers such as Alberto Ginastera (1916–1983) and Silvestre Revueltas (1899–1940). He also composed his own work, such as chamber works and improvisations for piano and strings, including Improvisation No. 3 for Violin and Piano (1965).

▲ ***Eduardo Mata conducts the Phoenix Symphony Orchestra in 1975.***

KEY DATES

1942 Born in Mexico City, Mexico, on September 5.

1965 Becomes permanent conductor of the Guadalajara Symphony Orchestra.

1972 Becomes principal conductor of the Phoenix Symphony Orchestra.

1977 Becomes musical director of the Dallas Symphony Orchestra.

1993 Named conductor emeritus of Dallas Symphony Orchestra following his retirement.

1995 Dies in plane crash near Cuernavaca, Mexico, on January 4.

In 1972 Mata moved to the United States to become the principal conductor of the Phoenix Symphony Orchestra. A year later he became the orchestra's musical director. In 1977 Mata became musical director of the Dallas Symphony Orchestra (DSO), with which he was probably most associated. During this time he also conducted other major orchestras such as the Chicago and Boston symphonies, and the London Symphony Orchestra in England.

In 1993 Mata retired from the DSO, after which he was named its conductor emeritus. Returning to live in Mexico later that year, Mata concentrated on composing, teaching, and conducting. Less than two years later, Mata was killed when the plane that he was piloting crashed shortly after takeoff.

Further reading: http://www.colegionacional.org.mx/Mata0.htm (biography).

MATEO, Fernando

Entrepreneur, Community Activist

If one needed to name an example of the American dream come true, Dominican-born Fernando Mateo would fit the profile perfectly. Mateo is an entrepreneur, community leader, and philanthropist who has focused his attention on protecting the rights of Hispanic American communities across the United States. Mateo has headed programs to reduce the number of guns in New York, to retrain drug-free inmates, and to reduce violence against drivers and passengers in New York taxis.

Achieving the American dream

Born in the Dominican Republic in 1959, Mateo was raised in Manhattan. Aged 17, he began working as a carpet salesman. He established his own company and through a combination of hard work and contract bidding, he soon turned his company into a multimillion-dollar business.

After pushing his company to corporate status, Mateo turned his attention to community-oriented work. In 1990, while still active in business, he began the Mateo Institute of Training (MIT). A nonprofit organization, MIT's programs taught prisoners the skills needed to secure jobs upon release. Mateo received nationwide attention and was awarded the Points of Light Award for his work.

Amid the rise of gun-related crime in New York, in 1993 Mateo initiated the "Toys for Guns" program. Originally conceived by Mateo's son, the program encouraged people to hand over guns in return for gift certificates. It was very successful, and Mateo found himself in the spotlight again. The program was later taken up by the Dominican Republic. Mateo worked with the Dominican Catholic church, using the church's own station, TeleVida, to promote the campaign.

▲ ***When Fernando Mateo's carpet business turned into a multimillion-dollar enterprise, he decided to dedicate his time to improving his community.***

KEY DATES

1959	Born in the Dominican Republic.
1976	Starts carpet company at age 17.
1990	Initiates Mateo Institute of Learning.
1993	Initiates the successful "Toys for Guns" program.
1994	Receives the Person of the Year Award and the Ellis Island Medal of Honor; named "One of the Five Most Influential People in the Country" by the *New York Times.*
2002	Founds Hispanics Across America (HAA.)
2004	Speaks at the Republican National Convention, New York.

Doing good work

Throughout the 1990s Mateo continued to direct his efforts toward helping Hispanic American communities. In 1994 he set up the Fernando Express, which created hundreds of jobs for Hispanics across the New York area. In 1998 he became president of the New York State Federation of Taxi Drivers (NYSFTD). He addressed security issues while pushing the murder rate for taxi drivers to an all-time low.

In 2002 Mateo founded Hispanics Across America (HAA), an organization that serves Hispanic communities nationwide. An active Republican, Mateo has tirelessly defended Hispanic interests at political meetings.

Further reading: Torres-Saillant, Sylvia, and Ramona Hernandez. *The Dominican Americans.* Westport, CT; Greenwood Press, 1998.
http://www.haamerica.org/index.htm (Web site of Hispanics Across America).

MEDIA, SPANISH-LANGUAGE

The print and broadcast media—newspapers, magazines, books, radio, television, and cinema—have made a major contribution to the preservation of the Spanish language in the United States. They have also been a focus and a rallying point for Hispanic identity in a predominantly English-language culture.

Newspaper publisher Nicasio Idar (far right) poses in 1910 with staff at the Laredo, Texas, offices of La Crónica*, one of many Spanish-language publications of the time.*

Origins

The Spanish language came to Central and South America with the conquistadores in the 1500s. It later became established in the U.S. Southwest and in Florida, and has remained a significant presence in both regions ever since.

At the end of the U.S.–Mexico War (1846–1848), the northern half of Mexico was ceded to the United States, and approximately 100,000 Mexicans became U.S. citizens. The redistribution of territory was codified by the Treaty of Guadalupe Hidalgo (1848), which also made provisions for the maintenance and protection of the inhabitants' language and culture.

In practice, however, both were routinely disregarded when they were not actually suppressed. The subsequent history of the U.S. Southwest is full of instances of violations of Mexican American rights. For example, as recently as 1998, California passed Proposition 227, which banned bilingual education, a right that had been guaranteed by the treaty 150 years previously. In 2000, Arizona voters passed a similar measure, Proposition 203.

Although the situation there is not replicated throughout the United States and its dominions—in Puerto Rico, for example, linguistic maintenance is guaranteed—the Spanish language has remained under constant threat, particularly from Anglo-Americans, many of whom regard the English language as a defining characteristic of "Americanness."

Opposition to the use of Spanish in the United States has spawned resentment in the Hispanic community. However, it has often been counterproductive, because it has increased the determination of Latinos and Latinas to maintain their cultural heritage. Their resistance has been aided by the great advances in technology that have occurred since the mid-19th century.

Newspapers

As early as the 1850s, Spanish-language sections started appearing in U.S. English-language newspapers. One such publication, the *Los Angeles Star*, employed a reporter named Francisco Ramírez who, in 1855, launched a paper of his own, *El Clamor Público*, which documented the exclusion of Mexicans from the United States, and the racism they faced at the hands of newly arrived Anglo-American settlers. *El Clamor Público* was the most famous of several similar newspapers that emerged during the decade. They were all short-lived—with a four-

LA OPINIÓN AND *LA PRENSA*

La Opinión is one of the major Spanish-language newspapers in the United States today. It is one of the 100 most widely read U.S. dailies, and the nation's biggest-selling Spanish-language newspaper. Its founder, Ignacio Lozano, began publishing in Los Angeles, California, on September 16, 1926, the 116th anniversary of Mexico's independence from Spain.

Prior to the launch of *La Opinión*, Lozano and his family, who had left Mexico in 1910 to escape the violence of the country's revolution, founded *La Prensa* in San Antonio, Texas.

Ignacio Lozano remained in charge of *La Opinión* until his death in 1953, at which point his son, Ignacio Lozano, Jr., took over the paper and ran it until 1986. Lozano's wife, Alicia Elizondo de Lozano, ran *La Prensa* until 1959, when she sold her interest and moved back to Mexico.

The Lozano family still manages and publishes *La Opinión* under the parent company ImpreMedia. While the paper is still published in Spanish and has retained its Latino cultural focus, it has continued to evolve, most recently through the addition of *La Opinión Digital*, an online edition for an increasingly youthful and media-savvy market. *La Prensa*, meanwhile, moved to a bilingual Spanish-English format to attract the increasingly dual-language Tejano market. It is particularly known for distinguished guest columnists, such as U.S. Congressman Henry B. González.

year lifespan, *El Clamor Público* was one of the most enduring—but they reflected the resolve of Latinos to present their own views, rather than merely translate into Spanish the Anglo-American take on current affairs.

Proliferation and diversification

By the mid-1870s, in Tucson, Arizona, there were several Spanish-language papers, including *Las Dos Republicas*, *El Fronterizo*, and *El Tucsonense*. Like *El Clamor Público*, they not only reported news but also protested negative stereotypes of Mexicans, and advocated for the protection of their civil rights. In contrast to Ramírez's paper, however, some became firmly established: The Moreno family, which published *El Tucsonense*, remained in the news industry until 2003, when Arturo Moreno sold his interest to buy the Anaheim Angels, and thus became the first Latino to own a major league baseball team.

By the 1890s, Cubans in Florida had several Spanish-language newspapers, such as *La Igualidad* and *La Fraternidad*. Cuban Americans also advocated the formation of Spanish-language libraries and schools, and Mexican Americans soon lobbied for similar provisions in the Southwest. Black Cubans found their concerns represented in English-language papers such as the *Tampa Bulletin*, which was backed by the National Association for the Advancement of Colored People (NAACP)

At the start of the 20th century, there were also many Spanish-language house magazines and newsletters belonging to various unions, mutual-aid societies, and national and patriotic organizations. The tradition lapsed between World War I (1914–1918) and World War II (1939–1945), but was revived in the 1960s. Members of the Chicano movement self-published bilingual newsletters that also featured news stories, prose, and poetry. Significantly, some Chicano-owned magazines, such as *Lowrider*, crossed over and became successful with a wider, non-Latino audience. Chicano publishing houses, such as Quinto Sol, also emerged in the 1960s. Many of the books they produced had previously been rejected by Anglo-American mainstream publishers who were unsure of the commercial market for such works.

Libraries

One effect of the proliferation of printed material in Spanish was the creation of numerous Spanish-language libraries and bookstores. In the 1920s, several Spanish-language libraries opened in southern California, particularly in Los Angeles. They were stocked mainly with books donated by the Mexican government and Mexican bookstore owners. In 1926, the League of Mexican Culture opened a library in Belvedere that featured Spanish-language books and newspapers. Most of the books it carried focused on the lives of people in Mexico or Latin America, with only a small number of works on Mexican Americans. The tradition then established has since been maintained: Today, there are many Spanish libraries and bookstores throughout the U.S. Southwest and Florida.

Into the big time

From modest beginnings in the 1960s, the Spanish-language print media expanded significantly. Spanish-language newspaper circulation tripled between 1990 and 2005, during which period Anglo-Americans substantially reduced their newspaper purchases. Publishers were quick to capitalize on the new trend. The ImpreMedia conglomerate became the leading publisher of Spanish-language newspapers, producing titles in cities including New York (*El Diario/La Prensa*), Los Angeles (*La Opinión*), Chicago (*La Raza*), and Miami (*El Nuevo Herald*). ImpreMedia successfully merged several regional newspapers that focused on the three largest Latino groups—Mexicans, Puerto Ricans, and Cubans—into a single enterprise.

Glossy, Latino-focused lifestyle magazines have also emerged in bilingual Spanish-English formats. *Hispanic*, first published in 1987, and *Latina*, founded in 1996, have become popular with bilingual and bicultural upwardly mobile professionals. *Latina* has been profitably marketed through digital media, showbusiness events and promotions, and a line of fashion accessories launched in association with the retail company Sears, Roebuck.

El Consejo Electoral le exige a Chávez respetar su fallo 4A

el Nuevo Herald

El Plan 8 se abre a nuevas solicitudes 4A

Aprueba el Congreso bloquear el correo basura por internet 2A

En vigor la nueva ley del Medicare

Cubrirá las medicinas por receta a partir del 2006

ING OUR PROM TO SENIORS

El flu se ensaña con los niños

El Nuevo Herald *is one of several popular Spanish-language daily newspapers in Miami, Florida, a state with a large number of Hispanic citizens.*

Radio

Spanish-language radio in the United States began in the 1920s and 1930s in the Southwest. The earliest stations featured Spanish music, and news and public information programming in the language. By the end of the 1920s, radio broadcasts reached one-third of Mexican Americans.

During the Great Depression (1929–1939), millions of U.S. citizens lost their jobs. In a wave of xenophobia (fear of foreigners), many Mexicans and Mexican Americans were deported to Mexico so that they could not take work away from Anglo-Americans. During the period, there was much debate in the United States about whether Spanish-language radio was desirable; many U.S. citizens took the view that English should be the only language of the airwaves. Commercial interests prevailed, however: Even then, despite their poverty, Mexicans, Puerto Ricans, and Cubans represented a lucrative market that businesses were anxious to exploit. One of the earliest and most successful radio shows was *Pedro J. González and Los Madrugadores* (*see box on page 95*).

The first Spanish station

The first all-Spanish-language radio station in the United States was KCOR in San Antonio, Texas. It went on the air in 1946, and was originally owned and operated by a Chicano. San Antonio broker Raul Cortez had applied to the Federal Communications Commission (FCC) several years earlier for a license for a full-time Spanish-language station with the rationale that it would help mobilize Chicanos behind the war effort. Cortez and others, including Paco Sánchez from Denver, Colorado, became brokers for Spanish-language radio, personalities, and advertising. By 1960, Spanish-language radio accounted for two-thirds of all foreign-language broadcasting in the United States.

The expansion reawakened nativist fears that Spanish would usurp English as the language of the United States, and the federal government responded by restricting Latino freedom to broadcast. In response, a large border radio system emerged in Mexico, just south of the Rio Grande. From there, powerful transmitters broadcast back into the United States. The programs aired mainly music, not only that of Mexicans, but also of Mexican Americans who were banned from the airwaves of their own nation. Border radio allowed for a diversity in programming and formats not found in U.S. markets.

XEPN from Jalisco and XEAW in Reynosa broadcast Spanish-language musicians popular in the United States, such as Lydia Mendoza, known as "La Alondra de la Frontera" (the lark of the border). Polkas, *mariachi*, and *orquesta* were also in great demand, and Mexican singing cowboys such as Pedro Infante and Jorge Negrete became major stars in the United States. Their popularity on radio soon extended to movies, and their Spanish-language films became hits in the United States.

While Mexico imposed fewer broadcasting restrictions than the United States, its government was also concerned about the possible consequences of unregulated airwaves. For example, in 1937, Mexican president Manuel Avila Camacho compelled every border station to broadcast *La Hora Nacional* (The National Hour), a program produced by his government's ministry of press and media.

Despite opposition, the practice of producing programs in one country and broadcasting them abroad but not at home became common. Today, Radio and TV Marti go out from Florida into Cuban airspace 90 miles (144km) from the U.S. mainland. The aim of such broadcasting—to infiltrate and possibly to undermine the culture of a foreign power—was used by Latinos to subvert U.S. government regulations long before the government used the tactic against its opponents.

In addition to individual Spanish-language radio shows, entire networks emerged, including the Hispanic Broadcasting System (1949) and the Spanish Broadcasting System (1960). They were followed by radio information networks. *Latino USA*, distributed by

Outside the county court house in San Antonio, Texas, a journalist files a live report for one of the city's numerous Spanish-language television stations.

LOS MADRUGADORES

The earliest Spanish-language broadcasts on U.S. radio went out on established stations during off-peak hours. One of the most famous pioneer shows, *Pedro J. González and His Madrugadores* (early risers), was first aired on radio station KELW out of Burbank, California, from 4:00 A.M. to 6:00 A.M., targeting Mexicans getting up early for work. The show did not cut into broadcast hours, but merely extended them. González not only sang live on the air, but also provided news, features, and human-interest stories. The show carried Spanish-language advertising on behalf of local and national sponsors. González's show became so popular that it was extended until 7:00 A.M. Lunchtime and evening hours were subsequently added.

Unlike readers of newspapers such as *La Opinión*, radio listeners did not have to be literate in order to be informed. When González spoke out in the 1930s against the repatriation of Mexicans from Los Angeles during the Great Depression (1929–1939), he became the target of false charges by Los Angeles district attorney Buron Fitts. In 1934, after an unjust trial based on perjured testimony, González was found guilty of sexual assault on a minor and sentenced to 150 years' imprisonment. The Latino community formed a defense committee to help him, but to no avail. González was released from San Quentin Prison in 1940 after serving six years of his term, but immediately deported to Mexico. He returned to the United States 30 years later, but was never exonerated of the charges against him, even though the complainant had admitted lying on oath.

National Public Radio (NPR), a weekly half-hour program, is currently the only English-language radio transmission for Latinos, but it is nonetheless an indication that the cultural importance of Latinos now extends beyond dedicated Spanish-language stations. In the late-20th century, Latinos also gained acceptance as broadcasters on mainstream English-language stations. One of the best known examples is Juan González, cohost with Amy Goodman of the radio show *Democracy Now!*

On average, Latinos listen to radio in Spanish for 22 hours per week, about 6 hours more per week than non-Latinos tune in to English-language stations. Other major markets outside the Southwest include New York, Illinois, and Florida. WSKQ in New York is the largest Spanish-language station in the city, consistently ranking in the advertisers' top 10. In Miami, several stations vie for the top spot, including WAQI and WQBA. Anti-Castro WQBA station director Emilio Milian was injured when a car bomb exploded outside his radio studio in 1976. In 2000, the same station led massive protests against the deportation of nine-year-old Cuban castaway Elian González, indicating the political power of Spanish-language radio. In Chicago, WOJO and WLEY are in the top 10 as well. While New York and Florida stations target more Dominican, Cuban, and Puerto Rican listeners, most other stations focus on Mexican and Mexican American listeners.

Television

Spanish-language television in the United States began in the 1950s in major Latino population centers such as San Antonio and Los Angeles. KMEX-TV was the Spanish-language TV station in Los Angeles. Ruben Salazar worked there at the time of his death during the Chicano Moratorium of 1970. Today, KMEX Channel 34 is one of the largest stations in southern California. Its 6:00 P.M. and 11:00 P.M. newscasts have more viewers than any English-language station.

KMEX is now owned by Univision, a media conglomerate whose history reflects the growth in the power and influence of the U.S. Hispanic community. Until 1987, Univision was the Spanish International Network (SIN), which opened in 1955 in San Antonio. From the outset, it was a full-service station, with news, children's programs, game shows, dramas, and situation comedies. In its current, greatly expanded form, Univision is estimated to be worth more than $8 billion, an amount that does not include its purchase of the Hispanic Broadcasting Company radio group for $3 billion in 2003. Univision owns more than 50 stations and 40 affiliates.

Antonio Valverde reads a morning news bulletin at Univision 34's main studio in Los Angeles, California. Univision is the largest Spanish-language media company in the United States.

KEY DATES

1926 *La Opinión* newspaper is first published in Los Angeles, California, on September 16; the League of Mexican Culture opens a Spanish library in Belvedere, California.

1946 KCOR, the first Spanish-language radio station in the United States, begins broadcasting in San Antonio, Texas.

1955 The Spanish International Network (SIN) begins Spanish-language television broadcasting in San Antonio, Texas.

1986 Telemundo television station begins broadcasting.

1987 *Hispanic* magazine is launched.

1996 *Latina* magazine is launched.

2000 Azteca America, a Latin American broadcast conglomerate, launches a TV channel in the United States.

Univision covers the whole gamut of modern Hispanic life: Politics, religious events, natural disasters, and sports in Latin America are featured nightly. There is no comparable coverage on English-language television. As long as there continue to be such differences in content, Spanish-language television will continue to thrive. Viewers with limited Spanish-language skills also are tuning in in growing numbers to see more international coverage of the news than that provided by cable news stations.

Other Spanish-language networks have appeared, such as Telemundo in 1986, and, in 2000, Azteca America, a division of the Latin American TV Azteca. There Latinos work in all functions, a development that attracted the attention of the major U.S. networks. In 2001, NBC, with its parent company General Electric (GE), bought Telemundo for $2.7 billion, thus becoming the first English-language network to invest in Spanish-language television. Telemundo has 15 stations and 32 affiliates. The GE acquisition was a clear indication that Latinos have had a major impact on commercial television in the United States.

The rapid expansion of Spanish-language television presented new challenges to Anglo stations, which responded by increasing their coverage of Latino events. During English-language coverage of the Latin Grammies and the Alma Awards, the annual Hispanic heritage achievement ceremony, advertising appears in Spanish. Among the regular features in the breaks during those shows are advertisements for the U.S. Postal Service. Some commentators have noted the irony of the U.S. government endeavoring to reach the Latino market through the mass media in a language that they tried for so long to discourage.

Conclusion

The mass media have provided Latinos with news and entertainment since 1848, when the United States took over a large part of Mexico. The effectiveness and popularity of newspapers, magazines, books, and, more recently, radio, television, and cinema have depended to a large extent on their use of Spanish as the medium of communication. Although the choice of language has been criticized by those who believe that U.S. citizens should speak English, the rapid increase in the Latino population, together with its growing economic power, have attracted publishers, broadcasters, and advertisers. The firm and lasting establishment of Spanish as a U.S. language is reflected by the fact that televisions are now hardwired to include a Spanish-language adapter. Networks such as ABC are actively using and promoting this technology to attract the Spanish-speaking community.

See also: González, Henry B.; González, Juan D.; González, Pedro J.; Idar Family; Mendoza, Lydia; Moreno, Arturo; Salazar, Ruben

Further reading: Bender, Steven W. *Greasers and Gringos: Latinos, Law, and the American Imagination*. New York, NY: New York University Press, 2003.
Berg, Charles Ramírez. *Latino Images in Film: Stereotypes, Subversion, Resistance*. Austin, TX: University of Texas Press, 2002.
Greenberg, Bradley S. (ed.). *Mexican Americans and the Mass Media*. Norwood, NJ: Ablex, 1983.
Mayer, Vicki. *Producing Dreams, Consuming Youth: Mexican Americans and Mass Media*. New Brunswick, NJ: Rutgers University Press,
Wilson, Clint II, Felix Gutiérrez, and Lena Chao (eds). *Racism, Sexism, and the Media: The Rise of Class Communication in Multicultural America*. Thousand Oaks, CA: Sage Publications, 2003.

MEDINA, Harold R.

Judge

Harold R. Medina was a judge of the U.S. Court of Appeals for the Southern District of New York and the U.S. Court of Appeals for the Second Circuit. In the late 1940s, he became known as "the patient judge" after he presided over the trial of 11 communist leaders. A greatly respected lawyer, Medina had a brilliant and incisive mind. He spoke several modern languages, and was a talented Latin and Greek scholar.

Early life

Born in Brooklyn, New York, on February 16, 1888, Harold Raymond Medina was educated at Public School No. 44, after which he went on to study at Holbrook Military Academy. A gifted student, he went to Princeton University, where he studied under Christian Gauss (*see box on page 99*). He graduated in 1909, after which he received an LLB at Columbia Law School in 1912, graduating first in his class.

A dedicated man

After leaving Columbia, Medina worked hard to establish himself in the world of law. He undertook several jobs over the next few years, including writing a new edition of

▲ ***Harold R. Medina was an influential lawyer and judge. A cultured man, Medina was also known for his love of the classics.***

KEY DATES

1888	Born in Brooklyn, New York City, on February 16.
1909	Receives degree from Princeton University.
1912	Receives LLB from Columbia Law School.
1915	Becomes associate professor at Columbia Law School, until 1940.
1918	Establishes private practice in New York, until 1947.
1947	Nominated to U.S. District Court, Southern District of New York, by Harry S. Truman in May; confirmed by the Senate in June.
1949	Presides over the trial of 11 people accused of communist activity.
1950	Nominated by Harry S. Truman to a seat on the U.S. Court of Appeals for the Second Circuit; confirmed in June.
1980	Retires from the bench.
1990	Dies in Westwood, New Jersey, on March 14.

a lawyers' manual, creating a series of law lectures for which he became famous (1912–1942), and teaching law at Columbia University (from 1915). In 1918, he opened his own law practice, Medina and Sherpick, which specialized in appellate (appeal) court work. He spent the next years building up a formidable reputation as a lawyer.

In 1932 Medina took part in his first criminal trial, involving officers of the Bank of the United States; this resulted in further trial work. He remained in private practice until 1947, when President Harry S. Truman successfully nominated him as U.S. district judge for the Southern District of New York.

The patient judge

Medina presided over several cases, but none received as much press attention as the 1949 trial of 11 leaders of the American Communist Party (ACP). The 1940 Alien

INFLUENCES AND INSPIRATION

The scholar and dean of Princeton, Christian Gauss, was among the people who most influenced Harold R. Medina.

A respected teacher and critic, Gauss was born in Ann Arbor, Michigan, in 1878, the son of South German immigrants. While studying at the University of Michigan, Gauss worked in a variety of jobs to support himself, including serving as a baker's boy, farmhand, bill collector, and drug clerk. After working as a journalist in Paris, France, he returned to the United States to teach at Michigan. He began teaching at Princeton in 1905, and became a full professor at the age of 29. In 1912 Gauss was promoted to become chair of the department of modern languages. He served in that position until 1936. He was also dean of the college (from 1925) and was later named the first incumbent of a chair in modern languages.

Gauss's classes were legendary. His courses on Dante and the Romantic writers influenced many Princeton students. Medina said that Gauss taught him how to think: He recalled that Gauss "led and guided with so gentle a touch that one began to think almost despite oneself." Gauss died in 1951.

Registration Act, also known as the Smith Act after Representative Howard W. Smith of Virginia, the man who had introduced it, made it illegal for anyone living in the United States to "advocate, abet, or teach the desirability of overthrowing the government." The men were charged with breaching the act in organizing "as the Communist Party" and advocating and teaching the principles of Marxism-Leninism. They were also accused of advocating those principles through the publication and circulation of books, articles, magazines, and newspapers. Among those arrested in 1948 were Eugene Dennis, the general secretary of the ACP, William Z. Foster, a labor activist and former leader of the ACP, and Benjamin Davis, an African American lawyer, member of the New York City Council, and member of the ACP.

During the nine-month trial, the prosecution found it difficult to prove that any of the accused men had actually done or said anything to support the charges. Instead, it used passages from Karl Marx and testimonies from former ACP members to incriminate the accused.

Adverse criticism

The trial and Medina inevitably received a lot of public attention. Some commentators accused Medina of being biased. He was also called a racist, especially after he called Davis "boy" in the course of the trial. Medina was labeled an anticommunist and was accused of having made up his mind that the men were guilty before the trial started. His supporters, however, claimed that Medina presided over an extremely difficult trial with heroic calm. He was called "the patient judge" in the media.

The 11 men were subsequently found guilty: 10 were sentenced to five years in jail and had to pay fines of $10,000 each, but the eleventh man, Robert G. Thompson, received a shorter sentence of three years. Thompson was subsequently killed in prison, battered to death by Yugoslav fascists.

Medina became a media star almost overnight. The Associated Press named him "Man of the Year" in 1949. In a 1951 appeal, Abraham J. Isserman, one of the trial lawyers, accused Medina of judicial misconduct and of favoring the prosecution: Both accusations were dismissed and the appeal was denied.

On June 11, 1951, President Truman nominated Medina to a seat on the U.S. Court of Appeals for the Second Circuit. On June 21 of that year, the Senate confirmed Medina's appointment to the bench. He assumed senior status on March 1, 1958, serving in the position until 1980, when he retired.

Other interests

Medina wrote several books and articles, mainly on matters of legal procedure. He received public acclaim for *Judge Medina Speaks*, a book that contained a range of his writings, from speeches to essays on such subjects as "The Pursuit of Happiness" and "Why Study Latin?"

A member of several associations and societies, a charter trustee of Princeton, a fellow of the American Academy of Arts and Sciences, and the recipient of many honors and awards, including several honorary doctorates, Harold R. Medina died on March 14, 1990, in New Jersey.

Further reading: Hawthorne, Daniel. *Judge Medina: A Biography.* New York, NY: W. Funk, 1952. http://www.findarticles.com/p/articles/mi_m1282/is_n7_v42/ai_8903629#continue (brief obituary from the *National Review*).

MEDINA, Pablo

Writer

The Cuban-born writer Pablo Medina has lived in the United States since 1960. While teaching full time, Medina is also a novelist, poet, and essayist whose work concentrates on the experience of being an exile.

Cuban childhood

Medina was born in Havana, Cuba, in 1948. He describes his upbringing in a middle-class family in the city in his 1990 autobiography *Exiled Memories: A Cuban Childhood*. His life revolved around his immediate family—his father Pablo, his mother Bela, and younger sister Silvia—as well as a large extended family of grandparents, aunts, uncles, and cousins, many of whom lived close to the family home in Havana.

During the 1950s, Medina attended the Cathedral School, a U.S.-sponsored school in Havana, and later the Ruston Academy, an American college in the city. At the Cathedral School, he learned English sufficiently that by the third grade he could read books in English. Mark Twain became a favorite author, along with any science fiction.

Exiled

After the 1959 Cuban Revolution and the communist Fidel Castro's ascent to power, Medina's family, like many other Cubans, left the island. They took one of the last scheduled flights bound for the United States.

The family settled in New York City. In his autobiography, Medina describes the shock of arriving in New York, aged 12, and seeing snow for the first time. In an effort to overcome his homesickness, he sought out any Cuban connections within the city. Medina also had a thirst for knowledge, and spent many hours in the New York Public Library. After completing high school, he earned a master of arts' degree from Georgetown University in Washington, D.C.

KEY DATES

1948	Born in Havana, Cuba.
1960	Moves to New York City.
1990	Publishes *Exiled Memories: A Cuban Childhood.*
2005	Publishes *The Cigar Roller.*

In his autobiography, Medina explained that the reason he had written about growing up in Cuba 30 years after he had left was because he wanted to remember what it was like. In his memoirs, he described his childhood obsession with all things American, and his desire to have a suburban American life. As an adult, having achieved his dream, he reflects on falling between two worlds: "Life in the United States for me has not been a search for roots (that presumes their loss), but rather a quixotic attempt to become a creature I never was nor ever can be—an American as I understood, or misunderstood, it to be. I thought that changing nationalities was as easy as changing clothes, speech patterns, or books to read."

Inspiration found

The dilemma of positioning oneself between two worlds has continued to interest Medina, and the fiction that followed his autobiography reflects his position as an exile. *The Return of Felix Nogara* (2000) describes the return to the fictional island of Barata, closely modeled on Cuba, of a Baratan exile and United States citizen who now lives in Miami, Florida. In a recent novel, *The Cigar Roller* (2005), Medina recounts the life of Amadeo Terra who, as he is dying from a massive stroke in a Tampa, Florida, nursing home, remembers his early life in Cuba and later life in the United States.

Medina writes his fiction in English and his collections of poetry, which blend past and present, in both English and Spanish. His poetry has appeared in numerous publications, including *The American Poetry Review* and the *Antioch Review*. He has also translated many Spanish-speaking poets into English, including the Spanish poet Federico García Lorca.

Medina has received many awards, including the 2002 award from the CINTAS foundation and the Woodrow Wilson/Lila Wallace Reader's Digest fund. He lectures widely both in the United States and overseas. He also works as a professor at the New School in New York City and in the MFA (Master of Fine Arts) program for writers at Warren Wilson College in North Carolina.

Further reading: Medina, Pablo. *Exiled Memories: A Cuban Childhood*. Austin, TX: University of Texas Press, 1990. http://www.postroadmag.com/Issue_2/Etcetera2/Letters_To_My_Father/E.medina.html (a letter from Medina to his father).

MELENDEZ, Bill
Animator

Bill Melendez is among the most revered cartoon animators working in the Unites States today. He is best known for his long-standing work on the Charlie Brown television specials based on the comic strip *Peanuts,* written by Charles M. Schultz (1922–2000).

The Aztec exile

Melendez was born José Cuauthemoc Melendez in 1916 in Hermosillo, Sonora, in Mexico. His father—a Mexican general—gave all his children grandiose-sounding Aztec names. In later life, José Cuauthemoc became known simply as Bill. Political unrest in Mexico led Melendez's mother to take her four children to Douglas, Arizona, where they received their education. After high school, Melendez studied at the Chouinard Arts Institute (later the California Institute of the Arts) in Los Angeles.

In 1938 Melendez went to work for the Walt Disney Studio, where he contributed to such classic features as *Fantasia* (1940) and *Bambi* (1942). In 1941, when Disney was hit by strikes, Melendez moved to Warner Brothers Studios, where he helped create some of the popular Bugs Bunny and Daffy Duck shorts.

In the wake of World War II (1939–1945), the style of animations became less realistic, using limited movement and greater abstraction in color and form. Melendez followed this trend, briefly working at United Productions of America (UPA), the pioneers of "limited animation."

A long collaboration

During the 1950s, Melendez won acclaim for his work as a director and producer of industrial films and commercials. He first met Charles Schultz while working on a Ford Motor Company television commercial featuring the *Peanuts* characters. In 1965 he was invited by Schultz to animate the first Charlie Brown television special for the

▲ ***Bill Melendez has animated all the* Peanuts *television shows since 1965. He also provides the voice for Charlie Brown's dog, Snoopy.***

CBS network. At first the network expressed reservations about Melendez's quirky animation style, largely a result of the low budget and short production time. Nevertheless *A Charlie Brown Christmas* proved a great success, drawing half of all American viewers when it was first aired on December 9, 1965. The show subsequently won both an Emmy and a George Foster Peabody award.

Melendez has continued to create the Charlie Brown television animations ever since—including more than 75 specials, a miniseries—*This Is America Charlie Brown* (1988–1989)—and four feature films, working alongside Schultz (until he died in 2000) and producer Lee Mendelson. His personal favorite is *What a Nightmare, Charlie Brown!* (1977), in which Snoopy has a dream about being a sled dog in Alaska.

In addition to the Charlie Brown animations, Melendez's production company, Bill Melendez Productions, has been responsible for producing numerous commercials and feature-length animations, including the Emmy-winning *The Lion, the Witch and the Wardrobe* in 1979.

KEY DATES

1916	Born in Hermosillo, Sonora, Mexico, on November 15.
1938	Begins work at the Walt Disney Studio.
1965	Animates first Charlie Brown television special.
1979	Wins Emmy for animated feature film of *The Lion, the Witch, and the Wardrobe.*

Further reading: Schultz, Charles M. A., Bill Melendez, and Lee Mendelson. *Charlie Brown Christmas: The Making of a Tradition.* New York: HarperResource, 2000.
http://www.billmelendez.tv (Bill Melendez Productions Web site).

MENDIETA, Ana

Artist

Ana Mendieta was an artist who used photography, video, and performance to explore feminist themes. One of the recurring themes of her work was violence on the female body. Mendieta died in violent circumstances after falling 34 stories from a window. The cause of death was the fall. Why she fell is unknown.

Early life

Ana Mendieta was born in Havana, Cuba, in 1948. She went to the United States at the age of 12, as part of Operation Peter Pan. This was a mass emigration of children from Cuba following Fidel Castro's revolution. Parents in Cuba feared for the future of their children, and sent them unaccompanied to the United States in the hope of giving them a better future. At first, Cuban children as young as five arrived at airports with notes pinned to them pleading for help. Later, the exodus became more organized with the U.S. Catholic community offering school scholarships to Cuban children. The federal government also stepped in to provide the young arrivals with foster homes.

Mendieta traveled with her older sister, just two of 14,000 Cuban children to make the journey. The chances of seeing her homeland again were remote, but Mendieta did make a return visit to Cuba in 1980. Mendieta was fostered in Iowa. She later received a master of fine arts degree at the University of Iowa, Iowa City.

Artistic career

Mendieta's art ranged from earthworks to photography and performances. From the beginning she showed an interest in gender politics and identities. In her university thesis, *Facial Hair Transplant*, Mendieta presented an image of herself with facial hair as a form of drag.

Mendieta frequently represented herself in her works. One of her better-known pieces is *Rape Piece* (1972), a performance that she created in response to crimes and brutality against women, and especially in response to the rape and murder of a student at the University of Iowa.

The themes of orphanhood and exile also play a significant role in Mendieta's work. During the 1970s she traveled on an archeological expedition to San Juan Teotihuacán, Mexico, and also to Europe. Her trips to Mexico and the study of its cultural legacy had an impact on her work.

KEY DATES

1948 Born in Havana, Cuba.

1960 Arrives in the United States.

1972 Produces *Rape Piece.*

1973 Produces *First Silueta*, the first of several silhouettes created over the next decade.

1985 Marries Carl Andre in February; dies in a fall from his New York apartment window on September 8.

1988 Andre is acquitted of Mendieta's murder.

1996 Mendieta's work begins world tour.

2004 Retrospective exhibition held at Whitney Museum of American Art, New York City.

From the 1970s to the 1980s, she produced a series of "siluetas" (silhouettes) for which she would become known. *First Silueta* (1973), a color photograph, presents a female body lying down on rocks while the face and most parts of the body remain covered by flowers.

In many of Mendieta's works, there is an interest in primitivism and myths. She often used earth in her work to represent these themes as she searched for connections with Hispanic and Native American cultures.

Violent death

In 1985 Mendieta married Carl Andre, a minimalist sculptor. Andre was accused of pushing his new wife from his 34-story apartment in Manhattan. Three years later, Andre was tried for her murder but was acquitted. In evidence, Andre repeatedly told the court that Mendieta's death was suicide. In the summer of 2004, the Whitney Museum of American Art presented the exhibition *Ana Mendieta: Earth Body.*

Further reading: Blocker, Jane. *Where Is Mendieta? Identity, Performativity, and Exile*. Durham, NC: Duke University Press, 1999.

Mendieta, Ana. *Ana Mendieta: A Book of Works*. Miami Beach, FL: Grassfield Press, 1993.

http://www.guggenheim.org/artscurriculum/lessons/movpics_mendieta.php# (biography and educational resources on Mendieta's work).

MENDOZA, Lydia

Singer

Very few Mexican American artists have had the universal appeal and influence of Lydia Mendoza. Mendoza entertained millions of music lovers on both sides of the Mexico–United States border and far beyond in a career that spanned nearly 70 years. Mendoza's musical legacy has been compared to that of other American musical pioneers, such as Leadbelly and the Carter Family. Mendoza was variously known as "The Meadowlark of the Border," "The Songstress of the Poor," and "The Glory of Texas."

Early life

The Mexican Revolution of 1910 to 1921 had a strong impact on the lives of all Mexicans. Mendoza's parents, Leonor Zamarripa and Francisco, were no exception. In order to avoid the chaotic situation during the revolution, and to get a better standard of living, the Mendozas migrated north from Monterrey, Mexico, to Texas and settled in Houston. Lydia Mendoza, the second oldest child of the family, was born in Houston in 1916.

Mendoza credits her mother with instilling a love of music in her and giving her the ability to remember countless songs. From an early age Mendoza exhibited a musical gift. She played the mandolin and violin with other members of her family. This family group was one of the ways the family earned a living. In the late 1920s the Mendoza family, under the name Cuarteto Carta Blanca (The Carte Blanche Quartet), performed regularly at La Plaza del Zacate, a public square in San Antonio, Texas. The money raised by these performances allowed the family to move to Detroit, Michigan, where there was work available for agricultural laborers. Mendoza's beautiful singing voice was soon discovered by other workers, and she and her family were paid to sing at family gatherings.

During the Great Depression of the early 1930s, the Mendoza family, like many others, struggled to survive. In 1933 the family returned to Texas and to playing for spare change in Houston and San Antonio.

KEY DATES

1916 Born in Houston, Texas, on May 21.

1933 Wins singing competition and begins to sing on radio.

1934 Records her first solo hit, "Mal Hombre."

1954 Begins solo tour of the United States, Mexico, and Latin America.

1977 Performs at the inauguration of President Jimmy Carter.

1982 Teaches as a guest lecturer at California State University at Fresno.

1988 Retires from performing and recording.

1998 Receives the National Medal of the Arts from President Bill Clinton.

▲ ***Lydia Mendoza's career spanned nearly 70 years, in which she sang for farm laborers and presidents.***

INFLUENCES AND INSPIRATION

Mendoza composed very few songs herself. Instead her success stemmed from her unique interpretation and adaptation of the songs composed by others. Her collaborators included Agustín Lara (1897–1970), Chucho Monge (1910–1964), María Grever (1894–1951), Rafael Hernández (1892–1965), and José Alfredo Jiménez (1926–1973) from Mexico; and Tony De La Rosa (1931–2004), Beto Villa, Narciso Martínez, and many others from Texas.

The biggest influence in Mendoza's life, however, was her mother, Leonor Zamarripa Mendoza. Leonor's love for music shaped Mendoza's own interest in music.

Mendoza herself influenced many musical artists, including the Tejano band Little Joe y La Familia. Mendoza's greatest influence was perhaps felt by the Mexican and Chicano working classes, whom she entertained with a vibrant voice and stirring lyrics after their hard days of struggling for survival.

A family affair

Mendoza won a singing contest in 1933 and began making popular appearances on radio. In 1934 she recorded her first solo record hit, "Mal Hombre," which made her very popular among the Mexican American audience, bringing attention to her unique style. "Mal Hombre" became her signature song and catapulted her into a performing career that took her and her family on tours throughout Texas. In 1937 they were hired to play in California.

At the time it was uncommon for a Latina singer to accompany herself on the guitar, and this helped compound Mendoza's fame. Her success was triggered by her versatility in performing a range of musical styles. Inspired by the songs that she heard on XEW, Mexico City's leading radio station, Mendoza performed the latest songs of composers like Agustín Lara, Maria Grever, Rafael Hernández, and others. Mendoza performed these popular and familiar songs in her own style, accompanying herself with a 12-string guitar. Her singing style was so striking that audiences often failed to recognize the songs and thought they were listening to new musical pieces composed by Mendoza.

In 1935 Mendoza married Juan Alvarado, with whom she had three daughters. Unfortunately for the Mendoza family, the recordings and touring were heavily curtailed in the years leading up to and during World War II (1939–1945) because gasoline was expensive and in short supply.

After the war Lydia resumed recording and touring with her family. She released "Celosa," "Amor de Madre," "Pajarito Herido," "Al Pie de tu Reja," "Besando la Cruz," "Joaquín Murrieta," and other songs that also became hits.

A female troubadour

In 1954 Mendoza's mother died, and the traveling family show finally disbanded. Mendoza began solo tours of the United Sates, Mexico, and across Latin America. She performed in theaters and at festivals such as the Smithsonian Festival of American Folklife in Montreal, Canada, and at university campuses.

After her first husband's death in 1961, Mendoza married Fred Martínez. In 1977 President Jimmy Carter invited her to play at his inauguration celebrations. In 1982 Mendoza was invited to be a guest lecturer in music at California State University at Fresno. In 1988, at the age of 76, Mendoza announced her retirement from performing and recording. In 1998 she received the National Heritage Fellowship Award from President Bill Clinton.

A national treasure

Mendoza's success came from her powerful voice and ability to apply it to a range of musical styles. She sang in the following genres of music: tango, paso doble, bolero, corrido, ranchera, a canción, rumba, danza, tonado, danzón, huapango, vals canción, canción clave, fox canción, and canción redova. Today Mendoza's music is available on Arhoolie Records from El Cerrito, California.

Mendoza was at the forefront of a number of Tejano (Mexican Texan) artists who would compete in quality and quantity with musicians from Mexico in their attempt to cater to the musical market on the American side of the border.

In an interview with Yolanda Broyles-González in 2001, Mendoza stated: "There are very few Mexican women who have cultivated an uninterrupted career in music and who have dedicated themselves to it body and soul."

See also: Martinez, Narciso; Villa, Beto

Further reading: Broyles-Gonzalez, Yolanda. *Lydia Mendoza's Life in Music*. New York, NY: Oxford University Press, 2001.
http://www.npr.org/templates/story/story.php?storyId=4109900 (biography).

MENÉNDEZ, Robert

Politician

New Jersey senator Robert Menéndez is one of the United States's leading Democratic politicians. In 2006 he was one of three Hispanic Americans serving in the U.S Senate. Before entering the Senate, Menéndez had served for 13 years in the U.S. House of Representatives, where he eventually rose to become the third most senior Democratic member. Through his career, Menéndez has been a proponent of liberal values; he has always been a powerful and proactive advocate of minority rights.

Menéndez is a well-known and popular figure in the Hispanic American community nationally and makes regular appearances on Spanish-language television networks, such as Telemundo. In the non-Latino population outside New Jersey, however, he has a much lower profile. Nevertheless, most political commentators believe that he is likely to play an important role in any future Democratic administration.

KEY DATES

1954 Born in New York City on January 1.

1976 Earns bachelor's degree from Saint Peter's College, Jersey City, New Jersey.

1986 Serves as mayor of Union City, New Jersey, until 1992.

1987 Serves as member of the New Jersey state General Assembly until 1991.

1991 Serves as member of the New Jersey state Senate for two years.

1993 Serves as a Democratic member of the U.S. House of Representatives for New Jersey's 13th Congressional District until 2006.

2005 Is appointed to the U.S. Senate as member for the state of New Jersey and is sworn in in 2006.

▼ ***Robert Menéndez has been a New Jersey politician since 1986. He currently represents the state in the U.S. Senate.***

From lawyer to mayor

Robert Menéndez was born in New York City in 1954, the son of working-class Cuban American parents who had immigrated to the United States one year before. He was raised and educated in Union City, New Jersey, which during the 1960s became a haven for many Cuban immigrants fleeing the Marxist regime of Fidel Castro. After graduating from Union Hill High School, Menéndez attended Saint Peter's College in Jersey City, New Jersey. He earned a bachelor's degree in political science in 1976 and went on to study law at Rutgers School of Law in Newark, New Jersey, graduating from there in 1979. In the early 1980s, Menéndez began working as a lawyer in a private practice.

Menéndez had become involved in politics even before he reached college. Chosen by his school for an honors program, he organized a petition against the Union City Board of Education when he discovered that it did not pay for honors students' textbooks. His campaign eventually forced the election of a new board, and in 1974 Menéndez, who had just turned 20, found himself elected as one of its members.

INFLUENCES AND INSPIRATION

Menéndez's formative political influence was the Democratic politician and lawyer William Vincent Musto (1917–2006), who from 1962 to 1970 and again from 1974 to 1982 served as Union City's mayor. During his time in power, Musto pioneered affirmative action in the city and tried to reach out to the growing Hispanic community. He also nurtured the early careers of several young Hispanic politicians, including that of Menéndez. Commentators often compared the two politicians' relationship to that of father and son.

In the early 1980s, however, Musto was accused of corruption, and in the subsequent court case Menéndez testified against his former mentor. In 1982 Menéndez even went so far as to stand against Musto in elections for city mayor. The citizens of Union City were divided on the question of both Musto's guilt and Menéndez's motivation. The majority, however, voted for the incumbent, even though by now he was on his way to jail. The affair had little lasting impact on Menéndez's career. Four years later he stood for mayor once again; this time his campaign proved victorious.

During his time on the board, Menéndez became increasingly active in Democratic politics. He became the protégé of the Union City mayor, William Vincent Musto (*see box*). In 1986, at the age of just 32, Menéndez was himself elected as mayor of Union City, which at the time was home to the largest population of Cuban Americans outside Miami, Florida. Menéndez's popularity among the largely Hispanic American—and Democratic—electorate was confirmed when in 1987 he was elected to the New Jersey General Assembly and again in 1991 when he was voted into the New Jersey Senate. Finally, in 1992, Menéndez was elected to represent the New Jersey 13th Congressional District, which includes Union City as well as part of Jersey City, in the U.S. House of Representatives.

In the House of Representatives

Over the following 13 years, Menéndez was reelected as a representative six times. He often reached office by winning with 75 or 80 percent of the vote.

Menéndez quickly established himself as one of the most distinguished and respected Democratic politicians in Washington, D.C. During the administration of President Bill Clinton, from 1993 to 2001, Menéndez was the only Cuban American in Congress. He became an influential voice on Hispanic American affairs and was especially well known for his strong opposition to the Castro regime. In 1996 he led Democratic support for the controversial Helms-Burton Act—a Republican-spearheaded law that sought to tighten the U.S. trade embargo on Cuba. Many commentators now question the efficacy of the law, which they say has further increased hardship for ordinary Cubans. In the 2000 presidential election, Menéndez's popularity in the Hispanic community led to him to being considered as a running mate for Democrat Al Gore.

In 2003 Menéndez was elected chairman of the Democratic Caucus, making him the third most senior-ranking Democrat in the House of Representatives. He was also chosen to chair some of the Democratic Party's most important committees, including the task force on education and the task force on homeland security.

Despite being a popular politician both in Washington and in New Jersey, Menéndez's tough-minded approach has sometimes led him into conflict with other politicians, including fellow Democrats. For instance, he conducted an aggressive and long-running feud with the African American former mayor of Jersey City, Glenn Cunningham. This has arguably lost him the support of many African Americans in his district.

New Jersey's first Hispanic senator

Late in 2005 New Jersey senator Jon Corzine was elected state governor; in December he appointed Menéndez to his vacated seat in the U.S. Senate. Menéndez was sworn in on January 17, 2006, becoming both the first Hispanic American and first member of an ethnic minority to represent New Jersey in the Senate.

As the new junior senator, Menéndez was quick to make his mark. In February 2006 he cosponsored legislation with New York senator Hillary Rodham Clinton that would make it illegal for companies sponsored by foreign governments to buy U.S. port operations. Senator Menéndez was due to stand for election for his seat in the Senate in November 2006.

Further reading: http://menendez.senate.gov (Menéndez's Web site).
http://bioguide.congress.gov/scripts/biodisplay.pl?index=M000639 (official U.S. Senate biography).

MENENDEZ DE AVILÉS, Pedro

Conquistador

The first Spanish colonial governor of Florida, Pedro Menendez de Avilés had a busy naval career, clearing the Mediterranean coastline of French pirates, fighting in the Azores and the English Channel and, above all, commanding the Spanish fleet of the Indies (Caribbean) during the 1550s and 1560s.

During his campaigns in the Americas, Menendez de Avilés conquered various strategic locations for the Spanish crown and also built several fortresses at major Caribbean ports. They helped maintain Spain's military superiority in the area for more than two centuries. Today's Florida shows vestiges of Menendez de Avilés's explorations, and his first settlement, Saint Augustine, is one of the oldest continually inhabited towns in the United States.

Active youth

Born in the small fishing town of Avilés in Spain, Pedro Menendez de Avilés y Alonso de la Campa was one of the 19 children of an aristocratic family. When his father died at an early age, Menendez de Avilés left home to be brought up by foster parents, with whom he lived until he turned 14. An adolescent Menendez de Avilés then ran away to be a sailor. By the time he was 30, he had married, fathered three daughters, and built a reputation as an unruly but courageous naval commander.

After his first years at sea, Menendez de Avilés became an officer in the navy at the royal court of Spain. His first military assignment came in 1549, when Menendez de Avilés was put in charge of the fleet of Charles I (1500–1558) to fight against the French pirates who terrorized Spanish shipping in the Atlantic. Menendez de Avilés's services soon proved his worth and earned him the respect of the king. In 1554 Menendez de Avilés was given command of the Armada de la Carrera, the Spanish naval force in the Caribbean. In the same year, Menendez de Avilés was entrusted with the company of the royal prince, the future Philip II, in his failed trip to England to marry Queen Mary. In addition, Menendez de Avilés was given the responsibility of supervising the convoys that exchanged goods between Spain and its American territories. Menendez de Avilés guaranteed Spanish merchants safe passage from the Caribbean ports, especially Havana, Cuba, which was established by the Spanish in 1519.

▲ ***Pedro Menendez de Avilés was a Spanish naval commander. He is best remembered for ousting the French from Florida and making it a Spanish colony.***

KEY DATES

1519	Born in Avilés, Spain, on February 15.
1549	Led the Spanish fleet against French pirates.
1554	Named captain-general of the Caribbean fleet.
1563	Arrested for allegedly disobeying orders at sea.
1565	Defeats French forces in Florida.
1566	Signs a treaty with the Calusa Indians.
1574	Dies in Santander, Spain, on September 17.

Independent spirit

Although Menendez de Avilés's reluctance to accept bribes and his success in bringing back treasure gained him the approval of his officers, its also caused conflict with the Casa de Contratación. This board, which governed trade with the American colonies, was accustomed to receiving money in exchange for favors and objected to Menendez de Avilés's appointment. The tense relationships worsened

INFLUENCES AND INSPIRATION

As an explorer of his time, Menendez de Avilés was greatly influenced by the first series of conquistadores who crossed the Atlantic Ocean to establish thriving ports that would increase the wealth of the Spanish empire in the 15th and 16th centuries. Given his military appointments in the Caribbean, however, Menendez de Avilés was inspired in particular by Castilian explorer Juan Ponce de León, who was the first European to set foot in Florida and the founder of the oldest settlement in Puerto Rico.

With the passing of time, Menendez de Avilés also became the model to follow for future generations. He was particularly admired by his fellow countrymen in Avilés, his hometown, which began to be known as the Villa del Adelantado (town of the governor). Today the people of Avilés still regard Saint Augustine as their patron, and the town harbor also has a statue of Menendez de Avilés that oversees departing sailors.

when Menendez de Avilés was handed the care of the fleet of galleons that traveled from Mexico to Spain, and then to Flanders to supply the Spanish troops in the war against France in the early 1560s.

The members of the Casa of Contratación managed to take their revenge on their enemy in 1563. When Menendez de Avilés returned to Seville from America, they convinced the authorities that the commander had abandoned his responsibilities to the fleet to search for a lost vessel carrying his relatives. Menendez de Avilés was arrested and sent to prison for 20 months.

Revenge was only temporary, however. In 1565 Menendez de Avilés was released after paying a fine of 1,000 ducats. He was immediately reinstated and commissioned by King Philip II to colonize Florida. This area had been claimed for Spain by Juan Ponce de León, but by the 1560s several French settlements had been founded there threatening the Spanish claim.

Conquest of Florida

Menendez de Avilés was promoted to the rank of *adelantado* (governor) and supplied with 11 ships, 2,000 soldiers, and 15,000 ducats to establish a colony in North America. On August 28, 1565, Menendez de Avilés came ashore at today's Mission of Nombre de Dios in northeastern Florida. Initially, Menendez de Avilés had planned to disembark in the vicinity of Fort Caroline, but the presence of the French fleet in the Saint John's River forced him to seek shelter to the south.

In order to secure his position, Menendez de Avilés formed an alliance with the Timucuan peoples. He then founded a fortified settlement named Saint Augustine of Florida on September 8, 1565.

Menendez de Avilés's precautions were crucial to the lives of the 800 men who had survived the long sea journey. Thanks to their defensive location, the Spanish forces succeeded in confronting the French fleet that soon besieged Saint Augustine under the command of Jean Ribault. Sheltered by the natural harbor, Menendez de Avilés's men were able to destroy almost all the enemy ships, despite being heavily outnumbered. This single naval battle made Spain the most powerful force in Florida and put an end to the territorial ambitions of France.

At the same time that the French attacked Saint Augustine, the Spanish force attacked the nearby French colony of Fort Caroline. In the raid, Menendez de Avilés ordered the murder of everyone without exception. By the end of the fighting, Jean Ribault had been killed, along with hundreds of his countrymen.

Menendez de Avilés renamed Fort Caroline San Mateo and began to establish outposts and a string of ports up and down the Atlantic coast. Having situated the capital of Spanish Florida in Santa Elena, Menendez de Avilés set about developing the economy of his new domain. He built watchtowers at what later became Cape Canaveral and Biscayne Bay to protect merchant ships and alert the population against raiding pirates. In order to avoid disputes over resources with the Native American peoples in Florida, Menendez de Avilés also signed a treaty with the Calusa tribe. The Calusa agreed to sell food, clothes, and other supplies that the Spanish army might need.

Menendez de Avilés made a visit to Spain in 1574, and was commanded to prepare a fleet to fight the English at Santander, Spain. He was fatally wounded in the ensuing battle.

See also: Ponce de León, Juan

Further reading: Lyon, Eugene. *Pedro Menendez de Avilés.* New York, NY: Garland Publishing, 1995.
http://www.staugustine.com/king/pedro_menendez.shtml (Saint Augustine's tribute to Menendez de Avilés).

MENUDO

Musical Group

Formed in 1977 in Puerto Rico, the quintet Menudo became the biggest Hispanic American boy band of the 1980s. Organized by Edgardo Díaz (1960–), Menudo mainly consisted of Puerto Rican teenage boys. At first no member was allowed to stay in the group beyond the age of 15. This rule was eventually broken by Ricky Melendez (1967–), Charlie Masso (1969–), and Ricky Martin, who all stayed into their 16th year. Menudo, whose name is taken from a traditional Mexican spicy soup made from tripe, became successful first in Puerto Rico, then Venezuela and Mexico, before achieving success in the United States.

Making it big

Menudo's first U.S. appearance was a sell-out performance in New York City's Madison Square Garden in 1983. In 1984 Menudo released its first album sung in English, *Reaching Out*, which included "Like a Cannonball," the title song of the car-chase comedy *Cannonball Run 2*.

In 1989 Mexican teenager Adrián became Menudo's first non-Puerto Rican member. By the early 1990s Menudo became truly a Latin American group, boasting members from the United States, Venezuela, Cuba, and Puerto Rico.

Controversy

The beginning of the end for the group came in the late 1980s, when a number of members were caught with marijuana at different times and places. The scandal reached its apex when accusations of sexual abuse were lodged against manager Díaz, the band's choreographer, and others in the organization. Many of the protagonists in the scandal appeared on the Hispanic American television talk show *Cristina* to tell their sides of the story. Owing to the allegations and Menudo's declining popularity, Díaz sold the band to Vanxy Inc., a Panamanian company, in 1997. The new owners relaunched the band as MDO.

KEY DATES

1977 Band is formed.

1978 Band begins its own television show, *La Hora Menudo*, which continues until the early 1990s.

1984 Ricky Martin joins the group.

1997 Menudo changes its name to MDO and releases a self-titled album, *MDO*.

1998 The members of Menudo's most popular era reunite to tour Latin America under the name El Reencuentro.

2004 Menudo's management holds a talent contest to find the next members of the band.

▲ ***Menudo on stage during a recording of a television show in New York in 1984. The members at the time were (left to right) Ray, Charlie, Robby, Roy, and Ricky.***

Menudo legacy

There are now more than 30 ex-members of Menudo and MDO. Many of them have gone on to further successes. Some have continued acting in films and soap operas or have had successful musical careers. The most successful ex-member is Ricky Martin, a multiplatinum-selling artist. Martin joined Menudo in 1984, when he was 12 years old. As a solo artist he won a Grammy in 1998.

Menudo will always be a Latino musical phenomenon, with 35 albums released as Menudo and six as MDO. Few pop groups can claim to have recorded in as many languages—Spanish, Portuguese, English, Italian, and Tagalog (a Filipino dialect).

See also: Martin, Ricky

Further reading: Greenberg, Keith. *Menudo*. New York, NY: Pocket Books, 1984.
http://www.mdo.org (official Web site).

MIGUEL, Luis
Singer

Although he was initially adored by fans as a teen idol, Luis Miguel later managed to establish himself as the quintessential Latino crooner, singing dreamy romantic songs. He has sold more than 65 million records around the world and has won three Grammys.

Early life

Nicknamed "El Ídolo" (The Idol), Miguel was born Luis Miguel Rey Basteri in San Juan, Puerto Rico, in 1970. His father was Luisito Rey, a successful Puerto Rican singer from the 1960s. Miguel's mother, Marcela Basteri, was an Italian actress. As a child, Miguel was raised in Mexico.

Miguel's singing career started when he was 11. This was when he was discovered by a Mexican music executive while performing at a party in Veracruz. He was promptly signed as a recording artist and, thanks to the support of his parents, who were familiar with the music business, he soon became a successful teen star.

In 1985 Luis Miguel won a Grammy Award for a duet with British singer Sheena Easton. In the same year, he earned the Antorcha de Plata award at Chile's renowned Festival de Viña del Mar. In 1986 Miguel's fifth album, *Soy Como Quiero Ser*, established him as a superstar.

Adult star

In 1988, as Miguel grew into manhood, he decided to target a more mature audience. He switched labels and signed with Warner Music. That year he released the album *Un Hombre Busca Una Mujer* (A Man Looks for A Woman). The hit single from this album, "La Incondicional," marked a departure from the teen idol years.

By 1990 Luis Miguel had become an international phenomenon at the tender age of 20. However, the 1991 album *Romance* strongly reinforced the position by embracing a softer, more melodious style that moved

▲ ***With his good looks and sophisticated fashion sense, Luis Miguel is often referred to as a Latino Frank Sinatra.***

away from pop. It sold more than seven million copies worldwide, and became the first ever platinum-selling Spanish-language album in U.S. history. This hit album was soon followed by *Aries* (1993). Miguel was born under the sign of Aries, to which he has attributed his musical gifts. In 1994 Miguel released a second album of bolero songs, called *Segundo Romance*. This record sold 34 million copies worldwide.

Also in 1994, Miguel performed a duet with Frank Sinatra for the latter's album *Duets II*. This is the only English recording in Miguel's career so far. The singer has continued to record, releasing his third bolero album, *Romances*, in 1997.

KEY DATES

1970 Born in San Juan, Puerto Rico, on April 19.

1985 Wins a Grammy Award for duet with Sheena Easton.

1991 Releases first bolero album, *Romance*.

1994 Releases second bolero album, *Segundo Romance*, which sells 34 million copies.

Further reading: http://www.luismiguel.net (Miguel's Web site)

MILITARY

In the last 150 years, tens of thousands of Latinos and Latinas have served their country in the U.S. armed forces. Forty-two Latinos have been awarded the Congressional Medal of Honor—the United States's most prestigious military medal—while the ubiquity of Hispanic names on war memorials across the country bears witness to the sacrifices made by Latino communities. A single, short street in Silvas, Illinois—now renamed "Hero Street"—was home to 84 young Latinos who fought in World War II (1939–1945), the Korean War (1950–1953), or the Vietnam War (1964–1975). Eight of them gave their lives in the service of their country.

All Hispanic groups have played their part as members of the armed forces in protecting and maintaining the interests of the United States. Mexican Americans have fought in every major conflict since 1848, when the United States annexed the Mexican territories of the Southwest. Puerto Ricans have served in the U.S. military since Puerto Rico became part of the United States in 1898, and have taken a leading role in defending U.S. interests in the Caribbean and Central America. In addition, many Hispanics who do not have U.S. citizenship have served in the nation's armed forces. It is estimated that, at the start of the 21st century, 13,000 enlisted U.S. military personnel were "green-card soldiers," non-naturalized immigrants from the nations of Latin America.

Fighting for acceptance

Historically, this long and distinguished record of service has taken place within the context of a culture of discrimination and injustice in which Hispanic Americans have often been viewed as outsiders and foreigners. For many Latinos and Latinas, enlisting in the military has been a way for them to demonstrate their patriotism, their desire to assimilate, and their right to belong in the United States. It has also been a route out of poverty and social exclusion. In that respect, the history of Hispanic American participation in the U.S. military has been closely intertwined with the community's struggle for civil rights, increased educational opportunities, and a better life.

The Civil War

The Hispanic contribution to U.S. military efforts goes back to the birth of the republic, when the Spanish colonies in North America gave armed support to the revolution. Large-scale participation by Hispanic Americans began during the Civil War (1861–1865), in which some

Lieutenant General Ricardo S. Sanchez reviews U.S. troops under his command in Iraq in 2003.

KEY DATES

1864 During the Civil War, Joseph H. Decastro becomes the first Mexican to win the U.S. Congressional Medal of Honor.

1899 Formation of the Puerto Rican 65th Infantry Regiment, popularly known as the Borinqueneers.

1948 Mexican American Hector P. García founds the GI Forum; President Harry S. Truman signs Executive Order 9981, which calls for equality for all military personnel.

1964 Horacio Rivero becomes the first Latino four-star (full) admiral in the U.S. Navy.

1976 Richard E. Cavazos becomes the first Latino to attain the rank of lieutenant general in the U.S. Army.

1989 David Bennes Barkley, who was killed in 1918 during World War I, and awarded the Congressional Medal of Honor the following year, is recognized as the first Mexican American winner of the award.

2003 Latino Lieutenant General Ricardo S. Sanchez takes charge of U.S. ground forces in Iraq.

10,000 Latinos took part on both the Confederate and Union sides. Initially mistrusted by the U.S. military, soldiers of Mexican origin, such as Manuel Antonio Chaves, proved their loyalty to the United States during the conflict, and were sometimes promoted to senior positions. Three Mexicans—Joseph H. Decastro, John Ortega, and Philip Bazar—won the Medal of Honor, which was first awarded in 1861.

World War I

The United States entered World War I in April 1917. Some 200,000 Hispanic Americans enlisted voluntarily or were conscripted. The vast majority were Mexican Americans, but some 18,000 were from Puerto Rico, the male inhabitants of which first became subject to the draft in 1917.

Discrimination was rife in the U.S. armed forces. Although Latinos were not compelled to serve in segregated units, as African Americans were, they were often assigned menial jobs. Nevertheless, two Hispanic Americans—Private France Silva of the Marine Corps and David Bennes Barkley of the U.S. Army—won Medals of Honor for their outstanding courage in the face of the enemy.

World War II

More than 500,000 Hispanic Americans—including 65,000 Puerto Ricans—saw active service in World War II. Most of them were conscripts. Because draftees were usually inducted into regiments based in the place where they entered the military, many U.S. Army companies from the Southwest included large numbers of soldiers of Hispanic origin. Some of their units subsequently achieved outstanding distinction in battle. For example, the Arizona National Guard 158th Infantry Regiment—30 percent of whose soldiers were Mexican Americans—spearheaded the final assault on Japan in 1945. The regiment was singled out for special praise by General Douglas MacArthur, who described it as "the greatest fighting combat team ever deployed for battle."

Since many units were composed of soldiers who had grown up together in the same town, local communities sometimes suffered devastating losses in a single engagement. For example, E Company of the 141st Regiment of the 36th Texas Infantry Division—which was made up almost exclusively of Mexican Americans from the El Paso area—lost more than half of its men while contributing to the success of the Allied landing in Italy in 1944. The contribution and sacrifice made by the Hispanic community can be gauged by the number of Medals of Honor won by Hispanic American soldiers during the war. The community's total of 12 was proportionately higher than that of any other ethnic or racial group.

World War II was the first conflict in which Latinas played an important role. Women were not subject to the draft, but many volunteered for service in the Women's Army or the Nurse Corps. Latinas who wanted to enlist often faced strong opposition from the Hispanic community, which usually had conservative ideas about what constituted a woman's "proper" role, and wanted to minimize its casualties. One of those who overcame such objections was Anna Torres Vásquez of East Chicago, Indiana, who resisted pressure from her family and became a wartime air-traffic controller at a flight school in Florida.

The GI Forum

The racism experienced by Latino soldiers during World War II caused lasting resentment, and in the aftermath of the conflict there was a widespread determination that something must be done to prevent it from recurring. In 1948, Hector P. García founded the GI Forum to promote recognition of the military contribution of Mexican Americans. The following year, the GI Forum launched a national protest campaign after a funeral home in Three Rivers, Texas, refused to handle the body of Felix Langoria, a Hispanic soldier killed in the Philippines. The protest brought the issue of anti-Hispanic discrimination into the headlines, and during the 1950s the GI Forum's high profile enabled it to extend its campaigns into other civil rights areas, such as education and voting.

A changing military

Also in 1948, President Harry S. Truman signed Executive Order 9981, which called for the equality of all persons in the armed services, regardless of their ethnicity. The military immediately undertook sweeping reforms to end discrimination and segregation.

The changing ethos of the U.S. armed forces during the postwar period created a climate in which Hispanic Americans were able for the first time to participate equally in military life. Some outstanding Latino servicemen emerged during the late 1940s and early 1950s. Among them were Horacio Rivero, the first Latino four-star admiral in the U.S. Navy, and General Richard E. Cavazos, the first Latino four-star general in the U.S. Army.

Korea and Vietnam

Soon after Executive Order 9981, the U.S. military faced another major conflict, the Korean War, during which 168,000 Hispanic Americans saw service, mainly in the Army and the Marine Corps.

Despite the progressive policies implemented by the military, discrimination persisted. The Vietnam War was one of the most contentious conflicts in U.S. history, not least because of the large numbers of casualties suffered by Hispanic Americans and other minority communities. At the time, Latinos made up just 4.5 percent of the total U.S. population, but during the conflict they suffered more than 19 percent of the casualties. More likely to be drafted than their Anglo-American counterparts, Hispanic Americans were also more often assigned to the most dangerous combat roles. As a consequence, resistance to the draft and antiwar protest rapidly became an important focus of the Chicano movement, which became prominent in the 1960s and early 1970s.

After the United States withdrew from Vietnam in 1973, the character of the U.S. armed forces changed again. The draft had been ended in 1973, and the U.S. Army in particular became a much more compact organization, dependent on highly trained, professional volunteers. Although many Hispanic Americans had objected to their treatment in Vietnam, once entry into the armed forces ceased to be compulsory, life in the military became more attractive to them. Latinos—and, increasingly, Latinas—played an important role in post-Vietnam U.S. military actions. In the First Persian Gulf War (1990–1991), 20,000 Latinos and Latinas participated in the liberation of Kuwait. In 1997, one-third of the U.S. troops taking part in the peacekeeping mission in the former Yugoslavia were of Hispanic origin.

A Mexican American brigade parades at Fort Benning, Georgia, in 1943, just before despatch to the front line in World War II.

21st-century U.S. forces

Since the 1990s, the number of Hispanic Americans serving in the U.S. Army has increased by more

BORINQUENEERS

One of the most celebrated Hispanic-dominated outfits in the U.S. military is the Puerto Rican 65th Infantry Regiment, nicknamed the "Borinqueneers" after the native people of the island. The regiment was first formed in 1899, shortly after the U.S. annexation of Puerto Rico, and saw service during both world wars, when it was used principally to defend the strategically important Panama Canal. It was during the Korean War, however, that the Borinqueneers became a byword for military valor and determination. Early in 1951, they undertook a three-day assault on Chinese positions near the South Korean capital, Seoul. This bitterly fought enterprise ended when the Puerto Rican soldiers, with fixed bayonets, launched a sudden and ferocious charge, causing the enemy to flee.

than 30 percent. By 2001, Latinos and Latinas made up almost 9.7 percent of the Army, 10.5 percent of the Navy, 5.6 percent of the Air Force, and 14 percent of the Marine Corps. Increased participation reflects the growth of the Hispanic American population, and is also the result of a sustained program of targeted recruitment. As enrollment rates among other ethnic and racial groups, including African Americans, declined, military administrators in the Pentagon realized that the growing Hispanic population made up an important and relatively underexploited part of the military "market" in the United States.

21st-century conflicts

The increasing contribution of Latinos and Latinas to the military became evident in the Second Persian Gulf War of 2003, and in the subsequent occupation of Iraq. The U.S. Marines—in which Hispanic Americans have a high profile—took the leading role in the invasion, and suffered a disproportionately high percentage of the casualties. The first U.S. Marine killed in combat was Lance Corporal José Antonio Gutiérrez, a 28-year-old Guatemalan immigrant from Hawthorne, California, who was posthumously awarded U.S. citizenship. Such devastating losses and the stories behind them brought home the sacrifices that were regularly made by Latinos and Latinas—not only U.S. citizens, but also foreign nationals who had volunteered to fight for a cause in which they believed.

Political repercussions

The high numbers of Hispanic casualties in Iraq have provoked widespread criticism of the U.S. military, which has been accused of exploiting an especially vulnerable sector of the population: impoverished, youthful Mexican Americans and recent immigrants eager to improve their prospects and prove their patriotism. Critics point out that servicemen of Hispanic origin are much more likely to find themselves in combat roles, since they currently constitute 18 percent of frontline personnel, more than any other ethnic group.

Expanding role

In 2005, the percentage of Latinos and Latinas in the U.S. armed forces was lower than 13 percent, which is their share of the total U.S. population. However, over the coming years the number of Hispanics in uniform looks set to increase quickly, as the Hispanic population itself continues to grow and becomes one of the most demographically youthful sectors of the U.S. population. Opportunities for education and training, the prospect of a secure and well-paid career, and the influence of strong role models such as Lieutenant General Ricardo S. Sanchez, the former commander of the coalition forces in Iraq, will continue to attract large numbers of young Hispanics into the services.

See also: Barkley, David Bennes; Chaves, Manuel; Garcia, Hector; Sanchez, Ricardo S.

Further reading: Ramos, Henry A. J. *The American GI Forum: In Pursuit of the Dream*. Houston, TX: Arte Publico Press, 1998.
Mariscal, George (ed.). *Aztlán and Viet Nam: Chicano and Chicana Experiences of the War*. Berkeley, CA: University of California Press, 1999.
Rivas-Rodriguez, Maggie (ed.). *Mexican Americans and World War II*. Austin, TX: University of Texas Press, 2005.
www.neta.com (Latino and Latina contributions to the U.S. military).

MINAYA, Omar
Baseball Manager

Omar Minaya is the first Latino general manager in the history of Major League Baseball. Minaya earned that distinction when he was appointed as general manager of the Montreal Expos in February 2002. He then became executive vice president of baseball operations and general manager of the New York Mets.

KEY DATES
1958 Born in the Dominican Republic.
1985 Joins the Texas Rangers as an amateur scout.
2002 Becomes general manager when he takes over at the Montreal Expos.
2004 Rejoins the Mets as general manager.

Player to manager

Minaya was born in a small village in the Dominican Republic in 1958. His family immigrated to the New York City borough of Queens in 1967. He grew up in the Corona district among a community made up of many different ethnic groups. Growing up in this environment greatly enhanced Minaya's later ability to scout and sign players from a diversity of backgrounds.

▼ ***As general manager of the New York Mets, Omar Minaya has signed many top Latino players to the team.***

Minaya had a short baseball career as a player. He was drafted as an outfielder by the Oakland Athletics in the 14th round of the 1978 draft. Minaya played with the A's for one year before being released. He was also in the Seattle Mariners system for a year, but was again released and gave up his playing career. "I wasn't a good enough hitter to play professionally. I was fast and athletic, but I wasn't a good hitter," Minaya explained. "A lot of guys got released and always had an excuse. I would not have an excuse. I wasn't going to be one of those guys who came home and said the coach didn't like me or they were racist, all those excuses I heard over the years. I was going to be honest. If you were good enough to play the game, you'd be playing."

Baseball manager

In 1985 Minaya joined the Texas Rangers as an amateur scout in the Dominican Republic. He soon showed he had an eye for finding talent. In 1989 Minaya was promoted to director of Latin American scouting. In 1997 he joined the New York Mets as an assistant general manager, and helped recruit Dominican Sammy Sosa to the team.

In 2002 Minaya took charge of the Expos. The team was in disarray, with low attendance at games and a constant threat of going bust. Minaya had to recruit almost an entire staff. After successes in Montreal, Minaya returned to the Mets in 2004 as general manager. In that capacity, he has lured several stars to the team, including pitcher Pedro Martinez and outfielder Carlos Beltran.

See also: Martinez, Pedro; Sosa, Sammy

Further reading: Fox, Bucky. *The Mets Fan's Little Book of Wisdom.* Lanham, MD: Taylor Trade Publishing, 2006.
http://www.hispanicheritageawards.org/hispanic_det.php?id=89 (biography).

MINOSO, Minnie
Baseball Player

Minnie Minoso is one of the longest-serving major league baseball players in history. A seven-time All-Star and three-time Gold Glove winner in left field, Minoso is one of only two major league baseball players to appear in five different decades.

Minoso debuted in 1949 with the Cleveland Indians, and played throughout the 1950s and 1960s with the Chicago White Sox, the Indians, Washington Senators, and St. Louis Cardinals. Minoso was called up twice briefly by the Chicago White Sox in 1976 and 1980 to help him achieve his goal of playing in five decades. In 17 seasons from 1949 to 1980, Minoso finished with a career .298 batting average, 1,023 runs batted in, and 186 home runs.

Baseball career

Minoso's full name is Saturnino Orestes Armas Minoso Arrieta. He was born in 1922 in Havana, Cuba. Like many young Cubans, Minoso excelled at baseball. He was signed as an amateur free agent by the Cleveland Indians in 1948, and made his major league debut one year later. Minoso hit his first major league home run in just his second start, on May 5. However, he appeared in only nine games that season, and did not appear during the 1950 season.

Minoso was traded to the White Sox in a complex three-team deal in 1951. The very next day, Minoso became the White Sox's first black player. The game was against the New York Yankees, during which Yankee legend Mickey Mantle hit his first major league home run. The Mantle-led Yankees and Minoso-led White Sox would be great rivals for most of their careers.

Minoso finished his rookie season as the American League leader in stolen bases (31) and triples (14), and had the second-highest batting average (.326). He played six more full seasons with Chicago before being traded back to the Indians for two seasons. In 1960 Minoso returned to the White Sox for two years. He played with the Cardinals in 1962, the Senators in 1963, and briefly with the White Sox again in 1964, 1976, and 1980. Minoso never won a World Series as a player.

KEY DATES

1922 Born in Havana, Cuba, on November 29.

1949 Makes major league debut with the Cleveland Indians on April 19.

1951 Traded to the Chicago White Sox on April 30.

1960 Named to his seventh American League All-Star team.

1980 Appears in his final major league game with the White Sox on October 5.

▲ ***Minnie Minoso was selected as an All-Star seven times, all but once for seasons with the White Sox.***

Almost retired

Minoso tried to play during a sixth decade in the major leagues in 1990, but his request was denied. However, Minoso did eventually play in the 1990s. On June 30, 1993, the 70-year-old Minoso had one at-bat as a designated hitter for the St. Paul Saints of the independent Northern League. Minoso grounded out to Thunder Bay pitcher Yoshi Seo. Minoso later served as a community relations ambassador for the White Sox, and was with the organization as they won the 2005 World Series, the franchise's first title since 1917.

Further reading: Vanderberg, Bob. *Minnie and the Mick: The Go-Go White Sox Challenge the Fabled Yankee Dynasty, 1951–1964*. South Bend, IN: Diamond Communications, 1996.
http://www.baseballlibrary.com/baseballlibrary/ballplayers/M/Minoso_Minnie.stm (biography).

MIRANDA, Carmen

Singer

Carmen Miranda, known as the "Brazilian Bombshell" and the "Lady in the Tutti-Frutti Hat," was a Portuguese-born Brazilian entertainer who became popular with U.S. movie audiences in the 1940s for her stylized costumes, exotic accent, and charming personality. Miranda was the highest paid female star in Hollywood in her day and remains an enduring cultural icon of Hispanic America.

In the 1930s Miranda was a recording star during Brazil's golden age of samba. Her career coincided with significant technological innovations in mass media. She became a star on the radio, singing and recording numerous samba songs, many of which became hits during Rio de Janeiro's annual carnival. She achieved fame performing live on stage, but rocketed to worldwide stardom through film. Miranda was attempting to make a further crossover into the new medium of television when she had a heart attack and died, aged 46.

Brazilian childhood

Maria do Carmo Miranda da Cunha was born in Portugal in 1909. As an infant she traveled with her family to Brazil and settled in Rio de Janeiro. Miranda attended a Catholic school for needy children, but she was not able to graduate from high school. As a teenager, she found work in a women's boutique, where her ability to design and create original hats earned her good wages.

At the time, musical performance was considered an inappropriate endeavor for an unmarried woman from a respectable family. Nevertheless the young Miranda sought out opportunities to perform. Miranda was discovered by the composer and musician Josué de Barros (1888–1959). She first used the stage name Carmen Miranda in 1929, when she performed on Barros's radio program. Composer Synval Silva, who was a boarder at Miranda's family home, composed the samba "Adeus Batucada" for her. It was an instant hit and remained Miranda's favorite song.

In 1933, Miranda became the first Brazilian singer—male or female—to sign a contract with a radio broadcast company rather than be paid by the performance. By 1935

▲ ***Carmen Miranda poses with a tambourine during rehearsals for a show at the London Palladium in 1948. At the time she was earning $200,000 a year.***

KEY DATES

1909	Born in Marco de Canaveze, Portugal, on February 9.
1929	Makes first radio appearance.
1935	Becomes highest-paid Brazilian entertainer.
1941	Makes Hollywood debut in *Down Argentine Way*.
1947	Stars in *Copacabana* with Groucho Marx.
1955	Dies in Beverly Hills, California, on August 5.

INFLUENCES AND INSPIRATION

Through its global reach, the Hollywood movie industry projected an American vision of Hispanic culture through the roles of Carmen Miranda. To them she represented not just Brazilian traditions, but those of the whole of South America. Studios asked her to perform rumbas and fox-trots instead of sambas, and created elaborate Latin American settings that seemed exotic to U.S. audiences but offended many Hispanic Americans as cartoonish.

During World War II (1939–1945), the U.S. government implemented the Good Neighbor Policy to strengthen ties among all American nations both North and South, and to weaken any ties with the Axis powers of Germany and Japan.

A number of Miranda's Hollywood productions were meant to promote the ideal of a cohesive Americas, and yet the films presented to U.S. audiences offered a view of Latin American culture and society that lacked authenticity. Argentines complained when Miranda, a Brazilian, was cast in *Down Argentine Way*. Brazilians complained that Miranda was becoming too Americanized.

Nevertheless Miranda remains one of the most significant Latin American women of the 20th century. The influence of her career on empowering women in general and modernizing Brazilian society are hard to quantify.

she was the highest-paid performer in Brazil. Her greatest hit was probably her 1939 recording of "O que é que a Baiana tem?" (What is that that the baiana has?), composed by Dorival Caymmi.

Miranda was a pioneering performer not only because she was a woman, but also because in recording sambas for the dynamic radio market, she sang a form of Afro-Brazilian music that was dramatically different from the classical music preferred by the country's elites.

Famous look

At the time she was discovered in Brazil, Miranda had just created the costume that would later make her famous. Rather than following mainstream fashion trends, Miranda created a costume that reinterpreted the traditional clothing of the baianas, the Afro-Brazilian women from the northeastern Brazilian city of Bahia.

The baianas, who sold food in open-air markets and participated in public celebrations, wore a costume that dated back to colonial times. Miranda, a skilled seamstress in her own right, redesigned the baiana's traditional cotton blouse into a flirtatious, midriff-baring top, and accentuated the short sleeves with ruffles and sequins. Instead of a simple and modest skirt, Miranda's figure-hugging skirts were made with luxurious fabric and opulent decoration.

As a talented hat-maker, Miranda used the baiana's simple head-scarf as inspiration for eye-popping hats that usually featured a turban and elaborate decorations of feathers, jewels, and fruit. The baianas also wore strands of beads and good luck charms, and Miranda accessorized her costume with numerous colorful necklaces, bangles, and earrings. The final touch was added because of Miranda's petite stature—6-inch (15 cm) platform shoes. Wearing the baiana costume, Miranda set herself apart. She used choreographed dance steps and hand gestures to accompany her voice and created a unique performance. Miranda was a white woman dressed as an Afro-Brazilian woman and singing Afro-Brazilian sambas. She performed tirelessly in front of large and enthusiastic crowds.

American break

In the late 1930s, Miranda was recruited to perform in the Broadway musical *Streets of Paris*. She negotiated a contract that allowed her to bring her own band, Bando da Lua, and was a great success.

In the 1930s Miranda had appeared in several Brazilian films, but between 1939 and 1955, she made 14 Hollywood films. Her Hollywood debut was in *Down Argentine Way* (1941), with Betty Grable (1916–1971). In the film, her song "Down South America Way" made her an instant star. In the ensuing years she performed in numerous films, including *Weekend in Havana* (1941) with Cesar Romero (1907–1994) and *Copacabana* (1947) with Groucho Marx (1890–1977).

Miranda's crudely stereotypical roles alienated her from her Latin American audience. Nevertheless Brazilians were distraught by her untimely death, and some 500,000 people lined the streets during her funeral in Rio.

Further reading: Gil-Montero, Martha. *Brazilian Bombshell: The Biography of Carmen Miranda*. New York, NY: D. I. Fine, 1989.

http://www.carmenmiranda.net/home.php (Miranda's Web site).

MIRÓ, Esteban Rodriguez
Soldier, Politician

Esteban (or Estevan) Miró distinguished himself in the 18th century, first as an army officer in the American Revolution and later as governor of the Louisiana Territory and West Florida.

Esteban Rodriquez Miró y Sabater was born in Reus, Catalonia, Spain, in 1744. He joined the army when he was just 16, and saw action in later stages of the Seven Years' War (1756–1763). In 1765 he was sent to Mexico, where he quickly established a reputation as a distinguished soldier. He returned to Spain in the early 1770s.

KEY DATES	
1744	Born in Reus, Catalonia, Spain, on June 4.
1760	Joins the Spanish army.
1765	Sent to Mexico but returns to Spain in the early 1770s.
1785	Made governor of Louisiana.
1791	Resigns as governor and returns to Spain.
1795	Dies on June 4.

American battles
Following Spain's declaration of war on Great Britain in 1779, Spain officially entered the American Revolution (1775–1783). King Carlos III appointed Bernardo de Gálvez, the governor of Louisiana (Spanish territory west of the Mississippi River), as the general of the Spanish forces in North America. Miró, who had been stationed in Louisiana since 1778, became second in command. The 5,000-strong Spanish forces conducted a campaign against the British along the Gulf of Mexico and Florida coasts, and Miró led many successful campaigns to reclaim the territory of West Florida. In 1782 Gálvez appointed Miró acting governor of Louisiana.

▼ ***Esteban Rodriguez Miró was a Spanish soldier who governed the Spanish colonies of Louisiana and West Florida in the early days of the United States.***

Political power
Following the end of the war in 1783, the Mississippi River became the border between the new United States of America and Spanish Louisiana. In the following year Miró closed the lower Mississippi River to U.S. traffic, stifling the livelihoods of U.S. settlers to the north who used the river as a trade route.

Miró was made full governor of Louisiana after Gálvez was appointed viceroy of Mexico in 1785. He only allowed settlers from the United States to live in Louisiana if they swore allegiance to Spain and the Catholic church.

In 1787 General James Wilkinson approached Miró to enlist Spain's support in establishing an independent American state in the West. Wilkinson swore allegiance to the Spanish crown, but the authorities in Spain prevented Miró from supporting Wilkinson's scheme.

Miró was also occupied with administering New Orleans, the largest settlement in the colony. The city suffered from outbreaks of disease, and Miró quarantined parts of the city. In 1788 New Orleans was devastated by fire. Miró rebuilt the city, introducing much of the Spanish influence seen in the city's architecture. In 1791 Miró returned to Spain. He died in 1795 of an illness while serving as a field marshal in a war against France.

See also: Gálvez, Bernado de

Further reading: http://www.enlou.com/people/miroe-bio.htm (biographical timeline).

MOHR, Nicholasa
Writer

Nicholasa Mohr is one of the most important Hispanic American writers working in the United States today. She was one of the first Hispanic American, writers writing in English to be published by a major publishing house. Many of her books, some of which are aimed at children and young adults, concentrate on her experience as a Nuyorican, a Puerto Rican growing up and living for more than 40 years in New York City.

Early life

Mohr was born Nicholasa Golpe in New York City, the youngest child and only girl in a family of seven. Her mother, Nicholasa Rivera, arrived in New York from Puerto Rico in the 1930s at the age of 22, with four sons by her first husband. She met and married another Puerto Rican, Pedro Golpe, with whom she had two more sons and Nicholasa. The family settled in El Barrio (also known as Spanish Harlem), a predominantly Hispanic neighborhood in northern Manhattan.

Mohr's father died when she was eight, and her mother struggled to support her family alone, with her own health failing. The subsequent death of her mother left Mohr an orphan before she reached high school.

Artistic interest

Encouraged by her mother, Mohr had begun drawing well at the age of four and a half, copying cartoon figures such as Dick Tracy and Popeye. After graduating from Stabermore High School in Manhattan, Mohr studied at the Art Students' League and City College in New York City between 1953 and 1956, working different jobs to support herself in the meantime.

KEY DATES

1935 Born in New York City on November 1.

1973 Publishes *Nilda.*

1975 Publishes *El Bronx Remembered.*

1977 Becomes lecturer in Puerto Rican studies at the State University of New York.

1985 Publishes *Rituals of Survival: A Woman's Portfolio.*

1998 Publishes *Untitled Nicholasa Mohr.*

Having saved enough money to travel to Europe to study art, Mohr instead decided to go to Mexico City. There, she studied the works of the country's early 20th century artists Diego Rivera (1886–1957), Frida Kahlo (1907–1954), and Jose Clemente Orozco (1883-1949).

Rivera was a radical muralist whose work was highly political. He worked in Mexico, Europe, and in New York City, and painted for some of the most influential people in 20th-century history, including communist leader Vladimir Lenin and industrialist Henry Ford. Rivera and Kahlo had had a much celebrated and stormy romance, which included being married twice.

Kahlo is as much known as a Mexican feminist icon as a painter. Her body of work documents a lifetime filled with pain. She suffered from polio in her childhood and was severely injured by a bus in her late teens. Her tempestuous marriage to Rivera was also plagued by infidelities. She is rumored to have been a lover of Leon Trotsky, Lenin's erstwhile deputy, who fled to Mexico from Russia to escape Joseph Stalin.

Jose Clemente Orozco was another muralist. His work contrasted with Rivera's murals in that it depicted violence and chaos as he tried to represent the reality of political turmoil rather than its ideals. Mohr was deeply influenced by the different ways the three artists represented their Hispanic culture.

Study and marriage

Back in New York in 1957, Mohr studied at the Brooklyn Museum of Art School, the newly established New School for Social Research, and the Pratt Center for Contemporary Printmaking. She met Irwin Mohr, her second husband and the couple had two sons. Mohr's art studies culminated in a degree from the Pratt Center in 1969. Mohr began a successful career as a graphic artist, exhibiting her work with great success in 1971 in an East Village gallery.

Painting with words

Mohr's transition to becoming a writer came about because she liked to include words in her artwork. Her agent, noting the high literary content of her show, suggested Mohr try to write. Mohr wrote 50 pages about her life. In 1972, when a publisher commissioned her to design a book cover, she submitted her text along with the design.

INFLUENCES AND INSPIRATION

An important part of Puerto Rican life is a tradition of oral storytelling, or "*el cuento puertorriqueno.*" Mohr was brought up listening to a wide variety of stories, from folk tales to modern adventure stories, and recalls how they had the power to transport their listeners from their everyday lives.

As soon as she was able, at the age of seven, Mohr got a card for the public library and read as much as she could. Like many other minority and female writers before her, Mohr was soon aware that libraries and book stores held no books that described experiences similar to her own.

At school Mohr loved the writers Shirley Jackson, Carson McCullers, and Katherine Anne Porter. From their example, she concluded that the more specific the writing, the more universal its appeal. It was for this reason that she later decided to write about what she knew best—being a Puerto Rican girl in New York City.

Two weeks later she was given a book contract. Supported by a visual artist fellowship, Mohr completed her first book, *Nilda*, which was published in 1973. Based on her life, the novel describes growing up in El Barrio during World War II (1939–1945), following the life of a young girl through her teenage years until the death of her mother. The novel exposes the tensions between the different ethnic groups of the Puerto Rican community of New York. *Nilda* was very popular among its teenage audience. It broke new ground, as few Latinas had yet written about their experiences as children belonging to an ethnic minority. Mohr also illustrated the book herself.

Full-time writer

With the publication of her second book in 1975, a collection of novellas, *El Bronx Remembered*, Mohr became a full-time writer. The stories were a frank examination of various Puerto Rican neighborhoods in New York that dealt with topics such as sexuality, racism, and religion. *El Bronx Remembered* won an Outstanding Book Award from the *New York Times* in 1975, as well as the Best Book Award from *School Library Journal*.

Mohr's next book, *Nueva York* (1977), dealt with different episodes from the lives of Puerto Rican adults living in New York. It, too, won the Best Book Award from *School Library Journal*. *Felita* (1979) was aimed at a younger audience, and told the story of a young Puerto Rican girl whose parents decide to move to a better neighborhood. There, Felita misses her old friends. Her new neighbors would not let their children play with her. Her family decides to return to their old neighborhood.

Teaching career

Following the success of her early books, Mohr decided to teach as a means to help her community. Between 1977 and 1980 she taught Puerto Rican studies in New York and creative writing for different educational programs across the country. She also worked as the head creative writer and coproducer of the popular television soap *Aquí y Ahora* (Here and Now).

Family loss

After the death of her husband in 1978, Mohr and her sons moved to Brooklyn. Three years later a brother, to whom Mohr was close, also died. Mohr did not publish anything more until 1985, when *Rituals of Survival: A Woman's Portfolio* appeared. A collection of six short stories, aimed at an adult audience, the book struggled to find a publisher because of its feminist content. The following year Mohr published a sequel to the popular *Felita*. In *Going Home*, Felita visits Puerto Rico and discovers that her family there has very different values from her family in New York.

Award winner

Mohr published consistently during the 1990s, continuing to examine the urban Puerto Rican experience. *All For Better: A Story of El Barrio* (1993) is a 22-volume nonfiction series that examines life in the Hispanic American communities in New York. *In My Own Words: Growing Up Inside the Sanctuary of My Imagination* (1994) was Mohr's memoir of her early life. Her work has won numerous awards. In 1996 she won the lifetime achievement award from the National Congress of Puerto Rican Women, and the following year she was awarded the Hispanic Heritage Award for Literature.

Further reading: Mohr, Nicholasa. *Growing Up Inside the Sanctuary of My Imagination*. New York, NY: J. Messner, 1994. http://books.scholastic.com/teachers/authorsandbooks/authorstudies/authorhome.jsp?authorID=63&&displayName=Interview%20Transcript (interview with Mohr).

MOLINA, Gloria

Politician

Mexican American Gloria Molina is one of the most influential Hispanic politicians active in the state of California. From 1991 she served on the powerful five-member Los Angeles County Board of Supervisors, where she focused her work on meeting the needs of ordinary working people. Molina's popularity among Hispanic voters made her an important national as well as statewide figure, and she played a prominent role within the Democratic Party.

Molina's community-rooted political beliefs and ideals were forged in the Chicano and feminist movements of the early 1970s, and her groundbreaking career encompasses a succession of firsts for Hispanic American women in California. Molina's rise to prominence broadly reflects the growing empowerment and self-confidence of California's Hispanic community during the late 20th century. Her straightforward, tough-minded, and sometimes confrontational style has won her both supporters and detractors.

▲ ***Gloria Molina is one of the most powerful Latina politicians in the United States.***

An eldest child

Gloria Molina was born in the East Los Angeles suburb of Montebello in 1948, the eldest of the 10 children of Mexican American immigrants Leonardo and Concepción Molina. The family later relocated to nearby Pico Rivera, where for a time they were the only Spanish-speaking family in the neighborhood. Molina was brought up with a belief in self-discipline, determination, and hard work. As the eldest child, she was expected to help care for her siblings and to act as their role model.

After graduating from Pico Rivera's El Rancho High School, Molina worked as a legal secretary while attending college at night. At first she studied at the Community College of East Los Angeles and later at California State University. However, the pressure to earn income for her hard-pressed family eventually led her to abandon her studies. In 1969 Molina joined the East Los Angeles Community Union (TELACU) as a youth employment trainer. TELACU's founder and director, the labor activist Esteban Torres, was a key influence on Molina's career.

KEY DATES

1948 Born in Montebello, Los Angeles County.

1982 Elected as the first Hispanic American assemblywoman in California.

1987 Elected the first Hispanic American councilwoman in Los Angeles, California.

1991 Becomes the first Hispanic American woman elected to the Los Angeles Board of Supervisors.

Community activist

By this time Molina was already deeply involved in community politics, and in particular the fast-emerging Chicano movement—a civil rights movement that sought social inclusion for Mexican Americans and other Hispanic Americans. While still at high school, Molina had been inspired by the example of César Chávez, the leader of the United Farm Workers, who was fighting for equal pay and rights for migrant workers—many of them from Mexico—in the United States.

Like other Hispanic American women, however, Molina became dissatisfied with the dominant role played by men in the Chicano movement. In 1970 she helped form the Sacramento-based Comisión Femenil Mexicana Nacional (CFMN; The National Commission of Mexican Women).

INFLUENCES AND INSPIRATION

The eight-year campaign against the building of a California State prison close to the Boyle Heights neighborhood of East Los Angeles marked a watershed not only in Molina's career but also in the political empowerment of the Eastside Hispanic community.

Molina quickly perceived that the site of the new prison had in part been chosen because the state government believed that the local people—many of whom lived in low-income households and only spoke Spanish—would not protest. She responded by undertaking a bilingual information campaign, handing out leaflets to residents, and organizing community meetings. At one public hearing held by the government, Molina protested the absence of a translator.

The Boyle Heights community mobilized against the prison on a large scale. The community's activism was focused on a group called the Mothers of East Los Angeles, which in the summer months of 1986 and 1987 organized weekly protest marches in the neighborhood, attracting considerable media coverage.

The political defiance shown by this Hispanic community helped transform California politics, waking a complacent political establishment to both the needs and the political power of Hispanic Americans. The state governor eventually abandoned the Boyle Heights project in 1992.

A succession of firsts

During the 1970s Molina pursued a successful career in political administration, serving in the White House as a deputy for presidential personnel in San Francisco, California, as a deputy director for the Department of Health and Human Services, and finally in the office of the speaker of the California State Assembly. She continued to be involved in party politics, however, and in 1981 she agreed to run as a Democratic candidate in the upcoming assembly elections. Despite vociferous opposition from local male Hispanic politicians, she was elected the following year, the first Latina ever elected to the California state legislature.

Molina followed her success in 1987 when she was elected to the Los Angeles City Council, another first for a Hispanic woman. In her roles first as assemblywoman and later as councilwoman, Molina was determined to keep in touch with the needs of the communities she represented. Her engagement with grassroots politics was nowhere more evident than in her leadership of the campaign to stop the building of a new California state prison in Boyle Heights, an impoverished and largely Hispanic American community in East Los Angeles (*see box*).

In 1988, the U.S. Department of Justice forced the Los Angeles County Board of Supervisors to redraw the boundaries of its electoral districts in order to create a Hispanic-majority district, and thus a safe Hispanic seat on the county board. In 1991 Molina gave up her seat on the city council and ran for office in the new 1st Supervisory District, which she duly won. Her election pushed Molina into the forefront of not only Los Angeles but statewide and national politics. Representing a population of some 10 million, and controlling an annual budget exceeding that of many U.S. states, the five-county board supervisors—nicknamed the "five little kings"—are among the most powerful figures in the region.

After her initial election, Molina was reelected to the board seven times before 2006. During her tenure, she channeled funds into the building of affordable housing and parks, improving child and health care, and tackling antisocial behavior. While the county board has traditionally been known for its governance by consensus, Molina gained a reputation for being plain-spoken and even obstinate.

A future governor

Since the early 1990s, Molina also played an increasingly important role within the Democratic Party at the national level. She served as a vice chair of the Democratic National Committee, the body that coordinates the party's campaigns. Because of her popularity among California's Hispanic American population, Molina wielded considerable influence during both local and national elections. For some commentators, her powerful political presence, engaging personality, and principled integrity make her a possible future candidate for the governorship of California, or even the vice presidency.

See also: Chávez, César

Further reading: Pardo, Mary S. *Mexican American Women Activists: Identity and Resistance in Two Los Angeles Communities*. Philadelphia, PA: Temple University Press, 1998.
molina.co.la.ca.us/scripts/gmbio.htm (official biography).

MOLINA, John John

Boxer

A world champion boxer and Puerto Rican social figure, John John Molina (born Juan A. Molina) has a record of 52 wins and 6 losses, with 33 wins by knockout.

Early life

Born on March 17, 1965, in Fajardo, Puerto Rico, Molina started boxing at an early age. With a rigorous fighting discipline, he received national attention after his first big victory at the age of 20, when he knocked out Kelcie Banks. Molina became a celebrity virtually overnight in Puerto Rico.

A professional career

Molina turned professional in 1986. In his first fight he beat opponent Job Walters. He went on to win his next 14 bouts, of which nine were knockouts. For Molina it seemed that the sky was the limit. In 1987 he lost to former lightweight champion Lupe Suarez, but went on to win his next five fights. Molina became the number-one challenger for the International Boxing Federation (IBF) championship. He won the title in 1989, the same year in which he won the World Boxing featherweight championship by beating Juan Laporte.

Molina's fights were repeatedly broadcast on national television. On January 28, 1990, he knocked out Suarez in the sixth round, but he subsequently lost to Tony Lopez, who recovered the world junior featherweight title when he fought him Reno. In 1992 Molina again won the IBF junior lightweight title in a match against Jackie Gunguzula.

A hero in Puerto Rico, Molina was featured on the covers of several national magazines, including *Vea*. His glamorous lifestyle and love of beautiful women also made him popular with the media.

By 1995, however, Molina's career was going downhill. He fought hard but lost a landmark fight against world lightweight champion Oscar De La Hoya in February. Over the next few years, many of Molina's matches were against less well-known fighters. He grew increasingly frustrated with his promoters' decisions to pit him against less well-known contenders.

On May 9, 1998, Molina fought U.S. boxer "Sugar" Shane Mosley in his second attempt at the world lightweight championship; he lost by a knockout. Molina's last world championship fight was in January 1999, when he faced Mexican American junior lightweight champion Roberto Garcia. Garcia retained his title after a bruising 12-round contest. Molina continued to box for the next couple of years; he announced his retirement in 2001.

▼ ***John John Molina fought many of the world's best boxers during his career, including Oscar De La Hoya.***

KEY DATES

1965	Born in Fejardo, Puerto Rico, on March 17.
1986	Wins first professional boxing match.
1989	Wins WBO feather lightweight and IBF lightweight titles.
1992	Wins IBF title in South Africa.
1995	Loses to Oscar De La Hoya.
1998	Loses to "Sugar" Shane Mosley.
2001	Retires from boxing.

See also: De La Hoya, Oscar

Further reading: Seltzer, Robert. *Inside Boxing.* New York, NY; MetroBooks, 2000.
http://www.boxrec.com/print.php?boxer_id=008492 (Molina's matches).

MOLINA, Mario
Chemist

Mario Molino is a Nobel Prize-winning chemist. The award recognized Molina's discovery that chemicals named chlorofluorocarbons (CFCs) were damaging the Earth's ozone layer. CFCs are gases that were developed for use inside refrigerators and spray cans. They were initially thought to be very unreactive. However, Molina showed that they reacted with the ozone layer, made from a special form of oxygen high in the atmosphere. Ozone protects the surface of the Earth from dangerous solar radiation, and CFCs were shown to be making a hole in the ozone layer. As a result of Molino's work, CFCs were banned by the Montreal Protocol in 1987.

Early life

Molina was born in Mexico City, Mexico, in 1943. His father was a lawyer and a university teacher, and served as the Mexican ambassador to Australia and the Philippines. Molina had an international education, being sent to boarding school in Switzerland when he was 11. He was exposed to a wide range of studies, but his strongest interest was in science. By the time he entered high school, his fascination with chemistry was evident. Molina created his own laboratory in his parents' bathroom, guided by his aunt Esther, also a chemist. By the time he entered college, Molina had decided he would become a research chemist.

Academic career

In 1960 Molina became part of the chemical engineering program at the Universidad Nacional Autonama de Mexico (UNAM). The program allowed Molina to take math courses along with his chemistry studies. He earned a postgraduate degree from the University of Freiburg, in what was then West Germany, in 1967, which enabled him to widen his background and explore which areas of research he wanted to pursue. He began looking at PhD programs in the United States. In the meantime Molina returned to

▼ ***Mario Molina won a Nobel Prize for his work, the first Mexican American to be so honored.***

INFLUENCES AND INSPIRATION

Molina has readily acknowledged Sherwood Rowland (1927–) as a mentor and supportive colleague. He acknowledged in his Nobel Prize speech that he and Rowland communicated often during their research on the CFC problem, and their collaborations in articles and testifying at hearings on CFC emissions standards showed him the potential for good that such research could produce. His other inspiration is his wife, Luisa, whose collaborations in many experiments helped him learn how to conduct his own research. Molina has said that her support and understanding of his work helped him through difficult periods of his research.

Mexico to work as an assistant professor at UNAM. While there he helped create the university's first chemical engineering graduate program. In 1968 Molina accepted a place in the University of California at Berkeley's physical chemistry program.

During his PhD studies at Berkeley, Molina had the good fortune to join a research group headed by Dr. George C. Pimentel (1922–1989), who was using lasers to investigate chemical reactions. Pimentel's research into the dynamics of the molecular bonds enabled Molina to investigate the distribution of energy in certain kinds of reactions. While he worked on Pimentel's team, Molina met Luisa Tan, a research scientist who was also studying with Pimentel. Tan would later become one of Molina's closest collaborators, and eventually his wife.

Discovery

Molina earned his PhD in 1972, and a year later both he and Luisa joined the research group in Irvine, California, headed by Professor Sherwood Rowland. Rowland was a pioneer in what was called "hot atom" chemistry, the study of how the energy released by nuclear reactions could promote unusual chemical effects.

In July 1972, Molina and Tan married, and the new postdoctoral fellow got down to serious work. The project that Rowland offered him was to discover what happened to certain industrial chemicals that were thought to be inert and therefore harmless to the environment. These chemicals, chlorofluorocarbons, were widely used in industry. Molina's task was to investigate the molecular dynamics of CFCs, and see whether or not they were destroyed in the atmosphere.

After three months of what Molina considered not particularly interesting research, he and Rowland developed what was to become the CFC-ozone depletion theory. Molina found that CFCs remained intact in the lower atmosphere. Only when they reached higher altitudes were they destroyed by solar radiation. However, Molina also found that chlorine atoms released from the CFC molecules were then destroying Earth's protective ozone layer. These findings were published in the June 28, 1974, issue of *Nature*.

KEY DATES

1943	Born in Mexico City, Mexico, on March 19.
1972	Earns a PhD in chemistry from the University of California at Berkeley.
1973	Marries Luisa Tan.
1974	Publishes discovery of the behavior of CFCs.
1989	Becomes a faculty member at MIT.
1995	Awarded the Nobel Prize in chemistry.

Greatest honor

Molina eventually quit Irvine to pursue other research. He joined the Molecular Physics and Chemistry section at Caltech's Jet Propulsion Laboratory near Pasedena, California, in 1972. His son, Felipe, was born in 1977.

In 1989, Molina began work at the Massachusetts Institute of Technology (MIT), doing research in the field of global atmospheric chemistry. Molina became a member of the National Academy of Sciences, the Institute of Medicine, and has served on the President's Committee in Science and Technology. In 1995 Molina was awarded the Nobel Prize in Chemistry, along with Rowland and Paul Crutzen for their work in atmospheric chemistry. Molina donated $200,000 of his prize to research into the environment. Molina said in his acceptance speech that he was both "heartened and humbled" to be able to do something that had such an impact on the environment.

Further reading: Guidici, Cynthia. *Mario Molina*. Chicago, IL: Raintree, 2006. http://teacher.scholastic.com/activities/hispanic/molinatscript.htm (interview with Molina).

MOLL, Luis

Educator

Educating Hispanic American students has been a persistent challenge for American teachers. Historically there has been little interest among white, middle-class teachers for working in schools that have predominantly Hispanic American students. The teachers are often apprehensive because of their lack of knowledge of the language and cultural background of the students.

For a long time, it has been understood that an education program developed for an English-speaking middle-class school population is not adequate for non-English-speaking students. As a result, the hopes of the majority of Hispanic American parents that their children will be educated to a higher standard than they were themselves have consistently been dashed.

Recently researchers have made strides in finding solutions to this unacceptable situation. One of these researchers is Luis Moll, a professor of education at the University of Arizona in Tucson.

Education and research

Moll was born in Puerto Rico in 1947. He began his career as an academic and educator after graduating from California State Polytechnic in Pomona in 1972. He continued his studies at the University of Southern California, graduating from there with a master's degree in social work in 1974.

KEY DATES

1947 Born in Puerto Rico on June 28

1972 Receives his bachelor of science degree from California State Polytechnic University, Pomona.

1974 Receives a master's in social work from the University of Southern California.

1978 Receives his PhD from the University of California, Los Angeles.

1995 Becomes professor in the Department of Language, Reading and Culture, College of Education, University of Arizona.

1998 Elected as a member of the National Academy of Education.

2004 Named associate dean for academic affairs at the College of Education, University of Arizona.

Four years later, Moll was awarded his PhD from the University of California, Los Angeles. His main research interests were the connections between culture, psychology, and education, especially as it relates to the education of Hispanic American children.

In his ensuing research career, Moll has analyzed the quality of classroom teaching and examined literacy instruction in English and Spanish. He has also studied how literacy takes its place in the broader social contexts of households and community life. He is presently conducting a study of bilingual literacy development in Hispanic American children.

Funds of knowledge

Moll's book, *Funds of Knowledge: Theorizing Practice in Households, Communities, and Classrooms* (2005), highlights one of his most important contributions to academe. According to Moll, teachers underestimate what Hispanic Americans and children from other minorities are able to contribute in the classroom. Furthermore, he believes that schools should use "hidden" resources that Hispanic American parents have passed on to their children in their day-to-day lives.

This contention was developed by Moll when researching barrio families in Tucson, Arizona, where he has been a professor since 1995. Combining techniques from anthropology, psychology, linguistics, and education, Moll trained researchers to interview parents to uncover the knowledge and skills that could be used by teachers in educating Hispanic American children in Tucson's schools.

The researchers passed on what they learned to teachers, who used it to activate students' prior knowledge about topics in the curriculum. This prior knowledge can help students make connections to new topics and have greater success in school. Moll contends his system of analysis can be performed by any teacher.

Further reading: Gonzáles, Norma, Luis Moll, and Cathy Amanti. *Funds of Knowledge: Theorizing Practice in Households, Communities, and Classrooms*. Mahwah, NJ: L. Erlbaum Associates, 2005.

Jones, Toni G., and M. L. Fuller. *Teaching Hispanic Children*. Boston, MA: Pearson Education, Inc., 2003.

http://www.ncrel.org/sdrs/areas/issues/students/learning/lr1luis.htm (biography).

MONDINI-RUIZ, Franco

Artist

Specializing in playful, site-specific work, Franco Mondini-Ruiz abandoned a successful career as a lawyer to become an artist. He is best known for his Infinito Botánica, an old Mexican folk-healing shop he bought and transformed into a "social sculpture."

Using humorous elements to disarm his audience, Mondini-Ruiz's work explores political correctness and cultural bias, and deftly blurs the line between "high" and "low" art.

Early life

Mondini-Ruiz was born in San Antonio, Texas, in 1961. His world was one of glaring class and cultural distinctions. Mondini-Ruiz's father was a Eurocentric, upper-middle-class Italian immigrant, while his mother came from a working-class Mexican family. As a teenager Mondini-Ruiz worked in an electronics store owned by his parents, developing a taste for collecting junk. He earned a bachelor's degree in English in 1982 and a juris doctoris degree in 1985 from St. Mary's University in San Antonio. He then began work at a prestigious San Antonio law firm, but was unfulfilled with his life as a "yuppie lawyer."

▼ **People and Paintings,** ***a 2005 acrylic painting by Franco Mondini-Ruiz.***

KEY DATES

1961 Born in San Antonio, Texas.

1995 Gives up practicing law to focus on art.

1999 Reestablishes an old Mexican folk-medicine shop as Infinito Botánica and Gift Shop, a contemporary boutique, art installation, and salon.

Becoming an artist

For Mondini-Ruiz, making the transition from corporate lawyer to installation artist was gradual, partly conscious, and partly coincidental. A longing to live more expressively and revisit his Hispanic American roots prompted him to end his career as a lawyer in 1995. By coincidence, he had just discovered a treasure of artistic possibility—an 80-year-old botánica (a shop that sells herbs, charms, potions, and knickknacks) that was going out of business in San Antonio. He purchased the shop and used the existing inventory as part of an installation that integrated traditional botánica goods with cultural artifacts, his own sculptures, works by local artists, and craftspeople, and interesting junk. Always interweaving elements of class and culture, Mondini-Ruiz envisioned Infinito Botánica as a social rallying point where disconnected communities could come together.

Hispanic art

Mondini-Ruiz is inspired principally by the everyday art of his own Tejano culture. He has explained that Hispanic Americans have "a very sophisticated way of looking at and living with art ... I'm always amazed at how people decorate their yards, their houses, their food. They don't consider what they're making as art, because it's not affirmed as art."

His own installations are vibrant, kitschy, and humorous. Above all, they are affordable. Everything in Infinito Botánica is for sale, usually for less than $10. Mondini-Ruiz is based in New York City, and continues to bring his unique brand of social sculpture to different venues around the world.

Further reading: http://channel.creativecapital.org/project_327.html (introduction to Infinito Botánica and the work of Mondini-Ruiz).

MONGE, Yolandita

Singer, Actor

Singer Yolandita Monge first rose to fame as a child star, when she was known as the "Puerto Rican Judy Garland." Monge has had a string of hits as an adult, and has also become a successful actor.

Early life

Born in Trujillo Alto, Puerto Rico, in 1955, Monge was the daughter of Hector Monge and Delia Betancourt. Prior to Monge's birth, her parents and brother Hector had been living in New York, and the family returned to live in the United States shortly after Monge was born. They moved back to their native island seven years later.

Monge went to study at the Colegio Santa Cruz before attending the local public school. She sang in school choirs, and her musical talent quickly attracted attention. In 1969 Monge entered a singing contest run by a local radio show and won first prize. She went on to star in several television shows, including *Tribuna del Arte* and *Los Alegres Tres*. She was also a regular guest on popular programs such as *Luis Vigoreaux Presenta*.

▼ ***Yolandita Monge is known in Puerto Rico as a singer and actress.***

KEY DATES

1955	Born in Trujillo Alto, Puerto Rico, on September 16.
1969	Wins first prize in a radio singing competition.
1970	Releases *Puerto Rico's Poignant, Powerful, Incomparable: Yolandita Monge.*
1975	Has hit with "Cierra los Ojos" (Close Your Eyes).
1996	Honored by the Puerto Rican senate.

A Latin star

In 1970 Monge recorded her first album, *Puerto Rico's Poignant, Powerful, Incomparable: Yolandita Monge*. It was extremely successful, producing several hit songs, including "Las Olas" and the Spanish version of the Italian song "Vida," which became a summer hit in Puerto Rico. A popular child star, Monge sang with some of the leading Latin musicians of the time.

In the early 1970s, Monge lived in Mexico for a short while. Signed to TECA Records, she had more hits with songs such as "La Voz del Silencio." In Puerto Rico, Monge was part of La Nueva Ola (the New Wave), a group of musicians who sang popular music influenced by folklore. In 1975 Monge had an international hit with "Cierra los Ojos" (Close Your Eyes). The song boosted her reputation with music audiences in South and North America.

Monge signed with Sony Records in the early 1980s. She released several albums, including *Luz de Luna* (Moonlight, 1985). The record included "El Podor De Amor," a cover of "The Power of Love." Luz de Luna became a gold-selling album. Monge built on this success with the Grammy nominated *Laberinto de Amor* (Labyrinth of Love, 1987), which went platinum. Monge's success continued with such albums as *Vivencias* (Anecdotes, 1988), *Portfolio* (1990), the Puerto Rican folk album *Mi Encuentro* (1997), and *Sexto Sentido* (Sixth Sense, 2002).

Monge also established a successful career as an actor, appearing in *La Mentira*, *Escandalo*, and *La Viuda de Blanco*. The recipient of many awards, Monge entered the Guinness Book of Records in 1993, when she performed in three different Puerto Rican cities in one day.

Further reading: www.yolandita-monge.com (Monge's Web site).

MONROIG, Gilberto
Musician

Puerto Rican musician Gilberto Monroig was one of the leading singers of boleros—a Spanish style of music performed in triple time. Monroig sang with the orchestras of great Hispanic American bandleaders such Rafael Rivera and Tito Puente. In his 50-year career, he also released more than 30 albums, many of them as a solo artist. Monroig was inducted into the International Latin Music Hall of Fame in 2002, joining such musical legends as Astrud Gilberto (1940–) and Johnny Pacheco.

Early life

Born in Santurce, Puerto Rico, on July 2, 1930, Gilberto Monroig grew up in a neighborhood filled with music. As a child he listened to the tangos of renowned French-born Argentine singer Carlos Gardel (1890–1935).

Monroig and his brother Luis learned to play the guitar when they were children, and it quickly became apparent that the young Monroig was an exceptionally talented musician. He began playing in local bands from the age of 13. By the age of 14 he was playing at the China Doll nightclub in Santurce, a respected venue that attracted leading musicians such as Tito Rodriguez (1923–1972).

KEY DATES

1930	Born in Santurce, Puerto Rico, on July 2.
1943	Begins performing publicly as a musician.
1944	Joins first nightclub band.
1945	Makes first radio performance.
1946	Joins the Super Orchestra Tropicana as singer.
1949	Begins performing at the Caribe Hilton Hotel.
1951	Joins Tito Puente's orchestra as singer.
1955	Begins solo career in Puerto Rico.
1959	The single "Egoismo" achieves gold record status.
1964	"Simplemente una Ilusion" sells more than 500,000 copies.
1996	Dies in Santurce, Puerto Rico, on May 3.
2002	Inducted into the International Latin Music Hall of Fame.

Still barely a teenager, Monroig impressed audiences and musicians alike. By 1945 he had joined William Manzano's orchestra. The position involved playing regularly on the WPRA radio station in Mayagüez, Puerto Rico.

Front man

In 1946 the pianist Rafael Elvira hired the young Monroig to sing with his celebrated Super Orchestra Tropicana. Monroig toured all over Puerto Rico with the band. Three years later he joined Pete Rivera's orchestra, the resident band at the newly opened Caribe Hilton Hotel in San Juan, Puerto Rico, at the time one of the most prestigious hotels in the Caribbean. When bandleader Rivera moved to New York City to pursue his career, Monroig followed.

Proving to be a popular singer, Monroig quickly attracted a large and devoted following in New York. Known primarily for his poignant singing of bolero songs, Monroig played in the city's leading Latin nightclubs, including the Escambrón Beach Club. The young singer also made tours around Latin America.

Hit singles

In 1951 Monroig returned to New York, joining mambo and salsa bandleader Tito Puente and his orchestra. Monroig made several records during this time, including the hit "Malcriada." Over the next four years Monroig toured the Americas extensively with Puente. By 1955 he had grown tired of life on the road and decided to move back to his native Puerto Rico to concentrate on a solo career there.

Monroig enjoyed great success first in Puerto Rico and later abroad. He worked with leading musicians and released several hit songs, including "Mujer." He was awarded two gold records, the first in 1959 for the song "Egoismo" and a second in 1964, following his return to the United States, for "Simplemente una Ilusion" (Simply an Illusion). Monroig continued to tour until his death from cancer on May 3, 1996.

See also: Pacheco, Johnny; Puente, Tito

Further reading: Salazar, Max. *Mambo Kingdom: Latin Music in New York*. New York, NY: Schirmer, 2003.
http://www.musicofpuertorico.com/en/gilberto_monroig.html (biography).

MONTALBAN, Ricardo

Actor

Ricardo Montalban rose to become one of Hollywood's shining stars. His intensity as an actor, blended with skills honed on the Broadway stage, made him sought after as a performer in the early days of his career. Montalban competed with the Argentine actor Fernando Lamas (1916–1982) as Hollywood's premier "Latin lover." However, Montalban yearned for more dramatic roles so he could be taken seriously as an actor, and his wish was granted in his later years.

Early life

Born Ricardo Gonzalo Pedro Matalban y Merino in 1920, in Mexico City, Mexico, Montalban could not have dreamed he was destined to leave his mark in Hollywood history. The family moved to Los Angeles, California, when Montalban was in his teens, but his inability to speak English well prevented him from attending his local high school. Four months of intensive study enabled him to communicate in the language of his new country, and Montalban was enrolled at Fairfax High School. Montalban appeared in several high-school plays. One of his performances was seen by an agent from Metro-Goldwyn-Mayer (MGM), who offered him a contract.

Romantic roles

Montalban's first feature film, *Five Were Chosen,* was released in 1942. He then appeared in more than a dozen Mexican films, and as a bit player in several other studio productions. Montalban was often cast in roles that called for a definite ethnic type, and again and again he found himself in roles as the "Latin lover." He played opposite the leading ladies of the day, including Cyd Charisse (1921–) and Esther Williams (1921–). He appeared more than once with Williams, where he acted, danced, and even swam alongside his costar.

Breaking the mold

Montalban's first chance to break away from the typecast roles that were being offered to him came in 1949, in the World War II drama *Battleground*. In the film, Montalban played Private Johnny Rodriguez. The role showed off Montalban's acting ability to good effect.

Montalban's performance as a Mexican government agent in the 1949 film *Border Incident* helped raise awareness about the abuse of illegal aliens in the United States, and brought his talents to a wider audience. Montalban was gradually building his reputation as a talented actor and as a Hollywood activist.

▼ *Ricardo Montalban appears in the 1953 movie* Latin Lovers *with Lana Turner.*

INFLUENCES AND INSPIRATION

Ricardo Montalban's greatest influence on others comes not from his roles on screen, but from his role as founder of Nosotros. The organization is an advocacy group for Hispanic American actors. It also provides guidance, professional training, and peer programs for new performers. Such stars as Eddie Olmos, Salma Hayek, and Lorenzo Lamas received the benefits of Montalban's commitment to supporting the Hispanic American acting community. Many of his fellow actors have been active in the organization. Generations of Hispanic American actors have had their voices heard because of Nosotros's work to give Hispanic people a place in Hollywood.

In 1950, Montalban again showed off his acting range, when he played boxer Johnny Monterez in the film *Right Cross*. In 1952, another well-received Montalban performance highlighted prejudice and racism. This was his role as Chu Chu Ramirez, a fruit picker who is victimized because of his race and his belief in labor rights in the film *My Man and I*.

More roles

Montalban continued to go beyond what Hollywood perceived a Hispanic American actor could be throughout the 1950s as one the few Mexican film actors. In 1951, he appeared in the movie *Across the Wide Missouri* as the Native American Ironshirt. He sustained an injury to his spine while making the film that would plague him through the rest of his life and eventually confine him to a wheelchair. Montalban continued to act in films and television, and some of his best roles were still to come.

In 1957, he produced a highly acclaimed performance as a Kabuki actor in the film *Sayonara*. In the later part of his career, Montalban also had great success on the small screen. In 1979, after he had already won the hearts of viewers as the inestimable Mr. Rourke in the series *Fantasy Island*, Montalban won an Emmy Award for his role as Santangkai, leader of the Sioux tribe, in the television miniseries *How the West Was Won*. Montalban remarked to the audience when he received his award, "I don't know about Mr. Rourke, but this certainly fulfills my fantasy."

In 1982, Montalban returned to the big screen to reprise a role that would leave a legacy among a new generation of his fans. Montalban appeared as Khan, the villain in *Star Trek II: The Wrath of Khan*. Again, his ability as an actor came through, and turned a lightweight role into one of Montalban's most memorable appearances.

Leading the way

Montalban's talent forced Hollywood to take him seriously as an actor. Having experienced typecasting himself, he worried about its dangers for other Hispanic American performers. In 1970, Montalban founded the Latin media organization, Nosotros. The name means "we" and "us" in Spanish.

The organization is still active. Its aims are to improve the image of Hispanic Americans as they are portrayed in Hollywood, and to provide Hispanic American actors with a wider range of opportunities.

Montalban has been married for more than 60 years to Georgiana Young, the half-sister of actress Loretta Young (1913–2000). He is the father of four. Despite being confined to a wheelchair, Montalban continues to act. His most notable 21st-century performances have been in *Spy Kids 2: Island of Lost Dreams* (2002) and the sequel, *Spy Kids 3-D: Game Over* (2003).

KEY DATES

1920 Born in Mexico City, Mexico, on November 25.

1941 Makes his U.S. screen debut in short film *He's a Latin from Staten Island.*

1942 Appears in first feature film, *Five Were Chosen.*

1944 Marries Georgiana Young on October 26.

1970 Founds the Hispanic American media advocacy organization Nosotros.

1982 Takes title role in *Star Trek II: The Wrath of Khan.*

2002 Appears in *Spy Kids 2: Island of Lost Dreams.*

2003 Makes second appearance in a *Spy Kids* film as Grandfather in *Spy Kids 3-D: Game Over.*

See also: Hayek, Salma; Olmos, Edward James

Further reading: Montalban, Ricardo, and Bob Thomas. *Reflections: A Life in Two Worlds.* Garden City, NY: Doubleday, 1980.
http://www.nosotros.org (Nosotros's Web site).

MONTERO, Mayra
Writer

Mayra Montero is one of the most successful Hispanic American writers working today. She has received a number of awards for her short stories and novels, and her work has been translated into nine languages.

Journalism career

Montero was born in 1952 in Havana, Cuba, and educated at a Catholic convent before the 1959 revolution. Her father, a television writer and actor, moved the family to Puerto Rico after the Castro regime took hold.

Montero pursued a journalism career in both Mexico and Puerto Rico, but subsequently chose to establish herself on the island in 1972. For the next decade, Montero worked as a sports journalist and later as editor at an advertising company. In 1979, she joined the editorial staff of *El Mundo*, the oldest newspaper in Puerto Rico. She traveled around Central America and the Caribbean as a correspondent, working on the newspaper column *What the Wire Service Didn't Say*. This received distinguished awards from the Overseas Press Club Association an impressive five times. In 1984 Montero was honored with the Excelencia Periodística Eddie López, the top journalism award in Puerto Rico.

▼ ***Marya Montero's novel* Captain of the Sleepers *was published in English in 2005.***

KEY DATES

1952 Born in Havana, Cuba.

1979 Joins the editorial staff of the newspaper *El Mundo.*

1981 Establishes her fiction writing career with *Twenty-Three and a Turtle.*

1996 Publishes her anthology of newspaper articles, *Widespread Heavy Showers.*

2000 Receives La Sonrisa Vertical award for *Deep Purple.*

Works of fiction

Montero began writing fiction in 1981, with a collection of short stories called *Twenty-Three and a Turtle*. In 1986 she published her first novel, *In the Braid of the Beautiful Moon*, which placed Montero as a finalist in the Herralde de Novela awards in Barcelona, Spain.

Since then Montero has published eight novels, among them *The Last Night We Spent Together* (1991), which also placed her as a finalist in La Sonrisa Vertical's awards. In 1992, *The Red in His Shadow* became a best seller in Germany and Italy. Montero's novels have erotic content, with settings in the Caribbean, in particular Haiti and the Dominican Republic. In 2000, Montero's *Deep Purple* won La Sonrisa Vertical's award for the best erotic novel of the year.

Montero's works have been translated into at least nine languages, making her one of the most celebrated Caribbean contemporary writers. Her English translator is Edith Grossman. Other publications include *The Messenger* (1998), *Captain of the Sleepers* (2002), *Vain Illusion* (2003), and *Being Almond* (2005). Montero's newspaper columns are now collected together in an 1996 anthology.

In 2006, Montero worked for the newspaper *El Nuevo Día*, writing the weekly column *Before Monday Rolls Around*. As a Cuban-Puerto Rican writer, Montero continues enriching Caribbean literature. Her nonfiction works appear in scholarly as well as in literary publications throughout the world.

Further reading: Montero, Mayra. *Captain of the Sleepers.* New York, NY: Farrar, Straus, and Giroux, 2005. http://www.bombsite.com/montero/montero.html (interview with Montero).

MONTEZ, Maria
Actress

In the early 1940s, Maria Montez became one of brightest stars of the Universal Pictures movie studio. Despite her limited experience as an actress, she appeared in more than two dozen films between 1940 and 1951.

From Hispaniola to Hollywood

Born Maria Africa Gracia Vidal in Barahona, the Dominican Republic, Montez was the daughter of a Dominican woman from the town of Baní and a businessman from the Canary Islands, Spain, who held the title of honorary Spanish vice-consul. While her date of birth is often given as 1917 or 1918, she was actually born in 1912.

Montez's first marriage in 1932 to the U.S. banker William McFeeters ended in 1939, when Montez moved to New York and began to work as a model. Shortly afterward, she accepted an offer from Universal Pictures in Hollywood. She adopted the screen name Maria Montez in homage to the dancer Lola Montez (1818–1861).

Montez played small parts in several Universal films and also appeared in 20th Century Fox's *That Night in Rio* (1941) with Alice Faye, Don Ameche, and the "Brazilian Bombshell" Carmen Miranda. Montez, who had a supremely self-confident, glamorous stage persona, was not satisfied with the small roles she was offered. She cultivated her appeal by emphasizing her accent and incarnating a stereotype of the sensual Latin lover.

"Queen of Technicolor"

In 1942 Montez played the title role in *The Mystery of Marie Roget,* based on the story by U.S. writer Edgar Allen Poe. However, the film that would launch her to stardom later that year was the extravagant Technicolor fantasy *Arabian Nights* (1942). After the success of the film, she costarred in many other escapist pictures with actor Jon Hall (1915–1979), including *White Savage* (1943), *Ali Baba and the Forty Thieves* (1944), *Gypsy Wildcat* (1944), and *Cobra Woman* (1944).

KEY DATES

1912	Born in Barahona, Dominican Republic, on June 16.
1939	Arrives in New York City.
1941	Appears as Scheherazade in *Arabian Nights.*
1951	Dies in France in September 7.
1996	Maria Montez International Airport opens in Barahona, Dominican Republic.

▲ ***Maria Montez stars in* Hans Le Marin *(Hans the Sailor), a French film made in 1948.***

The "Queen of Technicolor," as Montez became known, was a popular pin-up girl for soldiers in World War II (1939–1945). She used her fame to improve diplomatic relations between the governments of all American nations. Serving as a goodwill ambassador in connection with the Good Neighbor Policy aimed at boosting U.S. influence in Latin America, Montez accepted a medal of honor from the Dominican dictator, Rafael Leonidas Trujillo, in 1943. She attended Franklin Delano Roosevelt's birthday party as Eleanor Roosevelt's guest in 1944.

In the late 1940s Montez left Hollywood and settled in France. She acted in several European films before dying from an apparent heart attack in 1951.

See also: Miranda, Carmen

Further reading: Hadley-Garcia, George. *Hispanic Hollywood: The Latins in Motion Pictures*. New York: Citadel Press, 1990.

SET INDEX

Volume numbers are in **bold** type. Page numbers in *italics* refer to captions.

N

Picture Credits

c = center, t = top, b = bottom.

Cover: Corbis: Bettmann t, c; **Courtesy Indiana University:** b; **TopFoto.co.uk:** Revolution Studios/Phillip V. Caruso, SMPSP cb; **West Carolina University:** ct.

Courtesy of the Albuquerque Museum, PC1998.27.29, museum purchase, 1995 G. O. Bonds: 68; **Photo of Nicholas Kanellos is reprinted with permission from the publisher (Houston: Arte Público Press-University of Houston, ©2005) from APP Archive Files:** 6; **Photo of Tato Laviera is reprinted with permission from the publisher (Houston: Arte Público Press-University of Houston © 2005) from AAP Archive Files:** 19; **Bella Records:** 48; **Courtesy Dr. Hector P. Garcia Papers, Special Collections & Archives, Bell Library, Texas A&M University, Corpus Christi:** 33; **Center for Southwest Research, The University Libraries, University of New Mexico, Collection 000-021 0107:** 49; **Photo Courtesy of the Citizens' Committee for Historic Preservation, Las Vegas Photographic Archive ≠ 0941:** 73; **Corbis:** 23, Bettmann 35, 113, epa/Ali Haider 111, Ann Johansson 96, James L. Lance 17, Reuters 76, SABA/Najlah Feanny: 9, Ted Streshinksy 12; **Empics:** ABACA 54, AP: 5, 116, AP/Elise Amendola 80, AP/Mike Derer 91, AP/Damian Dovargane 122, Denis Doyle 81, AP/Alan J. Duignan 37, AP/Chris Garythen 115, AP/Andre Leighton 105, AP/Jose Luis Magana 110, AP/Chris Pizzello 36, AP/Jaime Puebla 125, AP/Lynne Sladky 124, AP/Mario Suriani 109, AP/ Nick Ut 101, AP/Sal Veder 56, Barratts/Alpha 8, Joe Raymond 7, Rich Pedroncelli 14; FGS Books: Primera Hora/Jose Cruz Candelaria: 133; **Getty Images:** 29, 44, 50, 61, 83, AFP 88, Frederick M.Brown 28, George De Sota 53; **© 2006 Philip Gould:** 77; **Luis Leal:** 21; **John Jota Leanos:** 22; **Library of Congress:** 18, **repro no.LC-USZ62-171504** 47, **repro. no.LC-USZ62-113376** 63, **repro no. LC-UZ62-102263** 107; **Collection of the Louisiana State Museum:** 119; **Cesar A. Martinez:** 72; **Elizabeth Betita Martinez:** 69; **Oscar Martinez:** 79; **Missouri Valley Special Collections, Kansas City Public Library, Kansas City, Missouri:** 31; **Munger, Tolles & Olson LLP:** 84; **Paw Photos, Seeley G. Mudd Manuscript Library, Princeton University:** 98; **Michael Provost:** 26; **Retna:** Kelly A. Swift: 45; **Rex Features Ltd:** Dezo Hoffmann 42, SNAP 131; **Eliezer Rodriguez Jr.:** 129; **Photo courtesy of Izzy Sanabria (SalsaMagazine.com):** 20; **Dorothy Sloan-Rare Books, Austin, Texas:** 55; **Portrait of Xavier Martinez, ca.1905. Originally photographed by Arnold Genthe. Image courtesy of the Macbeth Gallery records, 1838-1968, in the Archives of American Art, Smithsonian Institution:** 86; **Courtesy of Frederieke Taylor Gallery, NYC:** 128; **Tejano R.O.O.T.S. Hall of Fame:** 103; **Institute of Texan Cultures at UTSA: photo no. 084-0590 Courtesy of A. Ike Idar** 92; **University of Texas at Austin:** Mark Rutkowski 87; **TopFoto.co.uk:** 38, 67, 117, ArenaPAL/Clive Barda 90, The Image Works/Bob Daemmrich 95, The Image Works/Jeff Greenberg 94, The Image Works/Wanda J.Benvenutti 25, PA 65, Sony Pictures Classics 57, UPP 70, UPPA Ltd 41, Roger Viollet 134; **United States Department of the Treasury:** 59; **U.S. Department of Defense:** 40.